FROM LYNDA'S TABLE

For Aurélie

FROM LYNDA'S TABLE

Lynda Booth

DCS
PUBLISHING

INTRODUCTION

At some point in my early twenties, I became a collector of chefs. I had always collected recipes and cookbooks but it was dawning on me that this was not sufficient. At that time I was trying to get to grips with Italian cooking and wasn't making a great fist of it. I realised I needed a mentor. From somewhere in the back of my memory came a phrase from a long-lost review that the best Italian restaurant in England was in fact in Wales. That had stuck with me. It wasn't difficult to find out that the restaurant in question was the Walnut Tree and that the chef was Franco Taruschio. I was lucky in that when I phoned, I got through to his wife, Ann. She advised me how to approach him and promised me a room for the duration. And so I got on the boat to Holyhead and made my way down to Abergavenny and stood at Franco's side for a month. He didn't teach me directly. It was more that I watched him as he cooked, I tasted when he tasted and I made myself scarce when the going got tough. When service was finished, we talked to wind down. That was how I learned about Italian food and about Franco – and about opening the door of a chef. He never questioned why I had come or why he had agreed to such a one-sided arrangement. He recognised a yearning and it was natural to him that he would feed it.

For the next decade, I went travelling. I moved around the world from fine food restaurant to taverna to catering company – to anywhere they were passionate about food. It was often a much harder graft than it had been with Franco, but it was a similar quest. I found the buzz of a kitchen to be hugely energising. Slowly becoming part of a team compensated for the crazy hours. All the while, I was adding to my food memory. My palate was developing under such constant focus, but I was also building a sense of what could be achieved. It was the tastes more than the written recipes that I took with me.

It was fair to say that I was dogged in tracking down chefs I wanted to work with. I found it was possible to open almost any door, but success wasn't down to chance. Each chef needed a personalised plan of assault. For example, when my husband got posted to Oxford and I set my eyes on working with Raymond Blanc, there was a clear strategy of engagement. I knew that my slim CV would not likely set the heart racing in a Michelin two-star restaurant. I decided not to even darken the door. I lay patiently outside, walking up and down the gravel pathway. When at last Monsieur Blanc appeared, I pounced on him. It's hard to tell if he was more taken aback by my French or by my surprise attack, but fifteen minutes later, the deal was done.

When my travelling days were over, I could no longer hunt down my food heroes. However, as my cookery school grew, I realised that I could transfer the energy into luring them to come to me. Thus began a new set of adventures. Every time I went to a food festival or ate in a restaurant, I was on the lookout for someone who might come to teach at the school and shake us out of our familiar ways.

My hunch is that people who buy cookery books are also looking to keep learning, to continue extending themselves. This book certainly aims to meet that type of adventuresome spirit. It aims to give an understanding of technique and a confidence in using a whole array of ingredients. At times it tries to push boundaries. The hope is that when you open the fridge door, you will be flooded by new possibility.

I tend to take my very favourite cookery books up to my bedroom so that I can get stuck into them on a lazy Sunday morning. I enjoy getting the feel of cookery writers and seeing how they came up with or came across their recipes. I like a cookery book with plenty of reading. At some point, an idea will catch my fancy and there will be a flurry of coloured stickers to mark pages. Shopping lists will get drawn up. The day's adventure can start. My hope is that this book might become a part of your own food odyssey.

Chapter One

FOUNDATIONS

Master key techniques while rustling up some great food: bake a loaf, prepare a salad, whip up a stir-fry. And then get a handle on some key questions:

HOW TO WORK WITH YEAST · HOW LONG SHOULD I KEEP AN OLIVE OIL? · IS IT WORTH MAKING MY OWN STOCK? · WHAT IS THE EFFECT OF BLANCHING VEGETABLES? · WHAT IS THE BEST SECRET FOR COOKING PASTA? · WHY DOES PASTRY NEED TO REST? · WHEN DO I GET A REST?

NANCY SYME

If she were alive today, she would be well over a hundred years old. She had a remarkable impact on my career and yet I met Nancy Syme no more than a dozen times.

I was living in Vancouver twenty years ago, working crazy hours in an impressive, if rather soulless, kitchen. I decided that on Thursdays, my day off, I would give cooking classes from my kitchen. My husband was dispatched with posters and a marketing campaign that resulted in just a single call. Nancy hung up so quickly that I wasn't able to get her number. That rather committed me to running the class, although I had worked out that I would need a minimum of six students to break even. Nancy had the good grace not to comment on the fact that she was the only person to show up. Perhaps it never occurred to her that there might have been others.

Either way, we set to as if this was what we had both expected. I would have all the ingredients prepared and her menu printed, and we would cook together from mid-morning. I had more to say than I realised and she loved the combination of stories from where I had worked on the one hand and learning about cooking on the other.

We would usually have wine with our lunch. By four, she would tell me she would have to be getting along. She would gather her things together and scrape any leftovers into small containers she had brought with her. She did occasionally wonder out loud as to how I could be making anything at all. I was enjoying it too much to tell her that it would have saved me good money to take her out to lunch every week and forget the class entirely.

I found that my time with Nancy was occupying more and more of my thoughts. On the walk to and from work, I found myself thinking of ideas for the following Thursday. Would she need to know this, or would she enjoy that, or how would she impress her demanding sister (whom we jokingly referred to as Wicked Irene)? Over a period of months, my vague plans for the future were replaced by the very clear idea of my own cookery school. And that changed everything.

Nancy was a diligent pupil. She listened to every word, scribbled notes all over her recipes and told me that I needed to explain the steps in vastly more detail – which I duly did. She started shopping differently. She bought new knives and fresh vegetables. She started to enjoy cooking. She ate less by herself and took opportunities not to entertain in a formal sense, but to have others join her. We invited the formidable Irene for one lunch and she told me that Nancy had embraced much of my philosophy of food. That stunned me. It had never occurred to me that I had a philosophy of food. Irene described how Nancy diligently practised her chopping action, insisted on using foods I had endorsed and tried to eat with others at least once a day (apparently I had told her it was joyless to eat on her own). Irene told me how Nancy would mimic my accent as she strutted around the kitchen with her new confidence and her new priorities. But most of all, Irene talked of the new joy that Nancy got from a well-presented plate, the taste of a soup or the smell of fresh baking. Food had moved from being a chore to something life-affirming. I was mightily proud of her.

I can't remember exactly what Nancy and I cooked, but I have a fair idea. I learned not to presume too much and we covered important basics that she could build on – what she requested was a foundation, hence the title of this chapter. If she could prepare a salad, make a soup, rustle up a stir-fry, griddle some fish and prepare some pasta, she would have important rudiments as well as something worthwhile to eat. I do remember that early on we baked some bread because she told me the derivation of the word "companion" – *com pane*, with bread – and it has stayed with me. After sharing bread that morning, we were companions.

BREAD

Bread is a good starting point for this book. It requires rolling up your sleeves and feeling the flour between your fingers. Feel is an important sense to awaken and develop when dealing with food. A bread recipe is a guide but it can't be fully relied on when baking bread. How much liquid to use depends on factors such as the heat of the kitchen or the type of flour. There is no choice – you simply have to build a sense of the consistency you are seeking.

It appeals to start with bread, too, because bread forms an important part of my own food background. My very earliest food memory is of skipping across the fields to run into my Auntie Pam's kitchen and watch her make a brown soda bread. Out of the oven, still warm, with some butter and homemade jam, it is still one of my most evocative tastes. When I am out of the country long enough, it becomes the taste I most crave. Bread was also central to my first food job at Ballymaloe House. There was nothing I cooked more often than their brown yeast bread and nothing I enjoyed tucking into more at a break, with perhaps a few fresh prawns and some homemade mayo. Heaven.

MYRTLE ALLEN

Myrtle was my first boss. She had the measure of me. She had the measure of us all. She had an enormous presence both from the quiet force of her personality and from all she had achieved in Irish food circles. Being summoned on a fortnightly basis, to work out the next rota, was slightly fearsome because her praise meant so much and the occasional rebuke left you feeling abashed, that you had let her down. When she wasn't under time pressure, she would share some of the memories and challenges of how she had started and built up the business. My favourite image was her description of how, when Ballymaloe was still a family home for her five young children, she used to reverse her packed Renault 4 up the front steps and into the cavernous hall so that the mountain of groceries could be unloaded.

She understood that I wanted to work my way around the entire kitchen. I had to accept that over the summers, no rotation could be considered. As the season became quieter, I would be on the move again. I started off as the 'trolley dolly' (desserts) and worked my way through each section, finally getting to work on mains. It was a rich three years. Like so many before and after me, I took her honest, encouraging, but ever watchful leadership as the norm and saw the wild men I subsequently encountered in other top kitchens as the aberration. Wish that were true!

Brown
Yeast Bread
Page 18

Auntie Pam's Brown Soda Bread

This bread is all about the flour. I often throw in some bran, oatmeal or wheat germ, but it's the quality of the flour that matters. Compared to the over-refined flour in other countries, our own Irish stoneground will always win out. Eat a slice warm and try to stop cutting another.

Makes 1 loaf

450g extra coarse stoneground brown flour

60g plain white flour

1 rounded tbsp porridge oats

1 rounded tbsp bran

1 rounded tbsp wheat germ

1 rounded tbsp pinhead oatmeal (or replace with one of the above if unavailable)

1 level tsp bread soda, sieved

1 rounded tsp salt

1 rounded tsp caster sugar

475ml buttermilk, plus extra if required

sunflower oil, for greasing the tin

EQUIPMENT *900g loaf tin*
OVEN *Preheat the oven to 200°C, 180°C Fan, 400°F, Gas 6.*

Brush the loaf tin with sunflower oil. Sprinkle in some brown flour, tilting the tin so that it becomes coated with the flour. Shake out any excess.

Mix all the dry ingredients together in a large bowl. With your hand outstretched like a claw, mix most of the buttermilk into the flour in an anticlockwise motion. Add the rest of the buttermilk, as required, to make a dough that feels quite loose. The exact amount of liquid required will vary slightly each time.

Scoop the brown bread mixture into the tin and flatten it out with your hand. Place in the middle shelf of the preheated oven for about 45 minutes. Remove from the oven and run a knife between the bread and the tin. Turn the bread upside down, bang the edge of the tin on the counter and the bread should pop out. If you feel it requires further cooking, place it back in the tin and cook for 5 minutes. If you like a crisp crust (which I do), return the bread to the oven without the tin for a further 5 minutes. Cool on a wire rack.

Brown Yeast Bread

This is an old English recipe adapted from Elizabeth David's *English Bread and Yeast Cookery*. It's the simplest yeast bread imaginable, moist and full of flavour. It breaks all the rules for making good yeast bread. It requires no kneading and only a single rising. In bread making, a general principle is that the slower the fermentation, the better the bread. However, the higher proportion of yeast in this recipe ferments the bread much more quickly. The fast rising is also accelerated by the temperature of the water. The treacle adds a malty flavour to the bread. The addition of sunflower or pumpkin seeds, if you feel so inclined, would give the bread quite a different character. Good stoneground flour is essential.

When making the dough, the amount of liquid will determine the consistency of the bread. Too dry and the dough won't rise to the top of the tin in 20 or 30 minutes, or indeed at all. Too wet and it will rise over the tin or prove difficult to cook through. Like many yeast breads, this tastes best on the day that it is made. It gives a sense of accomplishment far out of proportion to the ease with which it is made.

Fresh yeast is available from any bakery or supermarket that has its own bakery. Alternatively, buy a tin of dried granules (they have a shelf life of about a year). The result will be every bit as good as with fresh yeast.

Makes 1 loaf

450g stoneground flour, preferably extra coarse

1 rounded tsp salt

2 tsp treacle

425ml water at blood heat, or more as required

30g fresh yeast or 1 tsp dried yeast granules

sunflower oil, for greasing the tin

EQUIPMENT *900g loaf tin*

OVEN *Preheat the oven to 200°C, 180°C Fan, 400°F, Gas 6 (conventional oven settings are better for bread if you have that option).*

Grease the inside of the loaf tin with sunflower oil.

Put the flour and salt in a large mixing bowl. In cold weather, warm the flour slightly by placing the bowl in the oven at the lowest setting, leaving the oven door slightly ajar. Mix the treacle with about 300ml warm water. Crumble in the fresh yeast, or if using dried, sprinkle the yeast granules on the surface. Leave to sit for about 5 minutes for the yeast to activate.

Stir the water, yeast and treacle together and pour into the flour. With your hand outstretched like a claw, mix the liquid into the flour in an anticlockwise motion. Gradually add more warm water until you have a wet, almost sloppy dough. Place the dough in the tin and spread it out evenly. It will only come halfway up the tin. Leave in a warm place to rise.

When the mixture has risen to the top of the tin – this usually takes 20–30 minutes – place in the oven for 40–45 minutes. Run a knife around the outside of the bread, tap the loaf tin upside down on the counter and it should pop out. If the crust feels quite soft, place the loaf back in the oven upside down without the tin for a further 5–10 minutes. Cool on a wire rack.

SALAD

At its simplest, a vinaigrette consists of some extra virgin olive oil, some wine vinegar and some salt. My usual balance is four parts oil to one part vinegar.

With so few ingredients, each matters a great deal. Take the oil, for example. A cold-pressed extra virgin olive oil from a good producer is extracted from the olive by pressure alone. Olives from different areas will have different characteristics. My current favourite is a Ligurian extra virgin olive oil, easily distinguishable by its gold foil wrapper that covers the whole bottle. It's fruity and full of character. However, there are lots of really good-quality olive oils on the market and it's a very personal choice. Some are more intense and are at their best when diluted with a neutral oil, such as sunflower oil. Half extra virgin olive oil, half sunflower oil generally works well, but try different proportions and make your own judgement.

There are many different types of vinegars on the market and they, too, vary in quality. It's interesting to try out different vinegars – red wine, white wine, cider, champagne, sherry and balsamic. Consider buying one or two to start with to get the experimenting off the ground. Balsamic and sherry vinegar are the two that I tend to use most often and, in both cases, it's well worth buying aged vinegars. Get used to tasting vinegars. Try the vinegar on its own or fill a small dish with vinegar and olive oil and dip some bread into it.

Lemon juice can also be added to dressings instead of vinegar, adding a freshness and a sharpness to a vinaigrette, which is particularly stunning drizzled over fish.

Once you have a feel for trying out different oils and vinegars, other options can be considered. Honey or a pinch of sugar can add a little sweetness. Herbs can add flavour. Some mustard (Dijon, wholegrain or tarragon) can add sharpness and depth. Garlic is another option, but use it sparingly and make sure that it's well crushed.

NUT OILS – HAZLENUT AND WALNUT

An interesting option is to vary the type of oil. Walnut oil and hazelnut oil are widely available and add another dimension to a vinaigrette. These oils are intense and need to be diluted by at least as much sunflower oil or a mild extra virgin olive oil. If I am using four parts oil to one part vinegar, then my choice is either half nut oil and half light olive oil/sunflower oil, or a quarter nut oil and three-quarters mild-flavoured oil. Nut oils should be kept in the fridge once they have been opened. They have a shelf life of about six months.

CHOOSING AND PREPARING THE GREENS

A combination of leaves can be more interesting than just one type of lettuce. If you have the opportunity to buy organic leaves that have been freshly picked, all the better. Some leaves such as chicory, radicchio and frisée lettuce have a natural bitterness, which makes for an opportunity to add sweetness to a vinaigrette in order to create a good balance. In this case, I might add some orange juice, honey or sugar.

Always wash the leaves carefully in lots of water. The easiest way to dry them is to fold the leaves in a dry tea towel and shake vigorously over the sink. When restaurants are dealing with a large volume of leaves, this method works well. A salad spinner is another option, but be careful not to overspin, as this can tear or bruise the leaves.

Choose a bowl that could hold about double the quantity of leaves you wish to dress so that it's easy to distribute the vinaigrette evenly. The amount of dressing required will depend on the vinaigrette and the type of leaves. Sturdy, crispy and coarse leaves generally need more vinaigrette than delicate ones. Dress the leaves by hand or carefully with some salad servers, just until the leaves glisten. I often taste a single leaf to help decide whether a little more vinaigrette is required.

HOW ELSE COULD I USE VINEGAR?

It's a pity to have an aged vinegar sitting there waiting for an occasional outing on a salad. With the depth developed from the ageing process, vinegars can transform food. Pearl onions or shallots cooked in aged sherry or balsamic vinegar can be served with fish, meat or as an accompaniment to a tart or salad. Vinegars can also be added to certain braising dishes to give depth or drizzled over roasted peppers.

A Classic French Vinaigrette

This is the typical French vinaigrette suitable for a salad of mixed greens to be served on its own or as an accompaniment.

2 tbsp white wine vinegar
salt
8 tbsp extra virgin olive oil or half
  extra virgin, half sunflower oil
grinding of black pepper

Pour the vinegar into a bowl and add the salt. Whisk in the olive oil and a little freshly milled pepper. Alternatively, shake all the ingredients together in a screw-top jar.

Put the salad greens in a bowl and whisk the vinaigrette for a final time. Toss the salad with just enough dressing that the leaves glisten. Mix the salad just before you go to table or the leaves will wilt.

My Preferred Basic Vinaigrette

My own preference is for a vinaigrette with a bit more punch, so I tend to include some mustard.

1 tbsp sherry vinegar or balsamic
  vinegar
¼ tsp Dijon mustard
4 tbsp extra virgin olive oil
½ tsp honey (optional)
pinch of salt

Pour the vinegar into a small bowl. Add the Dijon and whisk in the olive oil, followed by the honey. Season with salt. Alternatively, mix all the ingredients in a screw-top jar and shake vigorously.

Sylvie's Vinaigrette

Every summer, Sylvie leaves her home in Brittany and comes to pay our family a visit. She is the easiest person to have around, relating to each of us very personally. She is extremely practical and so for weeks before she comes, we all develop a list of things that we will ask her to attend to (holes in pockets, falling shelves and the like). She has many mixed-up English expressions that we can't bear to change and some have become part of our own lexicon, such as a "wash-disher".

Sylvie is also a great cook, with her own way of doing things. Ask her to make a vinaigrette and she will take my very smallest whisk (about the size of a teaspoon) and a small bowl with a rounded base. Then she whisks the oil into some vinegar and mustard (adding the oil oh so slowly) so that it emulsifies.

The end result is a thick vinaigrette that coats all the leaves. The salad must be dressed as soon as the vinaigrette is made, otherwise it may split. And on the rare occasion it does split, it will just have a different consistency but it will still taste great. So you do what Sylvie would do – give a Gallic shrug and bring it to the table.

2 tsp sherry vinegar
1 slightly rounded tsp Dijon
   mustard
85–110ml extra virgin olive oil
salt

Place the sherry vinegar in a small bowl along with the mustard – ideally a bowl with a rounded base so that you can whisk more easily. Whisk in the oil little by little. The oil should form an emulsion with the mustard, yielding a thicker vinaigrette. Season, pour the dressing over the salad leaves, toss and serve straight away.

Salad with Avocado, Pine Nuts and Shavings of Parmesan

Avocado, pine nuts and streaky bacon are a great combination for a salad – add Parmesan croutons and a few shavings of Parmesan and you get more textures and flavours.

Serves 6

20g pine nuts

2 tsp olive oil

170g bacon lardons

2 avocados

salt

18 baby cherry tomatoes

210g mixed lettuce leaves

a few shavings of Parmesan cheese (remove from a chunk of Parmesan with a vegetable peeler)

FOR THE DRESSING

1 tbsp white wine vinegar

2 tbsp hazelnut oil (or just replace with olive oil if you prefer)

1 tbsp sunflower oil

1 tbsp olive oil

salt

FOR THE PARMESAN CROUTONS

120g thick slices white bread, such as ciabatta

30g butter

1 tbsp olive oil

1 garlic clove, crushed

30g Parmesan, freshly grated

OVEN *Preheat the oven to 180°C, 160°C Fan, 350°F, Gas 4.*

To make the parmesan croutons

Cut the bread into 2cm cubes and place in a bowl. Heat the butter and olive oil in a small saucepan and add the crushed garlic. Pour this over the bread, tossing the cubes as you go so that they are all well coated. Mix in the grated Parmesan. Spread the croutons out on a baking sheet and place in the oven on a high shelf until lightly golden all over, about 10 minutes. The croutons may be made a few hours in advance and kept in an airtight container once cooled.

To make the dressing

Pour the vinegar into a small bowl. Whisk in the oils and season.

To prepare the salad

Heat a pan and when hot, add the pine nuts. Toss continuously for a minute or two to toast the nuts. Be careful, as they can scorch easily. Remove straight away to a cold plate. Alternatively, roast the pine nuts in a hot oven (180°C, 160°C Fan, 350°F, Gas 4) for 3–4 minutes.

Pour the olive oil into the frying pan. When the pan is hot, add the lardons of bacon and cook over a brisk heat, stirring regularly, until the fat renders out and the bacon becomes crisp. Drain on kitchen paper.

Remove the skin from the avocados, cut in half and remove the stone. Cut into cubes, season with salt and spoon over some dressing. Slice the cherry tomatoes in half and season with salt. Break the lettuce leaves into large bite-sized pieces. Place all the lettuce in a serving bowl and add the avocado, cherry tomatoes, lardons of bacon and pine nuts. Toss the salad leaves with just enough dressing to make them glisten. Scatter a few shavings of Parmesan and some croutons over each serving.

Chorizo and Roasted Pepper Salad with a Poached Egg

Chorizo sausage is one of those ingredients that enhances so many different types of dishes. In this salad, the chorizo is tossed off in the pan until it exudes its own oil. The new potatoes, which have been precooked, are tossed in the chorizo oil, which adds to their flavour. You can roast your own peppers but you can also buy beautiful tinned roasted peppers, marinated in olive oil. Look out for Spanish piquillo peppers, which are a great staple to have in the cupboard. These red peppers are smaller than our typical variety and are traditionally roasted over embers, which gives them a distinct sweet, spicy flavour.

Serves 4 as a starter

12 small new potatoes

175g chorizo, sliced

4 eggs

2 Little Gem lettuces, separated into leaves

60g green beans, blanched and refreshed (see page 41)

2 roasted red peppers (see page 28), cored, deseeded and cut into strips about 5cm wide

FOR THE SHERRY DRESSING

3 tinned anchovies, finely chopped

1 sliver of garlic, crushed

2 tbsp sherry vinegar

splash of Amontillado sherry (optional)

5 tbsp light olive oil

Maldon sea salt and freshly ground black pepper

To make the sherry dressing, place the anchovies, garlic, sherry vinegar and Amontillado sherry (if using) in a bowl with the olive oil. Season to taste and mix with a hand whisk.

Place the potatoes in a pot of boiling salted water and simmer until tender but still firm. Drain. The potatoes may be cooked in advance and pan-fried just before serving.

Heat a non-stick frying pan, add the chorizo and cook over a low to medium heat to release the oil. Remove the chorizo, leaving the oil in the pan. Cut the potatoes in half lengthwise and then add to the pan. Cook until well coloured on all sides and warmed through, 2–3 minutes. Set aside.

To poach the eggs, bring a large, deep pot of water to the boil. Turn down the heat so that the water is at a bare simmer. Stir the water to create a whirlpool effect in the centre. Crack each egg into a small bowl and once the water is swirling, slide the egg into the centre. You can poach 3 or 4 eggs at a time. Keep over a low heat. The eggs will take 4–5 minutes to cook. It's important that the yolk remains runny. Remove from the pot and place on a plate lined with kitchen paper.

Break up the Little Gem leaves into 2 or 3 pieces and place in a bowl. Add the potatoes, green beans and roasted peppers. Toss the salad with just enough sherry dressing to coat the leaves. Scatter the chorizo over each serving and top with a poached egg.

HOW TO ROAST PEPPERS

Preheat the grill to its hottest setting. Place the peppers on a baking tray under the grill and cook until the skin blisters and becomes charred. Keep turning until the peppers are partially blackened all over. Remove to a plate.

Remove the skins of the peppers while they are still hot with the help of a small fruit knife. After peeling, remove the stem, slice the pepper in half and remove the seeds and membrane.

Alternatively, roast the peppers in a hot oven. Preheat the oven to 220°C, 200°C Fan, 425°F, Gas 7. Rub the skins with a little olive oil. Roast on a baking tray until blistered and partially blackened. Peel as above.

HOW TO POACH EGGS IN ADVANCE

Use really fresh eggs for poaching, as the white will be firmer and will set more quickly. The white of older eggs is inclined to become more straggly, in which case you can cut off some of the white after cooking. Cook a maximum of 3 or 4 eggs at a time in a large pot.

Poached eggs can be cooked in advance and put straight into a bowl of iced or cold water to stop the cooking. As soon as they are cold, they should be drained on a tea towel. They can then be placed on a tray lined with kitchen paper, covered and put in the fridge. To reheat, bring a pot of water to the boil and add the egg just until heated through.

STOCKS

In the very first flat I shared with my husband, he was extraordinarily tolerant of my desire to buy kitchen equipment before almost anything else. However, even he raised a surprised eyebrow the day a small cabinet freezer was delivered. Did we really need this, he wondered from his perch on a tea chest.

A freezer is incredibly useful. It can become a liability if it's too easily filled with food that will never see the light of day and oddments that can never be identified. However, to keep something that I have made in too great a quantity, for certain fruits and for a range of foods that will quickly be turned around, it's hard to beat. Above all, it's home to my beloved homemade stock cubes.

Stock is surprisingly easy to make and, I believe, so worthwhile. Most cooks who haven't tried it think it must be a lot of bother. I remember during one rowdy class after I had been going on a bit about the virtues of stock, a voice from the back chirped, "Get a life, Lynda", which made everyone erupt with laughter. The fact is, though, that I don't see stock as a chore – all that's needed are chicken bones (carcasses or just wings), a few basic vegetables and some aromatics (for instance, bay leaf, peppercorns and sprigs of thyme). Thrown into a pot and covered with water, the stock simply bubbles away quietly on the back of the stove and requires minimal attention.

My stock usually comes about in two ways. I may have some bones to hand from roasting a chicken, so I chuck them in a pot and have stock for immediate use. Alternatively, I decide I want to make a big batch of stock so that I can hoard it for all sorts of uses over a longer period. This grander scale requires no more time and effort other than a trip to the butcher for some chicken carcasses or to buy a pile of chicken wings.

SEEKING OUT A BUTCHER

There are many reasons why I like to go to my butcher, John O'Reilly. I love going somewhere where I can have a chat. He provides a sense of community. He is enormously well informed, always suggesting different cuts and alternative ideas. Then there is the small matter of his meat being so much better than what I can buy in a supermarket because he has the patience and knowledge to hang it.

Chicken Stock

Though I offer quantities for a chicken stock here, they should only be used as a guideline. It is not necessary to be exact.

1kg chicken carcasses or chicken wings

enough cold water to cover the bones

1 onion, finely chopped

1 celery stalk, finely chopped

1 carrot, peeled and finely chopped

1 sprig of thyme

1 bay leaf

parsley stems

5 black peppercorns

Here are some general points about making a chicken stock.

Start with the chicken bones in cold water. The flavour is drawn out of the bones as the water comes up to a boil.

Bring to a rolling boil and then turn down to a very gentle simmer. If the stock remains cooking at a fast boil for too long, the fat may emulsify with the broth, resulting in a fatty and cloudy stock.

Skim the scum. This is an inelegant term for a quick job. Use a ladle to remove all the impurities that rise to the surface. Every time you pass by, cast an eye over it to see if further skimming is necessary. The stock will probably need to be skimmed three or four times during the cooking process.

Add the vegetables and aromatics. Some chefs cook the stock without any vegetables, so don't worry if you don't have everything to hand.

Simmer gently. Let the stock simmer for 4–5 hours.

Cool and strain. Leave to cool, then strain into a deep container. For immediate use, skim off the fat that rises to the surface. Otherwise, leave to cool completely and then place in the fridge for several hours or ideally overnight. Remove the layer of fat that sits on the top. This is much easier than trying to remove the fat at an earlier point. You can dab the surface with kitchen paper if it still looks a little greasy. Now you have a totally fat-free broth that can either be used as a basic stock for soup or risotto or reduced down further to add to sauces.

SOME DOs

If the water reduces below the level of the bones during the cooking process, top it up with extra cold water.

Chicken stock will keep in the fridge indefinitely if boiled up every two or three days to remove the bacteria. Allow to cool before returning to the fridge.

SOME DON'Ts

Never add salt to a stock. If you are reducing the stock, it will become too salty.

Reduce a stock only after it has been strained and degreased. Never reduce a stock by fast boiling while the bones are still in the pot (this applies to chicken, meat or fish). If you boil the stock with the fat, it will taste greasy.

REAL STOCK CUBES

Once you have made stock, it can be used immediately or stored for later use by making stock cubes for the freezer. To make the cubes, the stock needs to be concentrated. Pour the degreased stock back into a pot – the wider the pot, the quicker the evaporation – and then, at a rolling boil, reduce the stock to a fraction of its volume. Pour this concentrate into deep ice cube trays, allow to cool and then place on a tray in the freezer overnight. The next day, pour boiling water from the kettle over the back of the ice cube trays and pop out all the cubes. Store your homemade stock cubes in a ziplock bag, label and date them, and keep in the freezer.

To use these stock cubes for a soup, simply dilute a few of them per litre of water. For a sauce, I use the stock cubes undiluted with perhaps a few tablespoons of water.

A further advantage of having your own stock cubes means that the exact amount required can be used without any waste.

NO STOCK? NO PROBLEM!

There is no need for your heart to sink when you see chicken stock listed as an ingredient for a recipe. A homemade vegetable stock is a great alternative. It's easily made and can be used straight away. Another good option is to buy Marigold bouillon (preferably the low-salt version), a powdered stock that is made from organically grown vegetables. It's available in all health food shops and some supermarkets and just needs to be diluted with water. It's a very useful ingredient to have in the cupboard.

Vegetable Stock

All sorts of vegetables can be used to make a vegetable stock and the choice will somewhat depend on what it's to be used for. This is a good general recipe.

4 celery stalks, sliced

3 leeks, white part only and 3cm of the green, chopped finely

3 carrots, diced

2 large Spanish onions, coarsely chopped

2 bay leaves

2 sprigs of thyme

½ tsp black peppercorns

about 2 litres water

Put all the ingredients together in a saucepan. Bring up to the boil, lower the heat and allow the stock to simmer for 45 minutes. Skim during the cooking process, if necessary. Strain and allow to cool. Store in the fridge for up to 3 days. Boil to reduce the liquid if you wish to strengthen the flavour.

Celeriac and Carrot Soup

This is a hearty soup. You could use other root vegetables, but I favour including celeriac because it's used much less often. I'm not sure why, because it has a great flavour – perhaps it needs a good agent and marketing campaign to give it some publicity. Even keen foodies can find it a challenge to identify the two main vegetables as they get stuck into this soup.

Serves 4

2 tbsp olive oil

15g butter

1 large or 2 medium onions, chopped

salt

500g celeriac

250g carrots

1.2 litres chicken stock (page 30) or vegetable stock (page 32)

Heat the olive oil and butter in a large saucepan and add the onion. Season with salt, stir, cover with a lid and cook gently until the onion is completely tender, about 15 minutes.

Place the celeriac on a chopping board and remove the outer skin with a serrated knife. Chop into smallish chunks. Peel the carrots and chop into smallish pieces. Add the celeriac and carrot to the onion, season and continue cooking for about 5 minutes with the lid on. Add the stock and bring up to the boil. Simmer until the vegetables are tender, about 15 minutes.

Purée the soup in a blender or food processor and correct the seasoning.

Pea Soup with Broad Beans, Goat's Cheese and Mint

Pea soup is hard to beat and so quick to cook. Serve with some slivers of mint leaves, peas or broad beans as a garnish if you wish, and perhaps some creamy goat's cheese crumbled over the top.

Serves 6

25g butter

1 onion, finely chopped

salt

1.5 litres chicken stock (page 30)
  or vegetable stock (page 32),
  plus more if required

1.2kg frozen or fresh peas

1 garlic clove, peeled

3 tbsp chopped fresh mint

1½ tsp caster sugar

FOR THE GARNISH

30 broad beans

3 mint leaves

60g soft goat's cheese

To prepare the garnish

Bring a pot of salted water to the boil. Add the broad beans and cook for no more than 2 minutes. Remove them with a slotted spoon and run under cold water in a colander in the sink. Once cooled, remove the outer skin and set aside.

To make the soup

Melt the butter in a large saucepan. Add the onion, season and turn down the heat to low. Cook for about 10 minutes, until the onions are tender. They should be translucent but not brown. Add the stock.

Rinse the peas and drain. Add the peas to the pot along with the garlic clove, mint, sugar and seasoning. Turn up the heat and bring to the boil. Reduce the heat and simmer for 10 minutes. Blitz with a blender until smooth and put through a fine strainer. Return to the saucepan and bring up to the boil. Check the seasoning.

To serve, slice the mint leaves as finely as possible. Pour the soup into warmed bowls and top with some crumbled goat's cheese, broad beans and the finely sliced mint leaves.

Butternut Squash Risotto

I was once at a village celebration in northern Italy. Risotto was served from enormous vats. The villagers were a discerning group, so it had to be good. It was.

One of the old men regaled me with the story of the stained glass in Milan's most famous cathedral, the Duomo. The apprentice glassmakers were intrigued as to the shade of yellow that the master was able to achieve. It wasn't until he died that they found what he had been adding to his palate of colours. At this point the old man theatrically produced the last ingredient of the risotto – the saffron. It's a good story. It might even be true.

When I started teaching, I ran classes in Italian cooking. One of the dishes on the course was risotto alla Milanese (with, of course, the saffron). Over time, my risotto has evolved. I have added roasted butternut squash for colour and flavour. Sometimes I put Parma ham on the top (see page 38), cooked on a baking tray until crispy, or I add deep-fried sage leaves as a garnish.

Serves 6 as a starter

1 butternut squash

olive oil, for drizzling

sea salt and freshly ground black pepper

30g butter

1 onion, finely chopped

1 leek, white part only plus 2.5cm of the green, finely chopped

1.3 litres chicken stock (page 30) or vegetable stock (page 32)

400g risotto rice (Carnaroli or Arborio)

120ml dry white wine

pinch of saffron threads

TO FINISH

50–60g Parmesan cheese, grated, or to taste

30g butter

OVEN *Preheat the oven to 200°C, 180°C Fan, 400°F, Gas 6.*

Remove the skin from the butternut squash. Slice in half and scoop out the seeds and fibres with a teaspoon. Cut the flesh into large cubes and place in an ovenproof dish. Drizzle with olive oil, toss to coat and season with sea salt and black pepper. Roast in the oven until tender, about 30 minutes, turning over once or twice during the cooking. Purée in a food processor until smooth, adding a little stock or water if required.

Melt the butter in a heavy-based saucepan. Add the onion, season with salt and cook with a lid on over a low heat until completely softened. Add the chopped leek to the pot and continue cooking for a few more minutes. Meanwhile, heat the stock in a separate saucepan and keep this just below simmering point on the cooker.

Add the rice to the onion and leek and stir for a couple of minutes so that the grains of rice become coated with the butter. The risotto will take about 20 minutes to cook from this point onwards. Add the white wine and simmer, stirring, until the wine has evaporated. Add a ladleful of broth and simmer again until the stock has been absorbed, stirring regularly. Add in the saffron threads. Continue adding the stock, a ladleful at a time, for the duration of the cooking, allowing each batch of stock to be absorbed by the rice before adding another. Stir regularly. Taste the rice towards the end of the cooking. At the end, the rice should be tender but still retain a slight bite.

Stir in the puréed butternut squash. Mix well and add more stock if the risotto isn't loose enough. Finally, add the Parmesan and butter. Mix well and season to taste. If the risotto needs more flavour, add extra Parmesan. The final flavouring of the risotto can only be done to taste. Add a little more stock or boiling water, if necessary, to achieve a soft and slightly runny consistency. Serve immediately.

Preparing the risotto in advance

If the risotto is being reheated, cook the rice as above for 15 minutes as opposed to 20. (The cooking time of different types of rice may vary, so check the instructions on the packet before starting.) When par-cooked, pour the risotto onto a baking sheet and spread it so that it cools quickly. The risotto may be prepared to this point earlier in the day. When the rice has cooled, cover it and refrigerate if necessary.

Just before serving, reheat the stock. In a separate saucepan, heat a knob of butter and add the par-cooked risotto. Pour in a ladleful of hot stock and simmer until the stock has been absorbed. Add more stock, a ladle at a time, until the rice is tender but still with a bite. Add the puréed butternut squash, Parmesan and butter. Taste for seasoning and serve immediately.

Crispy Parma Ham

This is an optional garnish for the risotto.

1 slice of Parma ham per person

OVEN *Preheat the oven to 180°C, 160°C Fan, 350°F, Gas 4.*

Line a baking tray with a silicone mat or parchment paper. Place slices of Parma ham side by side on the tray and bake until crispy, 6–7 minutes. The Parma ham may be cooked a few hours in advance.

THE DOT OF THE RISOTTO

How do you determine when a risotto is cooked? The usual way is by taste. An interesting alternative is by looking carefully at the rice. Break open a grain after 10 minutes of cooking, or slice in half crossways, and you'll notice a large white dot in the middle – the outer coating of the rice is a different colour than the stark white core. Continue cooking, and as the rice becomes more tender, this white centre will grow smaller. By the end of the cooking, the outer coating of the rice will be relatively translucent, but there should still be a tiny white dot in the very centre indicating that the rice will still have a slight bite to it. Check for the dot. A risotto does not hold after it has been cooked to the point of perfection.

CONSISTENCY OF A RISOTTO

What I loved about crazy Italian kitchens was that the team really wanted me to understand each dish. My favourite chef, oblivious to the urgent tasks I was supposed to be attending to, used to signal for me to come and watch at critical moments. One that stands out was when he was making a risotto. Towards the end of cooking, he added in some cold butter and tossed the risotto in the pot rhythmically with the flick of his wrist. "*All'onda*," he kept saying until I grasped that he was "creating waves" as he flicked the risotto back on itself to emulsify the butter with the rice. The previous day he had noted that when I spooned my risotto onto a plate, it stayed firmly in shape. He told me that he would now demonstrate the correct consistency. He spooned some risotto onto a plate, tapped it gently from underneath with his fist and the risotto spread out flat across the plate. That was the consistency he was aiming for.

The butter and cheese, the final additions, actually thicken the risotto, so I like to reach the consistency I'm aiming for (with stock or water) before these are added. For an Italian chef, the consistency is as important as the flavour.

BLANCHING VEGETABLES

A question that often comes from the dining room to the restaurant kitchen is a surprising one. It's a query about how all the vegetables (particularly the green ones) have such vibrant colour and how their taste is so pure and intense. The usual answer is that the vegetables were blanched. It's a simple technique worth learning, whether the vegetables are to be used immediately or are being prepared for later use. In the summer, when there are many vegetables available, it's a great way to cook a selection of vegetables with the minimum of hassle.

The main principle is that the vegetables should be cooked as quickly as possible. This is best achieved by having a large pot on a fast rolling boil and not too many vegetables (certainly no more than 450g at a time) so that the temperature is not appreciably reduced when the vegetables are added.

It's important that the water should be heavily salted. The salt provides an even seasoning and is critical in setting the colour. The amount may seem high – 2 teaspoons of salt (11g) to a litre – but the vegetables don't stay long in the pot and are then refreshed in cold water. The only caution is that if there are many vegetables to be cooked, keep topping up the water or the proportion of salt will become unbalanced.

The cooking times will vary according to each vegetable, so the best way to test is by taste. Each vegetable should be cooked separately, as the timing will differ. In order to remove the vegetables in one go, ideally use a wire mesh basket that sits in the pot, but a strainer also works well for small quantities. After blanching, the vegetables are then refreshed in ice-cold water. If there are no ice cubes available, make sure to change the water with each set of vegetables. A large bowl works best to prevent the water from warming up. Leave the vegetables in the water until they are cold – just a few minutes – and then drain. Pat dry with kitchen paper to remove excess water. The vegetables may be stored for up to a day in the fridge. They should be layered between kitchen paper in a covered container in the fridge.

To reheat the vegetables, use a wider pot. Add a generous knob of butter (the exact quantity will depend on the amount of vegetables to be added to the pot) and enough water to cover the base of the saucepan. Bring to the boil and add the vegetables that take the longest to reheat first. Add in the other vegetables and cook until heated through. If the water evaporates before the vegetables are warm, add a little more so that the vegetables finish with a light glaze. It is this water and butter emulsion that is important. Taste and add seasoning.

GRIDDLE PAN

In one spell of my life on the food road, I worked my way down the Italian Riviera and found a small restaurant I very much wanted to work in. My poor Italian was not a good start. Though I got my foot in the door, I knew that there would be an early appraisal. After lunch service on my first day, there was a delivery of fresh fish, mostly unfamiliar to me. The head chef pointed at his three accomplices and said they wanted lunch in half an hour. A broad gesture indicated that the kitchen and all its ingredients were at my disposal. It was a dilemma: try to impress or keep it simple? I opted for the latter. I could sense the chef's eyes on me, assessing my technique, my speed and whether I would fit in with his carefully balanced band of brigands. I focused on the task: fillet the fish, warm a griddle pan, whip up a salsa verde, fish on the griddle for a couple of minutes either side. Simplicity won the day. I was given the nod of approval.

My abiding memory of my time there is not the food, good though it often was. It is being screamed at in Italian. Positively operatic.

SECRETS OF THE GRIDDLE PAN

A good cast iron griddle is often a great standby at home as well (when you buy one, make sure it's heavy cast iron and not a light pretender). It gives a much different result to pan-frying or roasting and is more akin to a barbecue. Throw on some fillets of fish, top them with some herb butter and you have a great meal.

The griddle is also a good way to cook vegetables such as aubergines (see page 85), peppers, courgettes or asparagus. Cooking vegetables on the griddle imparts a smokiness that gives such a distinctive flavour.

When using a griddle pan, there are just a few principles that have to be borne in mind.

PREHEAT THE GRIDDLE

The secret to using a griddle pan is to heat it for about 5 minutes before starting to cook. Once the smoke is rising from the griddle, turn the heat down slightly (but only slightly), open the window or turn on the extractor fan. The pan is now ready for cooking.

OIL THE FOOD, NOT THE PAN

Excess oil on your pan will start smoking and will burn. The solution is to oil the food instead.

LEAVE THE FOOD ALONE

It's important that you do not move the food around just after you have put it on the griddle, as it will stick. And sticking is what you are trying to avoid.

CHECK FOR EVEN COOKING

Throughout the cooking, it's important to keep an eye on the heat. If the meat, fish or vegetables are becoming too well done on the outside, then turn the heat down to allow the heat to penetrate more slowly. Bear in mind that the griddle pan will be hotter where it sits directly over your burner.

USE THE OVEN

Another option is to preheat the oven to 180°C, 160°C Fan, 350°F, Gas 4 before starting and to transfer the griddle to the oven (particularly with a thick piece of fish or chicken) to complete the cooking. This way, you can free up the hob as well as being sure that the meat or fish is evenly cooked throughout. Note that most griddle pans will have removable or ovenproof handles to ease the move to the oven.

A FRESH TWIST

A piece of fish coming hot off the griddle doesn't need a sophisticated sauce. A little herbed butter or aïoli (garlic mayonnaise) is a wonderful accompaniment. And I know that salsa verde goes down a treat on the Italian Riviera.

Griddled Fillets of Salmon with Herb Butter

This is a basic method for griddling fillets of fish such as cod, hake, halibut, haddock or salmon. As soon as the fish comes off the griddle pan, place a slice of flavoured butter on top. This will melt over the surface and add great flavour to the fish. A lovely supper dish – quick, easy, tasty.

When buying the fish, ensure that the skin has been left on, which will help protect the flesh when it's turned over.

Serves 4

4 fillets of fish, skin on, approximately 170–220g per person

salt

flour

butter, at room temperature, for spreading over the fillets

flavoured butter (pages 46–47), to serve

Remove the bones from each fish fillet with a fish tweezers. Dry the fish on both sides with kitchen paper.

Heat the griddle pan until very hot. Season the fish fillets, dip the flesh side in flour and shake off the excess. Lightly spread some butter on the flesh side, as if you were thinly buttering a piece of bread. (An alternative to the flour and butter is to season the fish and rub some olive oil on the flesh side.)

Wait until the griddle is beginning to smoke and then turn the heat down ever so slightly. Place the fish fillets, flesh side down first, on the hot griddle. The fish should sizzle as soon as it hits the pan. Do not be tempted to move the fish until the flesh begins to turn golden at the edges. Initially the fish will stick to the griddle, but as the caramelisation develops and forms a crust, the fish will release from the pan. The golden crust on the surface adds both flavour and texture. You may need to adjust the temperature of the hob at various points. Turn the fish over onto the skin side and cook for a few more minutes, depending on the thickness of the fish. The fish should be moist and slightly rare in the centre. Overcooking will dry out the flesh.

To serve, place a slice of herb butter on top of the warm fish, or use a pesto or sun-dried tomato butter, as outlined on pages 46–47.

Flavoured Butters

Herb Butter

Incorporating herbs into butter and adding a squeeze of lemon juice is a great way to add a burst of flavour. Make the butters into a sausage shape and wrap in cling film or parchment paper. They will hold for a few days in the fridge or a few months in the freezer. To accompany fish, I prefer to go with a single herb such as basil, dill, fennel, chervil or tarragon.

110g salted butter, at room
  temperature
good squeeze of lemon juice
bunch of basil, fennel, dill, chervil or
  tarragon, chopped

Place the butter in a bowl and mix in the lemon juice and chopped herbs. The butter should be heavily speckled with the chosen herb. Spoon the butter onto a piece of cling film or baking parchment and mould into a tight cylinder, twisting the ends like a Christmas cracker to form the shape. Refrigerate until ready to serve.

Pesto Butter

15g basil leaves
15g Parmesan cheese, finely grated
1 large garlic clove, crushed
3 tbsp olive oil
100g butter, softened

Put all the ingredients except the butter in a food processor and blend until smooth. Add the butter and blend together just until mixed. Wrap as above and store in the fridge or freezer.

Sun-dried Tomato Butter

100g sun-dried tomatoes

15g Parmesan cheese, finely grated

2 large garlic cloves, roughly
  chopped

3 tbsp olive oil

100g butter, softened

FOR THE SUN-DRIED TOMATOES

400g cherry tomatoes

olive oil

Maldon sea salt

caster sugar

1 tsp thyme leaves

OVEN *Preheat the oven to 140°C,
120°C Fan, 275°F, Gas 1.*

To prepare the sun-dried tomatoes

Cut the tomatoes in half crossways. Place them on a roasting tray in a single layer. Drizzle a few drops of olive oil over each tomato and season with a pinch of sea salt and sugar. Scatter the thyme leaves over the tomatoes. Roast in the lower part of the oven for approximately 75 minutes. Remove from the oven and leave to cool completely before using.

For the sun-dried tomato butter

Put all the ingredients except the butter in a food processor and blend until smooth. Add the butter and blend together just until mixed. Scoop out onto cling film and wrap up in a sausage shape. Twist the ends and refrigerate or store in the freezer.

Whipped Butters

Another interesting idea is to whip the butter with an electric whisk before adding the other ingredients. When whisked, the butter lightens in colour and expands in volume. You may then add the desired flavours and wrap as above.

Homemade Mayonnaise and Its Variations

A homemade mayonnaise to which you add some good-quality olive oil is a wonderful accompaniment to griddled or pan-fried fish, prawns or poached salmon and has countless other uses. For aïoli, a classic garlic mayonnaise, add crushed garlic cloves or try roasted garlic, mashed to a paste and then mixed into the mayo to give a mild yet distinctive taste. Another interesting variant is sauce gribiche. Instead of starting with a base of raw egg yolks, the eggs are hardboiled and the yolks are mashed with a little mustard. The oil is then drizzled into the yolks before adding capers, gherkins and some chopped herbs. Sauce gribiche is fabulous with fish or griddled asparagus or it can be added to cooked baby potatoes to make a potato salad.

Mayonnaise

2 egg yolks

1 tbsp white wine vinegar

¼ tsp Dijon mustard

225ml sunflower oil

75ml good-quality extra virgin olive oil

squeeze of lemon juice

¼ tsp salt

Place the egg yolks in a bowl with the vinegar and mustard. Using a hand or an electric whisk (electric is preferable), whisk in the sunflower oil in a cautious trickle at first, then gradually building up to a steady stream. The mayonnaise will become thicker as the oil is poured in. Finish by adding the extra virgin olive oil and a squeeze of lemon juice. Season with salt to taste.

If the mixture curdles (the mayonnaise becomes runny and does not thicken despite the addition of oil), place 1 egg yolk in a clean bowl and pour in the curdled mayonnaise drop by drop, whisking as you go.

To make mayonnaise in a food processor or liquidiser

Use 1 whole egg instead of the egg yolks. Put the whole egg, vinegar, mustard and salt into a liquidiser or food processor. Turn on the machine and then slowly add the oil through the hole in the lid until you have a thick emulsion.

Aïoli

For aïoli, pound 2 or 3 small garlic cloves in a pestle and mortar with a pinch of sea salt and mash to a paste. Add half the garlic paste to the basic mayonnaise recipe. Taste before deciding whether or not to add the remainder, as the pungency of garlic will vary according to the variety and the season. Another option is to add 2 or 3 chopped anchovies to the basic aïoli and a bunch of finely chopped herbs such as tarragon, chervil, mint or flat-leaf parsley. A combination of herbs provides interest. If the herbed aïoli sits for an hour or two, it improves.

Lemon Mayonnaise

Replace the vinegar in the basic recipe with 1 tablespoon of lemon juice and add the finely grated zest of a small lemon.

Mustard, Dill and Honey Mayonnaise

130g mayonnaise

2 tsp finely chopped dill leaves

1½ tsp wholegrain mustard

1 tsp Dijon mustard

1 tsp honey

salt

Combine all the ingredients in a bowl and season.

Sauce Gribiche

Serves 4

1 large egg

1 tsp Dijon mustard

70ml extra virgin olive oil

1½ tsp white wine vinegar

8–10 small capers, drained, rinsed and patted dry

2 gherkins

salt

3 tbsp finely chopped mixed herbs, such as flat-leaf parsley or tarragon

Cook the egg in boiling water for 10 minutes. Remove immediately from the heat and run under cold water to cool. When cold, remove from the shell and separate the egg and the yolk. Chop the egg white into dice the same size as the capers.

In a small bowl, mash the egg yolk with the mustard using a fork or the back of a spoon. Drizzle in the olive oil a little at a time, whisking continuously. The sauce will not emulsify (like a mayonnaise), so just whisk to combine well. Add the vinegar and whisk again. Add the capers, gherkins, chopped egg whites and seasoning, then add the herbs and mix well.

Griddled Lemon Chicken with Salsa Verde

What lifts this simple marinated chicken is the vibrant salsa verde. Salsa verde is stunning with lamb, beef, chicken, potatoes, white fish, on bruschetta with fresh mozzarella – the list goes on. Even those who think they don't like capers or anchovies seem to love the depth and freshness of this piquant sauce. All chefs have their own little twist. At the cookery school we might add extra herbs, a little mustard or some lemon zest. I thought that I knew every addition until I recently saw New Zealand chef Ruth Pretty add sourdough breadcrumbs, which gave real body to the salsa. As your confidence develops, you can start to develop your own variations.

Serves 4

4 chicken breasts

salt

3 tbsp olive oil (or use 2 tbsp olive oil and 1 tbsp chilli oil)

3 tbsp lemon juice

2 garlic cloves, flattened

FOR THE SALSA VERDE

4 anchovy fillets in olive oil, drained

2 garlic cloves, crushed

large bunch of basil leaves

small bunch of chives, chopped

small bunch of flat-leaf parsley

1 tbsp capers, drained

1 tbsp lemon juice

150ml extra virgin olive oil

salt

To prepare the chicken

The chicken will benefit from being marinated, ideally overnight. Season the chicken with salt. Mix the olive oil, lemon juice and garlic in a dish. Add the chicken, turning it once or twice to get it well coated with the marinade. Cover and leave to marinate in the fridge for as long as possible, ideally 24 hours. Turn once during this time.

Heat a cast iron griddle pan until very hot. Remove the chicken from the marinade and drizzle a little olive oil over the chicken breasts. Place the chicken on the hot griddle pan. Allow the chicken to cook without moving it at all until the underside of the chicken is turning a rich golden colour, 5–7 minutes. Turn the chicken over and continue cooking until the meat is tender. The exact timing will vary enormously depending on the size of the chicken breasts. If you prefer, the chicken can be transferred to a preheated oven at 180°C, 160°C Fan, 350°F, Gas 4 to finish the cooking. Allow the chicken to rest for at least 5 minutes before serving. Slice the chicken into 2 or 3 pieces and spoon over the salsa verde.

To make the salsa verde in a food processor

Put the anchovies, garlic, basil, chives, parsley and capers in the bowl of a food processor. Whizz for a minute or two, intermittently scraping down what is thrown up against the sides of the bowl. With the machine running, add the lemon juice and the oil in a thin stream. Capers are very salty, so taste before seasoning further.

The salsa verde will keep in the fridge for about a week if stored in a sterilised jar with a film of olive oil poured over the surface. After each use, clean down the sides of the jar and top with a fresh film of olive oil.

To make by hand

If you have a pestle and mortar, pound the basil leaves a few at a time. Add in the chives and flat-leaf parsley and pound to a rough paste. Next add in the garlic, capers and anchovies and pound together. Finally, mix in the lemon juice and olive oil. Taste and season.

PASTA

When I was growing up, there was a contraption for drying clothes over the range in the kitchen. It was a series of long wooden laths that you put the washing on, which was then hoisted up towards the ceiling, out of harm's way. Pulling it up and down caused many hours of amusement as all sorts of things were sent up to the high ceiling; it must have been made of sturdy stuff to survive. I hadn't seen one for years until I was working in a restaurant outside London. I was intrigued as to what it might be used for in that setting. The puzzle was only solved when the chef had finished making his pasta and he rolled down the line and hung the pasta over the laths to dry. With different vibrant colours (squid ink pasta, saffron pasta and so on), it was a striking sight to have high up over our heads.

We often make fresh pasta in the school (although regrettably, we don't have such an imaginative way of drying it), but dried pasta is a staple of every Italian household and claims equal respect. We may not have an innate Italian understanding of pasta, such as how to match sauces to shapes, but if we respect a few essential rules, we, too, can produce a proud plate of pasta. Here are three important principles.

SALT THE WATER

The first principle is salting the water sufficiently. This should be a measured rather than a random amount. Pasta is always made without any salt, and even if the sauce is seasoned, the pasta will be totally bland if the water is lacking salt. As a guideline for 400g of pasta, 1 tablespoon of table salt (not sea salt) should be added to 4 litres of water.

COOK UNTIL AL DENTE

The key to great pasta is in the cooking. This is the second vital principle. Overcook it and it not only goes limp, but it will no longer have enough body for the sauce to cling to. The timing for dried pasta is on the packet but should not be rigidly followed. Start testing the pasta a couple of minutes before the stated time, looking for that point when your bite is still gently resisted – hence the expression al dente (to the tooth).

RETAIN SOME PASTA WATER

Finally, the most useful tip I was ever given about cooking pasta was to retain some of the water the pasta was cooked in. I may not always need it, but there are so many times when returning a little of the pasta water to the pot completely changes the character of the dish. This is particularly true of an egg and cream-based dish like spaghetti alla carbonara, but also oil-based sauces like pesto. The pasta water adds starch as well as liquid and so both loosens the sauce and helps it cling to the pasta as it's stirred in over heat. A simple tip that can make a dramatic difference.

If you wish to reheat pasta on the hob, the most successful way is to put a good dash of pasta water back into the pot and then to toss the pasta around until it's hot.

Here are three additional points that may be useful when serving pasta.

PASTA PORTIONS

When deciding on portion size, the general guideline is 100g pasta per person for a main course and 60g for a starter. I find that 100g is more than I can manage, but this may be balanced out by some other hungry mouths.

PARMESAN

Parmesan is often one of the essential ingredients in a pasta dish (though it's not generally added to pasta with seafood). It's what gives the depth of flavour to the dish at the end. How much Parmesan you add can only be determined by taste and depends on the type being used. The best Parmesan available is Parmigiano Reggiano and in Italy you can buy different grades and different levels of maturity. I always have a chunk of Parmesan, which I keep wrapped in tinfoil in the bottom of the fridge. Never buy Parmesan already grated, as it has such a short shelf life – it's far better to grate it as required. A cheaper alternative to Parmigiano Reggiano is Grana Padano.

SPEED OF SERVING

Pasta does not benefit from sitting around. As soon as the pasta is ready, drain it, sauce it and serve it immediately in preheated bowls or plates.

Penne with Tomato Sauce and Fresh Mozarella

To my astonishment, I had an Italian student who once asked me how to make a tomato sauce. She was so used to the sun-ripened tomatoes of her homeland that she couldn't work out how to make a decent pasta dish with tinned tomatoes. My simple tip was to tell her to add some caster sugar.

The seeds are the bitter part of the tomato and are often discarded. Whole tomatoes that are sieved to remove the seeds and puréed are packaged as passata, which makes a good, rich tomato sauce when reduced and thickened. However, whether the tomatoes are tinned or bottled, I always add some caster sugar, as these tomatoes tend to be slightly acidic.

This is the fastest tomato sauce I make. No need to sweat off onions – simply reduce the passata with a little olive oil and sliced garlic and finish by adding a ball of fresh mozzarella. The mozzarella will melt into the sauce, making it mellow and creamy. Serve this with some smoked pancetta, chorizo or griddled vegetables.

Serves 4–6

3 tbsp olive oil

2–3 garlic cloves, sliced into strips

1 x 700g bottle passata or 2 x 400g tins tomatoes

1 tsp caster sugar

salt

120g fresh mozzarella in water, drained and coarsely chopped

6–8 basil leaves

400g penne

a fistful of freshly grated Parmesan, plus extra for serving

If you're using tinned tomatoes, purée them in a food processor or blender and pass through a sieve, discarding the pips.

Heat the olive oil in a frying pan over a low heat and add the sliced garlic. Cook the garlic for 10–20 seconds without allowing it to colour and then add the passata or sieved tomatoes. Season with the sugar and salt. Simmer until the tomatoes have reduced to a thick sauce. Just before serving, add the mozzarella and stir until it becomes creamy and has melted into the tomatoes. Shred the basil leaves with a knife and add to the sauce.

Meanwhile, bring a large pot of water to the boil and add some salt (about 1 level tablespoon of table salt to 4 litres of water). Add the pasta and cook until al dente. Drain, reserving some of the pasta water, and return the pasta to the saucepan. Pour over the sauce, add some grated Parmesan and a dash of pasta water and toss to mix. Taste and add more Parmesan if necessary. Serve immediately with a dusting of freshly grated Parmesan on the top.

Penne with Tomatoes, Gruyère and Pecorino Romano

Everyone loves to be able to rustle up a quick supper that's delicious and satisfying. The tomato sauce here takes about 15 minutes to cook. Pecorino Romano is an Italian sheep's milk cheese that supplies the interest.

Serves 4–6

a generous knob of butter

1 small onion, finely chopped

salt

8 whole tinned tomatoes (do not use the tomato juice from the tin)

175ml cream

400g penne

55g Gruyère, grated

30g Pecorino Romano, grated, plus extra for serving

Heat a knob of butter in a heavy-based saucepan and add the chopped onion. Season with salt, stir and then cover the pot. Turn down the heat to low and sweat the onions for 10–15 minutes, stirring occasionally, until softened. Chop the tinned tomatoes and add to the pot. Cook for a minute or so and then add the cream. Simmer for about 5 minutes over a gentle heat. The sauce may be prepared up to this point in advance.

Meanwhile, bring a large pot of water to the boil. For about 4 litres of water, you will need to add 1 level tablespoon of salt. Add the penne to the water, give it a stir and boil until the pasta is tender but still with a nice bite. Drain, reserving a little of the pasta water, and return the penne to the saucepan. Add the grated cheese and stir until it has melted. If the pasta appears to have absorbed all the cream, add a dash of pasta water and toss. Serve immediately with some extra grated Pecorino.

Tagliatelle with Parma Ham and Pistachios

Giusy was a spirited au pair who came from Sicily. Her strong interest in food sparked off a friendship from a very early point. She rustled up this pasta dish the evening she arrived with pistachios picked from her back garden earlier in the day. It remains a personal favourite. The sauce can be prepared in the time it takes to cook the pasta. After a hard day, that can be very welcome.

The amount of chilli you add will depend on personal taste. The hottest part of the chilli is in the seeds, which you may remove or not as you please.

Serves 6 as a starter

1 small red chilli

2 tbsp olive oil

2 large shallots, finely chopped

6 large slices of Parma ham, cut into strips about 1.5cm wide

225ml cream

60g roughly ground pistachios, plus extra for serving

400g tagliatelle or linguine

freshly grated Parmesan, for serving

Remove the stalk from the chilli and split it in half. Chop the chilli into fine dice. Heat the olive oil in a medium saucepan and add the chilli and chopped shallots. Cook for 1–2 minutes, until softened. Add the strips of Parma ham and toss for about 10 seconds. Add the cream and bring up to the boil, then reduce the heat and simmer gently for a few minutes. Add 3–4 rounded tablespoons of the ground pistachios to the sauce and simmer again for another minute or so. Set aside until ready to use.

Meanwhile, bring a large pot of salted water to the boil. For about 4 litres of water, add 1 level tablespoon of table salt. Add the pasta and cook until al dente. Drain, reserving a little of the pasta water, and return the pasta to the pot. Pour the sauce over the pasta and toss until well coated. Add a dash of the pasta water to loosen the sauce and toss again.

When serving, sprinkle some roughly ground pistachios over the top and a generous dusting of freshly grated Parmesan.

NOTE Particularly for the final sprinkling, make sure that the pistachios are not too finely ground. They add great texture when scattered over the pasta.

Mussels with Linguine, Garlic and Flat-leaf Parsley

A very simple and tasty sauce for pasta can be made by flavouring olive oil with garlic, chilli and flat-leaf parsley. This is an extension of this method, using the flavoured oil and then adding mussels that have been steamed open in white wine.

Serves 4

2kg mussels

350g linguine

100ml olive oil

4 garlic cloves, thinly sliced

2 red chillies, seeds left in and very finely chopped

20g flat-leaf parsley, chopped

2 tbsp dry white wine

Wash the mussels in plenty of changes of cold water. Knock off any barnacles with the back of a knife, then scrub the shells and pull off the beards (if they are obvious). Discard any mussels that don't close when given a sharp tap or any that are cracked.

Bring a large saucepan of salted water to the boil (use 1 level tablespoon of salt to every 4 litres of water) and cook the linguine for slightly less time than usual, as it will continue cooking with the mussels. Drain the pasta through a colander (reserving some of the pasta water) and mix in a drizzle of olive oil to stop it sticking together. Toss to mix.

At the same time as the pasta is cooking, heat the olive oil in a small frying pan. Add the sliced garlic and cook for about 20 seconds without colouring. Add the chilli and parsley to the hot oil. Cook for 10–20 seconds and then remove from the heat. Place the pot you cooked the pasta in back on the hob. Add the mussels and white wine, followed by the pasta. Cover the saucepan and cook over a medium heat until the mussels have all opened. As soon as the mussels have opened, remove the pot from the heat and add the chilli and parsley oil. Let the juices reduce for 2 minutes, then serve immediately.

OPENING MUSSELS

When cooking mussels, whether by steaming or in a broth, bear in mind that the mussels should be removed as soon as they open. If they are cooked for too long after that, they will shrink and become tough. In many recipes, they are removed from the pot and added in towards the end of the cooking.

CLASSIC STIR-FRY

Some of the restaurant kitchens I worked in were smaller than my own. Survival depended on organisation. Mise en place (literally 'put in place") was the order of the day. Everything that could be done in advance was done in advance. The single best domestic test of mise en place is cooking a stir-fry. Many stir-fries take only a few minutes to cook, but the timeframe doesn't allow for any hesitation or distraction. There is no question of leaving the stove. Every ingredient must not only be fully prepared, but to hand. The mere act of turning to get one ingredient from a chopping board is time you may not have, since if any of the ingredients burn, the whole dish will be tainted. With high heat, constant movement and a flurry of ingredients being thrown in from different bowls, this is your chance to feel like a chef.

The general principle is to heat the wok over a high heat without any oil for at least 2 minutes, then add the oil and swirl it around so that it coats the base and halfway up the sides. When the oil is hot, you are ready to go. Add the ingredients in the order given in the recipe. It's imperative to keep the heat really high and to keep tossing all the ingredients in the wok continuously to allow for even heat distribution. If there's any risk of burning, add a dash of water or stock to the wok. The liquid also creates a blast of steam and will accelerate the cooking briefly.

BUYING AND STORING WOKS

Asian markets are generally the best place to buy a good steel wok at a great price. After purchase, it needs to be seasoned before use. Start by washing the wok in hot soapy water to remove any film of grease or oil, then place over a high heat (or wok burner if you have one) until the whole interior changes colour to a deep blue/black appearance. Turn off the heat and wipe the interior with vegetable oil. Every time you use the wok, wash and dry it thoroughly and then lightly smear a little oil over the surface to prevent it from rusting.

Stir-fried Beef with Vegetables

Serves 4

450g beef sirloin

4 tbsp groundnut oil

100g shallots, thinly sliced

4 spring onions, washed and cut into 3cm pieces at an angle

3 garlic cloves, thinly sliced

2 red chillies, deseeded and diced

1 tbsp finely chopped fresh root ginger

60g shitake or button mushrooms, stems removed and thinly sliced

6 asparagus spears, woody ends removed (if thick, sliced in half lengthwise)

1 large red or green pepper, thinly sliced

3 tbsp light soy sauce

3 tbsp rice wine or dry sherry

1½ tsp caster sugar

FOR THE MARINADE

1 tbsp light soy sauce

1 tbsp rice wine or dry sherry

2 tsp sesame oil

Cut the beef into thin slices 5cm long, cutting across the grain. Put the beef into a bowl together with the marinade ingredients. Mix well and leave to marinate for about 20 minutes.

Heat a wok or large frying pan over a high heat until it's beginning to smoke. Add 2 tablespoons of oil, then remove the beef from the marinade with a slotted spoon and add to the wok. Stir-fry on the highest heat for about 2 minutes to brown the strips of meat. Remove to a plate and set aside. Clean out the wok with kitchen paper if there is any excess liquid left in the bottom.

Reheat the wok or pan over a high heat and add the remaining 2 tablespoons of groundnut oil. Add the shallots, spring onions, garlic, chillies and ginger and stir-fry for 20 seconds. Add the mushrooms, asparagus and peppers and toss again for a further 30 seconds. Add a dash of water if the bottom of the wok is beginning to scorch. Return the beef to the wok and toss to mix with the vegetables. Add the soy sauce, rice wine and sugar. Toss all together and then taste, adding more soy sauce and rice wine if necessary. Serve immediately.

Vegetable Stir-fry

The key vegetable in this dish is the cauliflower, as it seems to absorb all the flavours. Make sure to keep the cauliflower florets a reasonable size and attached to some stalk so that they don't fall apart during the cooking. Other vegetables such as asparagus, mangetout, pak choy or shitake mushrooms can be added. The cauliflower is transformed by the addition of the Indonesian sweet soy sauce called kecap manis, which is available in Asian markets.

Serves 4

1 small cauliflower, cut into florets

3 tbsp vegetable or sunflower oil

3 garlic cloves, finely chopped

2 red chillies, deseeded and sliced into rings

1 red pepper, deseeded and sliced into strips

4cm piece of root ginger, finely sliced and cut into shreds

6 spring onions, cut into 3cm lengths

150g baby spinach leaves

2 tbsp fish sauce

2 tbsp kecap manis

1 tbsp dark soy sauce

Cook the cauliflower in boiling salted water until tender but still with a good crunch. Transfer the cauliflower to a bowl of iced water, leave for a minute or two and then drain.

Heat the wok. When hot, add the oil followed by the garlic, chillies, red pepper and ginger. Sauté over a high heat for about 30 seconds. Add the cauliflower, spring onions, and baby spinach leaves and cook for a further 2 minutes, until thoroughly heated through. Add the fish sauce, kecap manis, soy sauce and about 2 tablespoons water. Continue to cook for another 30 seconds. Serve immediately.

SHORTCRUST PASTRY

For a year I worked at Lesley Stowe Fine Foods, which was both a catering company and a great deli in Vancouver. It was a very crisp operation. When we were beginning to finish for one day and making some preparations for the next, my favoured activity for winding down was to make some pastry. I have always found the action of making pastry relaxing. I would roll it out and line a row of tins, cover them with cling film and put them in the fridge, all ready for the next day. I still sometimes find myself making pastry the night before using it, which is probably a throwback to those days. To come home and find a quiche tin already lined lifts the heart and it's then no chore to whip up supper. While I'm baking the pastry blind in the oven, I can rustle up a filling with what is at hand, and in no time at all, I'm taking something out of the oven that will satisfy all the senses.

Pastry is about feel. If you have no experience of it, you can't have developed a sense of how it should be. So be patient with yourself. Understand the principles and, where possible, go and find your granny or somebody to whom it comes as second nature who can mentor your technique. It's an incredibly satisfying skill, so it's worth investing a little time into getting past the stage of mystery and frustration, which tends to mar early attempts.

LIGHT AND QUICK
Recipes for shortcrust pastry vary, but the general rule is that you use at least half the amount of butter to flour. Use plain flour, never strong flour. The butter should be just out of the fridge and cut into small cubes (half the size of your average dice). The aim is to work the butter into the flour quickly.

NEITHER CRUMBLY NOR STICKY
Once the butter has been mixed into the flour, beaten egg, egg yolk and water (or just water alone) are added to bind the pastry. For my basic quiche and tart pastry, I use beaten egg. This pastry can be made by hand or even more quickly in the food processor.

The amount of liquid used to bind the pastry is vital. Add too much and the dough becomes sticky and the pastry will be less crumbly. Add too little and the pastry will be dry and will develop cracks when you roll it out. After you have made pastry a number of times, you will get a sense of the consistency that you are seeking. Since the properties of flour vary so much, it's best to hold back some of the liquid, adding it by degrees, and work the dough as little as possible.

Once you have made the dough, bring it together into a ball using your fingertips, working quickly and deftly. This should take no more than 10 seconds. Try not to knead the pastry, as this would develop the gluten in the flour and make it more elastic, causing the pastry to shrink both at this point and, more pertinently, when it's in the oven.

TIME TO RELAX

Wrap the pastry in a piece of cling film and then flatten it into a disc about 2.5cm thick. Place in the fridge for at least an hour. Refrigerating the dough allows the gluten to relax and will make it much easier to roll out. Putting it out of harm's way allows you to relax too, which may be important if you are new to the next stage. Putting the pastry in the freezer for 15–20 minutes speeds up the resting process. However, be sure to set a timer, as if you leave the pastry in the freezer for too long, it will become too hard to handle and will have to be defrosted before rolling.

ROLLING OUT

When you take the pastry out of the fridge, feel how firm it is. If the pastry is rock hard, then it should be left out on the counter for a few minutes to soften. If the kitchen is very warm, the pastry will need to be that little bit firmer to start out with, as it will soften more quickly and become more difficult to handle. If it softens too much, it can be placed on parchment paper and then on a baking sheet and returned briefly to the fridge or freezer.

To roll out the pastry, dust the counter lightly with flour. The best technique is to throw the flour onto the countertop with fast horizontal flicks of the wrist, as if you were skimming stones on water. The aim is to prevent the pastry from sticking to the counter without changing the balance of butter to flour. If you want to roll the pastry into a circle, then shape it with your hands initially and tap with the rolling pin a few times to get it started.

Begin rolling the dough from the centre, turning the pastry clockwise after every couple of rolls. If you feel it sticking to the counter, loosen it with a metal palette knife or, if necessary, dust very lightly with a little more flour. If any cracks appear during the process, they can be pressed together. As the diameter of the dough increases, guide the rolling pin out from the centre.

A long metal palette knife is a good tool to have to hand to slide between the pastry and the counter if there are signs of sticking. Fold back the pastry and dust a little more flour on the countertop. Keep dusting the rolling pin lightly with flour, if needed. If you have too much flour on the pastry at the end, brush off the excess with a pastry brush.

Towards the end of the process, check the thickness of the pastry. It's unlikely to be of even thickness and the edges are at most risk of getting too thin. Stop short of rolling to the ends so that you achieve a uniform thickness of 3mm to 6mm.

To lift the pastry into the tin, put the rolling pin about a third of the way from the top of the circle of pastry. Flick the top end of the pastry over the rolling pin with the help of a metal spatula so that it wraps around the pin. Lift up the rolling pin, holding the pastry in place with your thumb and first finger, and unroll it loosely over the tin. Working very quickly, ease the sides of the pastry well down into the edges without stretching the dough. The edges of the pastry must be at a perfect right angle to the base.

Trim the excess pastry so that it's level with the rim of the tin. Wrap up the excess pastry in cling film and refrigerate. You may need some of this to patch up any cracks in the tart shell after baking blind. The pastry should be rested for a second time to further relax the gluten in the flour.

It's advisable to put the tin on a baking tray, particularly if you have a quiche tin with a removable base. It's all too easy to pick up the tin and inadvertently push the base up and dislodge the pastry.

Pastry should go straight from the fridge to a preheated oven.

BAKING BLIND

'Baking blind' is a term used to describe how a pastry shell is par-baked before the filling goes in. This prevents the base from becoming soggy during cooking. The pastry case is lined with baking parchment and filled with baking beans or dried pulses. When the pastry is half-cooked, the paper and beans are removed. The pastry base is returned to the oven to firm up the base before adding the chosen filling. Baking blind not only produces a firmer base, but a better-tasting pastry too.

Caramelised Onion Tart with Leeks and Feta

Onions cooked for a long time over a gentle heat and seasoned adequately will become soft and intensely flavoured. Cook them even longer and the juices of the onions will eventually caramelise on the bottom of the saucepan, providing a natural intense sweetness and turning the onions a rich golden colour. I manage to sneak leeks into dishes at every opportunity, so these, along with some cubes of feta, make a combination that I find hard to beat. Serve with a tossed salad.

Serves 6

FOR THE PASTRY

180g plain flour

100g cold butter, cut into cubes

1 egg, beaten

FOR THE FILLING

4 tbsp olive oil

1.2kg large onions, thinly sliced

salt

3 fat leeks, white part only
  plus 2cm of the green

30g butter

2 eggs, beaten

250ml cream or creamy milk

150g feta, cut into bite-sized cubes

EQUIPMENT *23cm quiche tin, about 3.5cm deep, with removable base*
OVEN *Preheat the oven to 200°C, 180°C Fan, 400°F, Gas 6.*

To make the pastry

Place the flour and butter in a food processor and pulse until it resembles fine breadcrumbs. While the machine is running, add three-quarters of the beaten egg and pulse again. Add the remaining egg, as required, to bring it together into a ball. Any excess egg should be reserved for later. The pastry should be neither too firm nor too soft. Remove the dough to a floured surface and knead gently for a few seconds just to bring it together. Wrap in cling film, press into a round disc and allow to rest in the fridge for 1 hour or longer.

Alternatively, to make the pastry by hand, place the flour in a bowl and add the butter. Rub the butter into the flour with your fingertips as quickly and as lightly as possible until it resembles coarse breadcrumbs. Add enough beaten egg just to bring it together into a ball. Continue as above.

Roll out the pastry to a thickness of about 3–5mm and line the quiche tin. Place the quiche tin on a baking tray, line the pastry with baking parchment or foil, fill with dried beans and bake for about 15 minutes. Check to make sure the paper will come away easily from the pastry. If not, leave in the oven for a few more minutes. Remove the paper and the beans. Using a pastry brush, paint the base of the tart with a little beaten egg and return to the oven for a further 5 minutes or so to dry out. Reduce the temperature of the oven to 180°C, 160°C Fan, 350°F, Gas 4.

To make the filling

Heat the olive oil in a large saucepan and add the sliced onions. Season with salt, cover with a lid and allow to cook over a gentle heat for about 30 minutes, stirring regularly. Remove the lid, turn up the heat a little and continue cooking. All the liquid will evaporate and the onions will begin to caramelise on the bottom of the saucepan. Allow this to happen and then scrape the caramelised bits on the bottom vigorously with a wooden spoon so that they become incorporated into the onions. Repeat this process until the onions are a rich golden brown colour.

Split the leeks in half, fan out the leaves and wash under a running tap. Slice the leeks crossways into rings. Melt the butter, add in the chopped leeks, season with salt and pepper and cover the saucepan. Cook over a low heat for about 10 minutes, or until the leeks have softened, stirring occasionally.

Mix together the eggs and cream (or creamy milk) and season with salt. Place the prepared tart on a baking sheet and fill with the leeks. Cover the leeks with a layer of onions and dot the cubes of feta around the tart. Pour in the egg custard, using a fork to mix it in with the onions. Bake for about 30 minutes, or until set and lightly browned.

Plum and Almond Tart

Frangipane tarts studded with fresh fruit always look so alluring. The frangipane in this tart is moist and the fruits can be varied according to what's in season. In the summer, peaches, raspberries, nectarines, cherries and blueberries offer alternatives to the plums suggested here. If I'm using raspberries or blueberries, I use much less fruit as they ooze so much more juice. About 200g raspberries placed around the tart, for instance, works very well.

Serves 6

FOR THE PASTRY

180g flour

100g cold butter, cut into cubes

2 tbsp icing sugar

1 egg, beaten

2 rounded tbsp plum or apricot jam

FOR THE FILLING

120g unsalted butter, at room temperature

120g caster sugar

2 large eggs

120g ground almonds

zest of 1 lemon

10 plums

icing sugar, to decorate

crème fraîche, to serve

EQUIPMENT *23cm quiche tin*
OVEN *Preheat the oven to 200°C, 180°C Fan, 400°F, Gas 6.*

To make the pastry

Place the flour, butter and icing sugar in a food processor and mix until fine. With the machine running, pour in about three-quarters of the beaten egg. Open the lid of the food processor and feel the pastry. If you think that it's moist enough to come together, pulse for another few seconds and turn out onto your countertop. You may well need all of the egg. At the end, the pastry should be neither too firm nor too soft. (If you happen to have any beaten egg left over, reserve it for later.) Remove the dough to a lightly floured surface and knead gently for a few seconds to bring it together. Wrap the pastry in cling film. Press into a flat disc about 2.5cm in depth and place in the fridge for about 1 hour.

If making the pastry by hand, put the flour, butter and icing sugar in a bowl. Chop the butter finely with a knife, then using the tips of your fingers, rub the butter lightly into the flour. Bind with just enough beaten egg to make the pastry come together. Refrigerate as above.

Roll out the pastry and line the quiche tin. Place a sheet of baking parchment over the pastry and fill with dried pulses. Bake the pastry in the preheated oven for about 15 minutes, or until it's just beginning to go golden around the edges. Very carefully remove the dried pulses and the greaseproof paper. Lower the

oven temperature to 180°C, 160°C Fan, 350°F, Gas 4. Brush the pastry base with a little beaten egg and return to the oven for a further 5–10 minutes, until the tart base looks crisp. Warm the jam slightly and paint it on the base of the tart.

To make the filling

Place the butter and sugar in a bowl and beat with an electric mixer until light and fluffy. Beat the eggs together and add gradually, mixing well between each addition. Add the ground almonds and lemon zest and fold into the mixture. Spread the filling evenly over the tart base.

Split the plums in half and remove the stones. Slice the plums and arrange them around the tart, slightly overlapping each slice. Return the tart to the oven and bake for 30–40 minutes. When ready, the top should be a light golden colour and the filling should be slightly springy to the touch.

Dust the tart with icing sugar just before serving. Serve with a spoonful of crème fraîche.

Chapter Two

GOING WEST

Find a wild lobsterman, feed a mob,
make a pizza base, bake a cake.

HOW TO SPICE UP A BARBECUE, CARAMELISE
AN ONION OR BUTTERFLY A PRAWN · WHAT IS
THE ULTIMATE BISCOTTI RECIPE? · HOW DO
YOU MAKE HARISSA? · HOW DO YOU KNEAD
A DOUGH? · WHAT ARE CANDIED SHALLOTS?

GOING WEST

Every summer we head off to Connemara for two weeks. There are rituals involved. It all starts with much discussion about how this year, unlike on all previous occasions, we will leave at the crack of dawn.

There is gleeful anticipation of 'beating the traffic' and 'gaining a day'. This hope is not officially abandoned until early afternoon on the day of departure. At this point, the front garden is piled with paraphernalia that dwarfs the not insignificant boot of our trusty estate car. There is one final attempt to find someone who might have an even larger roof rack than the huge one already mounted. And then the bartering begins in earnest. Each of us stands by our own stack and carries out high-level diplomacy with those who may back the cause for their own 'essential' items.

There is an understanding that although I can expect no favour for anything else, when it comes to kitchen equipment, the family will grant me a certain amount of leeway. They know too well the value of a happy cook. The only times I have been unhappy cooking on holiday are when I have been faced with dodgy ingredients or dodgy equipment, so I take precautions.

I go round my own kitchen, packing up a crate of whatever takes my fancy. Some oils, some spices, some knives. I would never go anywhere without my knives in their well-travelled bag. I love their weight, their balance, their sharpness. And then there is the equipment for this particular holiday: the griddle pan, the ice-cream maker, the pizza stone, the bread and muffin tins and the madeleine moulds. At this point, someone will bring up how many chefs pride themselves on using little other than a sharp knife, and I will reply that, with regret, I do not count myself among their number.

Once the 'food essentials' are in, they are covered immediately to minimise the chance of any renegotiation. The gear required for a spell in Connemara does just nicely: body boards, a few golf clubs, some wellies, suntan lotion, heavy jumpers, a couple of pairs of shorts and there is not a sign of anything culinary. Come hail or sunshine (and we are likely to get both), we will eat well, and at the end of the day, that is not to be underestimated. The unsuccessful items in this year's summer lottery are thrown into the porch, the front door is locked and we are on our way. Halfway there, someone wonders did we turn off the gas. The next set of rituals is just about to begin.

LOBSTER

WILD LOBSTER AND WILD FISHERMEN

When we arrive at our destination, my first food thoughts are of lobster. I don't have to go too far to get the best. Wild lobster is available from the wild fisherman who lives down the lane. I can feel that I am at an interview when I knock at the door. His voice comes from deep within and whichever child answers the door acts as intermediary, yielding a three-way conversation.

– Who is it?

– It's Lynda.

– She says she's Lynda.

– Where is she from?

– Where are you from?

– I'm from Dublin and I'm staying at the house up the hill.

– She's the one from Dublin and she's staying at the house on the hill.

So it goes on until finally he says, "Sure I know her well" and I am told to return the following day.

There is little relation between the number of lobsters I order and the number that are given to me when I go to collect my booty. Either way, 24 hours later, I will be walking back up the hill with three or four large lobsters and a huge grin on my face. My chef's mind is in overdrive, conjuring up all that I might do. I know that we will start off with hot buttered lobster that day and then move on to having it cold or tossed in pasta the next. Then I'm likely to move on to a shellfish sauce or a shellfish risotto. Cooking with lobster shells on holiday may not be practical for everyone, but I have packed my conical sieve, my sturdy old liquidiser, my muslin and the other accoutrements I would not head west without. If such an involved process may not be what most people would envisage doing on their holidays, then the recommendation is to try and find someone like me as a travelling companion.

Hot Buttered Lobster

There is a wonderfully large pot in the house. It was apparently used for making jam – but not today. It's so big that I can generally fit in two lobsters at once. Make sure that you have an adequate amount of water in the pot before you start. The water needs to be heavily salted. The recommended ratio is 150g salt to every 4.5 litres of water – as it turns out, this is the same as seawater! Bring to a rolling boil and put in the lobster, head first. Bring back to the boil if you are adding a second.

The lobster is cooked, tossed in clarified butter and then served in the shell. It needs nothing else. Hot buttered lobster and a glass of chilled white wine – this, for me, is as good as it gets to start my holiday.

Cook lobsters for 10 minutes for every 450g.

Serves 4

2 cooked lobsters, each weighing
 700–800g
clarified butter (60–100g)
 (see note on page 81)
sea salt
lemon wedges, to serve

To remove the meat from the lobster

Twist and remove the claws. Set aside. Place the lobster belly side down on a board, making sure that the legs are not directly underneath. With the head facing towards you, cut down through the shell between the eyes with a chopping knife. Turn the lobster around and finish cutting it in half through the tail. Remove the stomach sac from behind the eyes and discard. Separate the tail and the head. Remove any other pieces from the inside of the head and discard, but keep the shell for a shellfish stock or broth. Remove the intestinal tract from the tail – this is the black vein that runs the length of the tail – and discard.

Remove the lobster meat from the tail and any roe (the bright red coral). Chop the lobster into pieces about 2.5cm in size and break up the roe roughly.

Twist off the knuckle from each claw. Holding the claw in one hand, pull the lower pincer back and forth to break it and pull it out. Pull away the small piece of cartilage attached to the pincer. Crack the top of the claw with the back of a chopping knife and wiggle the knife to crack it open and loosen the shell. Remove the meat from the shell. For the knuckle, also crack the shell a little with the back of a chopping knife. Prise away the shell or use a lobster pick or skewer to take out the meat. Refrigerate any lobster meat that is not being used immediately.

To reheat the lobster in clarified butter

Place the half shells in the oven to warm for about 5 minutes. If you're cooking the meat from 2 lobsters, you will probably need to cook it in 2 batches, depending on the size of the pan. It's important not to overcrowd the meat.

Heat a couple of tablespoons of clarified butter in the pan and when it's very hot, add the lobster meat. Season with a touch of sea salt. Toss over the heat for a few minutes, just until the lobster is warmed through. Remove the shells from the oven and spoon the meat back into them. Add some extra clarified butter to the pan and heat through, scraping up any remaining bits. Add a squeeze of lemon juice. Spoon some over the lobster and pour the remainder into a preheated jug. Serve the lobster with a wedge of lemon and the heated butter.

CLARIFIED BUTTER

The milk solids in butter burn at quite a low temperature. Removing the milk solids means that the butter will have a much higher smoking point than regular butter (250°C, 480°F for clarified, 190°C, 375°F for regular butter). This decreases the risk of the butter burning and makes it good for sautéing. It can also be used as a seal on top of pâtés and terrines to prevent oxidisation. Clarified butter has a longer shelf life than regular butter and can be kept, covered, in the fridge for several weeks.

To make clarified butter, melt some butter in a saucepan and bring to the boil. Simmer gently until a foam settles on the top. Remove from the heat to allow the milk solids to settle at the bottom. Skim the foam (the whey proteins) from the top with a spoon and discard. The middle layer will be clear yellow butter. Strain the butter through a sieve or a strainer lined with muslin, pouring off the clear butter and leaving the milk solids behind. Discard the milk solids.

USING LOBSTER, PRAWN AND CRAB SHELLS

Lobster, prawn and crab shells can be used to make a shellfish broth or bisque. Always keep the heads from the lobster and prawns, as they are essential for this stock. If the shells are not being used immediately, wrap them tightly in cling film and store in a ziplock bag in the freezer. For details on how to make a shellfish bisque to accompany pasta or a piece of fish, see page 212.

Cold Lobster with White Soda Bread

On this holiday, I always like to have enough lobster left over from the first evening so that we can have some for lunch the next day. My favourite way to serve it is with warm white soda bread and a pot of homemade mayonnaise. Dill and mustard are the perfect additions to the mayonnaise for this feast (see page 49).

Makes 1 loaf

450g plain white flour, preferably unbleached

1 rounded tsp salt

1 tsp bicarbonate of soda (bread soda)

350ml buttermilk, plus a little extra, if required

OVEN *Preheat the oven to 220°C, 200°C Fan, 425°F, Gas 7.*

Sieve the dry ingredients into a large bowl and make a well in the centre. Pour in most of the buttermilk all at once. With your hand outstretched like a claw, mix the buttermilk quickly into the flour (hold back a little at first) to make a softish dough that's not too wet or sticky. Add a little more buttermilk, if necessary. When it all comes together, turn it out onto a floured work surface. Wash and dry your hands.

Knead the dough very gently just to bring it together. It's important not to overwork the dough. Pat the dough into a round about 20cm in diameter.

Place the dough on a lightly floured baking tray and cut a deep cross on the loaf. Bake for 15 minutes, then turn the heat down to 200°C, 180°C Fan, 400°F, Gas 6 for a further 20–30 minutes. Cool on a wire rack.

Soda bread is best eaten on the day it's made but will hold for a day or two longer.

HUNGRY HORDES

Meals are unpredictable on holiday. We might end up eating in a pub or at someone else's house, or then again, there might be twice as many children coming back to the house as left earlier in the day. Here are three dishes that have saved my bacon as the hungry hordes returned over the sand dunes.

Connemara Meatballs and Tomato Sauce

Simple homely fare, but very tasty. These meatballs are moist and succulent and, dare I say it, difficult to overcook. The bread, which is soaked in milk, is added to the beef and pork. This stops the meat from drying out too quickly. Is it the quality of the meat reared in this air or is it just the honest hunger from a day being blown around the beach that gives them so much flavour? Serve up with some buttered pasta noodles.

Serves 6 · Makes 50 meatballs

100ml milk

50g white bread, such as ciabatta, broken into chunks

500g minced beef (not too lean)

300g minced pork (not too lean)

1 small onion, grated

salt

60g grated Parmesan cheese

2 garlic cloves, crushed

1 egg, lightly beaten

1 tsp thyme or 1 tbsp oregano, chopped

pinch of cayenne pepper

2 tbsp olive oil

handful of fresh basil leaves, to garnish

FOR THE SAUCE

2 tbsp olive oil

2 onions, finely chopped

salt

4 garlic cloves, crushed

2 x 700g jar passata (puréed and sieved tomatoes) or 4 x 400g tins chopped tomatoes

2 tsp caster sugar

OVEN *Preheat the oven to 190°C, 170°C Fan, 375°F, Gas 5.*

To make the tomato sauce

Heat the olive oil in a saucepan and add the chopped onions. Season, cover with a lid and cook until the onions are completely tender, about 10–15 minutes. Add the garlic, stir for about 30 seconds and then pour in the passata or the tinned tomatoes. Season with salt and sugar and bring up to the boil, then lower the heat and simmer gently, reducing to a light sauce consistency. The sauce shouldn't be too thick, as the meatballs will be transferred to the oven.

To make the meatballs

Pour the milk over the bread in a bowl and leave to soften. Put the beef, pork and grated onion in a bowl and season. Squeeze the excess milk from the bread and add to the meat, breaking it into crumbs as best you can. Mix in the Parmesan, garlic, egg, thyme or oregano and cayenne. Mix well and form into meatballs.

Heat the olive oil in a large frying pan. When hot, add the meatballs to the pan in a single layer (you may have to do them in 2 batches so they aren't too crowded). Keeping the heat on medium-high, brown the meatballs all over. Remove to a gratin dish and cover with the tomato sauce.

Cover the dish with tinfoil and transfer to the oven. Cook for 30–40 minutes. Just before serving, chop the basil and scatter it over the top.

Aubergine and Lentil Moussaka

What happens if the hungry hordes include some vegetarians? This is the dish that has got me out of trouble most often. Perhaps it's the hint of cinnamon in the lentils that changes a humble dish into something more special.

Serves 6

675g aubergine

salt

olive oil

1 large onion, finely chopped

1 medium carrot, finely chopped

2 garlic cloves, finely chopped

200g Puy lentils or green or brown lentils

675ml chicken stock (page 30) or vegetable stock (page 32)

½ tsp ground cinnamon

¼ tsp cayenne pepper

FOR THE BÉCHAMEL

30g butter

30g plain flour

350ml milk

4–6 tbsp freshly grated Parmesan

salt

EQUIPMENT *20cm x 20cm ovenproof dish (or its equivalent)*

OVEN *Preheat the oven to 190°C, 170°C Fan, 375°F, Gas 5.*

Slice the aubergine into 7mm rounds. Layer in a colander, sprinkling each layer with salt, and leave for 30 minutes to 1 hour.

Meanwhile, heat 2 tablespoons of olive oil in a large saucepan. Add the onion, carrot and garlic and cook for about 10 minutes with the lid on. Add the lentils, chicken or vegetable stock, cinnamon, cayenne pepper and seasoning. Cover and bring to the boil, then reduce the heat and simmer for about 35 minutes, stirring occasionally. Remove the lid towards the end of the cooking if a large amount of liquid remains. If the lentils aren't quite cooked as the liquid evaporates, just add a little more stock or water. The lentils should have absorbed all the liquid at the end of the cooking. Taste and adjust the seasoning.

Rinse the aubergine and drain. Lay out on a tray and pat dry with a tea towel or kitchen paper. The aubergines may be griddled (my preference) or oven baked. Details of both methods are given below.

To griddle the aubergines

Preheat the griddle pan until very hot. When the griddle is beginning to smoke, turn down the heat slightly. Fill a small ramekin with some light olive oil. With a pastry brush, paint the aubergine slices on one side (do this in batches – I only paint as many as will fit on the griddle) and place them oiled side down on the griddle. Keep the heat high and cook the aubergine slices until golden on the

underside. Paint the top side with olive oil and season with salt. (All of the salt will probably have been washed off during the pre-salting process. However, if you have pre-salted the aubergine for as long as an hour, there may be a slight residue left, so always taste a small piece of aubergine before seasoning.) Turn the aubergines over and cook on the other side until golden and tender. The aubergines should no longer be white on the surface – when cooked properly, they become more translucent. Remove from the griddle and set aside until you're ready to put the dish together.

Roasting aubergine slices in the oven

Preheat the oven to 220°C, 200°C Fan, 425°F, Gas 7. Line a baking tray with parchment paper. Place the aubergine slices in a large bowl, drizzle olive oil over the slices and mix. Season with sea salt and mix again. Lay the aubergine slices on the tray in a single layer. Using a pastry brush, paint some extra olive oil on any slices that look dry. Roast in the oven for 20–25 minutes. Check after 15 minutes in case they need to be turned (one part of the oven may be hotter than the other). Remove from the oven when all the slices are well coloured. Leave to cool a little before using.

To make the béchamel sauce

Melt the butter in a medium saucepan and add the flour. Stir over the heat for about 1 minute. Gradually whisk in the milk and bring to the boil, then reduce the heat and simmer gently for a few more minutes. Add 2–3 tablespoons freshly grated Parmesan and seasoning.

To assemble the moussaka

Place half of the aubergine slices on the bottom of the baking dish, overlapping them slightly. Cover with the lentil mixture and top with the rest of the aubergine. Pour over the béchamel sauce and sprinkle the remaining Parmesan on top. Cook in the oven for approximately 30 minutes, or until heated through and lightly browned on top.

NOTE The moussaka may be made up in advance and refrigerated until ready to bake.

Caramelised Chicken with Oranges

This is one of those dinners that requires minimal work and makes for a great family meal. At the end of the cooking, the chicken pieces are golden and caramelised and have absorbed some of the orangey syrup. I generally serve this with rice and some crunchy vegetables on the side such as green beans, asparagus or purple sprouting broccoli, depending on the season. You may prefer to buy chicken legs and thighs instead of a whole chicken.

Serves 4

1 large chicken, divided into legs, thighs, wings and breasts, skin on

4 tsp Dijon mustard

salt

2 oranges, cut into wedges

½ onion, finely chopped

240ml orange juice

2 tbsp olive oil

4 tbsp soft light brown sugar

OVEN *Preheat the oven to 190°C, 170°C Fan, 375°F, Gas 5.*

Rub the chicken pieces with mustard and season. Place the pieces skin side down in an ovenproof dish large enough to hold them in a single layer. Add the orange wedges, onion, orange juice and olive oil. Place in the oven to roast for 20 minutes. Baste regularly.

Turn the chicken pieces over, skin side up. Sprinkle the brown sugar on the skin. Continue roasting and basting until the chicken is tender and golden brown. Chicken breasts will need about 30 minutes of total cooking time depending on thickness and thighs 40–45 minutes.

When the chicken is cooked, pour the chicken juices into a small saucepan. Tilt the saucepan and spoon the clear fat from the top and discard. If at this point there is still a lot of liquid, the sauce can be reduced by boiling it rapidly, which will also concentrate the flavour. Pour a little sauce over each serving.

PIZZAS

There are many things we love about the house we stay in when we are in the west of Ireland. It has a view of the crashing sea and is well placed to see incoming bright spells or storms. No house seems to adapt as well to the changing weather, offering us cosiness one minute and drawing us outside the next. We love the colossal fireplace and the greatest number of mismatched plates ever seen. We tolerate other features – such as the plumbing. Even the shortest burst from any tap leads to a loud scream from a scalded party in the shower. Sometimes this can help pass a few minutes on a rainy day.

The oven is something of a law unto itself but it does produce a great heat, and when you're making pizzas, a really hot oven is an important start. I dream of having a brick oven because of the extraordinary flavour it imparts to the dough. However, with a hot oven and a pizza stone, the base of the pizza will be cooked within a few minutes and will have a thin, crispy crust quite similar to that produced in a brick oven, so don't despair.

If you bake the pizza on a baking sheet, the dough will rise a little more in the oven, yielding a slightly thicker base with a more bread-like interior. This is still a very good pizza. Note that pizzas cooked on a baking sheet will take almost twice as long as times given in the recipes that follow.

My favourite pizzas seldom have a base of tomato sauce (though I always have some ready made for any requests). Grated Parmesan, pesto, crème fraîche or a syrupy red wine reduction can all be used as a base on which to scatter other ingredients. I like a light touch with the toppings and a light touch with the cheese. I don't want a pizza that fills me up with one slice.

Sundried
Tomatoes for a
pizza topping
Page 49

Basic Pizza Dough

Making pizza dough is straightforward and satisfying. The dough can be made by hand in a big bowl or whizzed up in a food processor. In either case, it will require a few minutes of kneading. The flavour and the lightness will be in a different league to any pizza base that you might buy.

Makes 750g prepared dough
  (enough for 3 x 25cm pizzas)

450g strong white flour

1 tsp salt

½ tsp caster sugar

7g fast-action dried yeast granules
  (1 sachet yeast)

olive oil

300–350ml warm water, or as
  required to make a softish dough

To make the dough

Place the flour in a food processor together with the salt, sugar and instant yeast. Turn on at full speed and add 2 tablespoons of olive oil through the feeder tube, followed by half the warm water in a thin stream. The dough will now have the consistency of breadcrumbs. Add the rest of the water little by little until the dough forms a ball and becomes soft and slightly sticky.

Alternatively, to make the dough by hand, place the flour in a large bowl with the salt, sugar and instant yeast and mix well. Drizzle in 2 tablespoons of oil and most of the warm water and mix by hand. Continue as above.

Scoop the dough out onto a lightly floured counter and knead for about 5 minutes, until smooth and elastic (see the 'How to Knead' section overleaf). When the dough has been kneaded, choose a bowl large enough to allow the dough to expand. Rub 1 teaspoon of olive oil around the inside of the bowl. Place the dough in the bowl and rub a drop of olive oil over the surface. Cover the bowl with cling film and leave to prove until it has doubled or tripled in size. This will take between 1 and 1½ hours. At the end of the proving time, the dough should look lighter, with air bubbles on the surface.

To preshape the pizza dough into rounds

Scoop the dough out onto a lightly floured counter. With a knife or a dough scraper, divide the dough into 3 or more pieces. 250 grams of dough is perfect for a 25cm pizza. Place one piece of dough on an unfloured section of the counter. Working with unfloured hands, cup your right hand over the dough and using a little downward pressure, move in an anticlockwise direction. The left hand is active too, guiding the movement with an open palm, aiding the rolling motion until the dough becomes perfectly smooth. Follow the same procedure with the remaining pieces of dough. Leave the dough on the counter to rest for about 10 minutes. If not to be used immediately, the dough can be put on a tray, covered and refrigerated for several hours. It should be brought back to room temperature over a period of at least a quarter of an hour before being rolled into shape.

Shaping the pizza by hand

Flour the work surface and flatten one piece of dough into a round, stretching with your fingers or using a rolling pin. The dough should be rolled quite thin if the pizza is to go on a pizza stone, a bit thicker if not.

If you are feeling more ambitious, then forgo the rolling pin and use your hands. Press the tops of your fingers into the dough just in from the edge to form an outer rim. Inside the rim, flatten the dough with the tips of your fingers and then, picking it up, gently use your thumbs to stretch the dough – not from the edge and not from the centre (you don't want to weaken the middle), but on that circle just inside the rim of the pizza. Don't get too hung up on making a perfect circle, but if a hole appears, pinch it together at an early point. You have the rolling pin at hand if your early attempts run into difficulty.

It's important to have all the toppings ready and to hand before transferring the dough to the pizza paddle (or light breadboard or quiche base), otherwise the dough may stick. Flour the paddle, place the dough on it and quickly add all the toppings. Shake the paddle to make sure that the dough will slide off easily. If it's sticking, loosen with a long metal spatula. Quick, confident, jerking movements of the wrist should make for an easy transfer. Practise with a small pizza if you are uncertain and you will be amazed at how proficient you will become.

HOW TO KNEAD

Kneading is a slow and rhythmic process. Flour the work surface lightly, dust your fingers even more lightly and you are ready to start. Put the four fingers of your working hand over the back of the dough, then lift and fold the dough towards you. Then, with the heel of the same hand, push the dough away from you. With your other hand cupping the side of the dough, give the dough a quarter turn. Then follow the same procedure, pulling towards you, pushing the dough away with the heel of your hand and each time giving it a quarter turn. Find your rhythm and keep going until all that stickiness is a thing of the past. Don't be tempted to continuously add more flour to the work surface – as you knead, the dough will become less sticky.

Pizza with Onions, Crozier Blue, Crème Fraîche and Rosemary Oil

Meltingly tender onions spread on a light base of crème fraîche form the base of this pizza, which is then topped with a blue cheese. A drizzle of rosemary oil just before serving adds a very special touch, but you could scatter some finely chopped rosemary over the pizza instead of the oil if you wish. Crozier Blue is the only blue cheese made from sheep's milk in Ireland. If you aren't a lover of blue cheese (though I strongly urge you to try this one – it's sensational), then substitute another type of cheese with a similar punch.

Makes 1 x 25cm pizza

250g pizza dough (page 93)

2 tbsp crème fraîche

about 40g grated Parmesan

140g slow-cooked onions
 (see below)

50g Crozier Blue cheese

rosemary oil (see recipe below) or
 ½ tsp chopped fresh rosemary

FOR THE SLOW-COOKED ONIONS
(makes enough for 2 pizzas)

800g onions

30g butter

1 tbsp olive oil

salt

OVEN *Preheat the oven to 250°C,
 230°C Fan, 475°F, Gas 9.*

If using a pizza stone, place the stone in a cold oven 1 hour before cooking and turn on the oven to its highest setting. A conventional oven setting is better for pizza, if you have the option.

To make the slow-cooked onions

Peel and halve the onions and slice into half rings. Heat the butter and olive oil in a large saucepan and add the sliced onions. Season with salt, cover with a lid and allow to cook over a gentle heat for about 40 minutes, stirring regularly. Remove the lid and continue cooking at a medium heat until all the liquid has evaporated. Scrape the bottom of the pot if the onions start caramelising on the bottom of the saucepan. Allow to cool. The onions will keep in the fridge, covered, for a few days.

To make the pizza

Preshape the pizza dough into a round (see page 94) and leave to rest for 10 minutes on an unfloured section of the counter.

Have all the topping ingredients ready. Roll out the dough to a 25cm round and place onto a heavily floured paddle or light wooden breadboard. Spread the crème fraîche over the base, leaving a 2cm border. Sprinkle a little Parmesan

over the crème fraîche and then spread the onions over the base. Put dots of Crozier Blue at intervals over the onions. As Crozier Blue is a strong cheese, only small amounts are required. Scatter over the chopped rosemary, if using. Dust the surface with some more Parmesan. Slide the palette knife under the dough to ensure that the dough isn't sticking, then quickly transfer the pizza to the stone. The pizza will take 5–7 minutes to cook.

When the pizza is cooked, remove from the oven and drizzle a little rosemary oil over the top. Serve immediately.

Rosemary Oil

200ml good-quality extra virgin olive oil
5–6 sprigs of fresh rosemary

Heat the oil and the rosemary together. Do not allow the oil to boil. When hot, turn off the heat and leave to infuse for 30 minutes. Strain the oil and discard the rosemary. Place a couple of sprigs of fresh rosemary into a bottle. Pour the infused oil into the bottle and seal. Keep in a cool place and use the oil within 6 months.

Pizza with Asparagus, Ricotta and Parmesan

This is a light, summery pizza making the best use of fresh asparagus. Spread some crème fraîche on the pizza base and add little clusters of ricotta flavoured with lemon and Parmesan. Other vegetables could be substituted for the asparagus, such as roasted peppers, griddled aubergine and blanched purple sprouting broccoli.

Makes 1 x 25cm pizza

100g ricotta

100g finely grated Parmesan cheese

20g chives, finely chopped

zest of ½ lemon

salt

12 asparagus spears (or if very thin, use 18)

250g pizza dough (page 93)

2 tbsp crème fraîche

OVEN *Preheat the oven to 250°C, 230°C Fan, 475°F, Gas 9.*

If using a pizza stone, place the stone in a cold oven 1 hour before cooking and turn on the oven to its highest setting. A conventional oven setting is better for pizza, if you have the option.

In a bowl, mix the ricotta with 50g of the grated Parmesan, the chopped chives and the lemon zest. Season and set aside.

Break off the woody ends from the asparagus and discard. Slice 3–5 of the asparagus spears crossways into fine slices and place in a bowl. Slice the remaining spears in half lengthways. If the spears are very thin, leave them whole.

Preshape the pizza dough into a round (see page 94) and leave to rest for 10 minutes on an unfloured section of the counter.

On a lightly floured counter, roll out the dough to a 25cm round and place on a lightly floured pizza paddle or breadboard. Spread the crème fraîche over the pizza base, leaving a 2cm border. Sprinkle half of the remaining grated Parmesan over the crème fraîche and then top with the sliced asparagus. Arrange the halved asparagus spears around the pizza. Divide the ricotta mixture into 6 balls and place around the pizza. Scatter with the remaining grated Parmesan.

Slide a palette knife under the dough to check that it hasn't stuck to the paddle. Transfer the pizza to the stone with a couple of jerking movements of the wrist. The pizza will cook in 5–7 minutes. Remove as soon as the base is lightly golden and serve immediately.

Pizza with Candied Shallots and Goat's Cheese

I love candied shallots. I often serve them as an accompaniment to meat dishes. The sweet and sour red wine jus that coats them is so intense that I wondered how it would work on a pizza. I tried it out with shallots and goat's cheese for a remarkable contrast and this is how I still like to make it.

Makes 1 x 25cm pizza

250g pizza dough (page 93)

1½ tbsp reduced red wine jus from candying the shallots

12 candied shallots (see page 102)

70g soft goat's cheese, such as St Tola

60g fresh mozzarella packed in brine, cut into very thin slices

3 tbsp freshly grated Parmesan cheese

OVEN *Preheat the oven to 250°C, 230°C Fan, 475°F, Gas 9.*

If using a pizza stone, place the stone in a cold oven 1 hour before cooking and turn on the oven to its highest setting. A conventional oven setting is better for pizza, if you have the option.

Preshape the pizza dough into a round (see page 94) and leave to rest for 10 minutes on an unfloured section of the counter.

Roll out the pizza dough to about 25cm in diameter and place on a lightly floured pizza paddle or breadboard. Drizzle a thin layer of the red wine jus on the base of the pizza, leaving a 2cm border. Coax the jus lightly, almost haphazardly, across the base. Arrange the candied shallots at intervals around the pizza. Place small knobs of goat's cheese in between the candied shallots. Scatter over the mozzarella and sprinkle Parmesan all over the pizza to finish.

Check with a palette knife to make sure that the base hasn't stuck to the paddle, then transfer the pizza to the stone with a couple of jerking movements of the wrist. Cook until the base of the pizza is golden, 6–8 minutes. Serve immediately.

Candied Shallots

Serves 4

16–20 shallots (ideally, small round shallots, not banana shallots, which are a lot larger)

15g unsalted butter

Salt

2 tbsp caster sugar

200ml red wine

60ml red wine vinegar

Peel the shallots carefully, leaving the root intact to keep the shallots from falling apart while cooking. Slice them in half through the root if they are large. Heat a medium saucepan over a moderate heat. Add the butter and when it begins to foam, add the shallots and season. Sauté gently until they turn golden in colour. Add the sugar and continue to cook for about 3 minutes, until the sugar begins to caramelise. Pour in the red wine and red wine vinegar. Cover with a lid and simmer for 10–15 minutes, or until the shallots are almost tender when pierced with a knife. Remove the lid and boil off any excess liquid so that the shallots become coated with the concentrated syrup. The syrup will still be a little runny at the end, though it will thicken as it cools. (If it becomes over-reduced, just add a tiny dash of water to loosen it.) Scrape onto a plate and set aside until cold. If the shallots are quite big, slice them in half through the root end.

NOTE Towards the end of the cooking, it's essential to watch the syrup like a hawk. If the syrup reduces too much, it can start to caramelise and burn.

Basic Tomato Sauce for Pizza

This is a basic, quick sauce that's handy to keep in small batches in the freezer so that you don't have to make it from scratch every time.

3 tbsp olive oil

2 garlic cloves, sliced into strips

1 x 700g bottle passata (crushed and sieved tomatoes)

1 level tsp caster sugar

salt

6–8 basil leaves

Heat the olive oil and garlic over a low heat in a frying pan. Do not allow the garlic to brown. Add the passata to the pan and season with the sugar and salt. Simmer until the tomatoes have reduced to a very thick sauce. Taste and fine tune the seasoning with salt and/or sugar, as required. Shred the basil leaves with a knife and add to the sauce.

Basil and Mint Pesto

A classic pesto is made with fresh basil leaves. The combination of basil and mint adds a stunningly fresh flavour.

140g fresh basil leaves

115g pine nuts

45–55g fresh mint leaves

70g Parmesan, freshly grated

225ml extra virgin olive oil (or more, depending on the consistency you need)

2 garlic cloves or 1 large clove, crushed (optional)

Whizz the basil, pine nuts and mint in a food processor just to the point at which they form a rough paste. Do not overprocess. Remove from the food processor and mix in the rest of the ingredients. Pack into a sterilised jar and keep covered with a layer of oil.

Alternatively, make the pesto in a pestle and mortar by first pounding the basil and mint leaves until they form a paste (it's easier to add the leaves in stages). Add in the pine nuts and crush them, then mix in the oil, garlic and Parmesan.

Pesto will keep in the fridge for a week or more if you keep it covered with a fresh film of olive oil. Always pack the pesto down with the back of a clean metal spoon and wipe down the sides of the jar with some kitchen paper after each use.

Harissa

This is a basic, quick sauce that's handy to keep in small batches in the freezer so that you don't have to make it from scratch every time.

250g long red chillies

3 garlic cloves

2 heaped tsp cumin seeds, ground

pinch of salt

100g piquillo peppers (or roasted and peeled red peppers)

2 tsp tomato purée

2 tsp red wine vinegar

4 tbsp olive oil

2 level tsp smoked paprika

Slice the top off the chillies, then halve them lengthways. Scrape out the seeds and discard. Blend the chillies in a food processor with the garlic cloves, ground cumin seeds and a pinch of salt until completely smooth. Add the peppers, tomato purée and vinegar and blend again until very smooth. Transfer to a mixing bowl and stir in the olive oil and paprika. Taste and adjust the seasoning.

Pour into a sterilised jar and pour a film of olive oil over the top. Harissa will keep for several weeks in the fridge if topped up with a fresh film of olive oil after each use.

Turkish Pizzas with Lamb and Harissa

I call this my "Turkish" pizza. It was inspired by a trip to Turkey when a mountain family shared their supper with me. I had found amazing bread at a market and, through gesticulation, I asked if I could see how it was made. It turned out to be quite a trip to the village. There were some hurdles as an unaccompanied woman, some time delays as they went to prayer and some language difficulties, all of which were generously overcome. After detailed explanations about the bread, it was actually the pizza they shared with me that caught my attention. The villagers had little in the way of material goods, but they had made a large communal brick oven, which reflected the priority they gave to their food. This is a variant of their meat pizza, with my own homemade harissa (see page 103). Bought harissa won't have the necessary depth of flavour.

Makes 3 x 25cm pizzas or 5 smaller
  pizzas

FOR THE DOUGH

about 225g natural yoghurt

150–180ml warm water

1½ tsp dried yeast

450g strong white flour

1 tsp salt

pinch of caster sugar

4 tbsp extra virgin olive oil

TOPPING INGREDIENTS FOR
3 X 25CM PIZZAS

1 onion

330g minced lamb

2 garlic cloves, crushed

3 tsp pomegranate molasses

¾ tsp ground cinnamon

¾ tsp allspice

¾ tsp ground cumin

salt

60g toasted pine nuts
  (see page 25)

120g fresh tomatoes, deseeded
  and finely chopped

6 tbsp homemade harissa
  (see recipe on page 103)

TO GARNISH

400g Greek yoghurt

fresh coriander leaves

2 red chillies, sliced into rings

OVEN *Preheat the oven to 250°C,
  230°C Fan, 475°F, Gas 9.*

If using a pizza stone, place the stone in a cold oven 1 hour before cooking and turn on the oven to its highest setting. A conventional oven setting is better for pizza, if you have the option.

To prepare the yoghurt dough

Heat the yoghurt in a saucepan or in the microwave until warm to the touch. Pour 150ml warm water into a jug and sprinkle on the dried yeast. Leave to dissolve for about 5 minutes and stir to mix. Place the flour, salt and sugar into a large bowl. Gradually mix in 4 tablespoons of olive oil, the yoghurt and the yeast and water mixture until the dough comes together into a soft ball, adding extra water as necessary. Remove from the bowl onto a lightly floured surface and knead for about 5 minutes. In a clean bowl (one large enough to allow the dough to expand), pour in 1 teaspoon of oil and rub all over the inside of the bowl. Place the dough in the bowl and rub a drop of olive oil over the surface of the dough. Cover with cling film and leave to prove until it has doubled or tripled in size. This will take between 1 and 1½ hours. At the end of the proving time, the dough should look lighter, with air bubbles on the surface.

To make the topping

Finely grate the onion and then drain the juices in a sieve. Place the lamb in a bowl and add the onion, garlic, pomegranate molasses, cinnamon, allspice and cumin. Season well and mix all the ingredients together. Add in the toasted pine nuts and chopped tomatoes. Refrigerate until ready to use.

To make the pizza

Once the dough has risen, remove from the bowl onto a lightly floured surface. Divide the dough into 3 or more pieces, depending on your preferred size. Preshape the pieces of dough into a round (see page 93) and leave to rest for 10 minutes on an unfloured section of the counter.

Roll or stretch the dough into a round, or if you're making smaller pizzas, shape in true Turkish style by stretching the dough into a teardrop shape. The dough should be about 3mm thick.

Place the dough on a lightly floured pizza paddle or breadboard. Spread harissa thinly over the base, leaving a 2cm border. Crumble over the mince mixture, breaking up any larger pieces.

Check with a palette knife to make sure that the base hasn't stuck to the paddle, then transfer the pizza to the stone with a couple of jerking movements of the wrist. Cook until the base of the pizza is golden, about 6 minutes on the stone. If cooking on a baking tray, the pizzas will take twice as long. Remove from the oven and place spoonfuls of yoghurt over the top. Scatter over coriander leaves and slices of red chilli as a garnish and serve immediately.

BARBECUE

There is a point in many Connemara evenings when it seems to go still. The wind dies down, the waves stop crashing and the light seems to glow against the hills. Someone will light the barbecue. It's not easy to cook a whole meal on a barbecue, but it's a wonderful ritual for cooking either the main attraction (perhaps some meat or fish) or a vegetable accompaniment.

At the cookery school we have gas barbecues, but over in the west of Ireland, I use charcoal. Is there a big difference in taste? I was surprised at the answer to this question. A few years ago, Weber invited me over to their barbecue school outside Oxford. They asked a group of us to do a blind tasting between gas and charcoal, and as they suspected, none of us could tell the difference – which was horrifying for the diehard charcoal users.

It's important to control the heat of a charcoal barbecue. This is partly achieved through mastering the air vents and partly through keeping the lid down so as to create convective heat – the heat radiating off the coals, bouncing off the lid and going round and round the food, cooking the food rather than just searing the outside. It's also important to know when to have coals on just one side of the barbecue. This offers the choice of a higher and direct heat on one side and a less direct heat on the other. This is vital for larger pieces of meat, which can easily burn on the outside and yet not be cooked all the way to the centre.

My main reservation with a charcoal barbecue has always been that at the critical moment, the coals can burn out, leaving me high and dry. My best investment has been a 'chimney', which is like a big metal jug with a wire rack at the bottom and holes up the side. The coals light easily and evenly and it allows you to add ready coals to the barbecue whenever you choose. It removes all worry that the heat source is about to die away.

A MEAT THERMOMETER

A meat thermometer is a very useful piece of kitchen equipment. It's the only accurate way of gauging the internal temperature of meat and is invaluable for testing large joints. To use, insert it into the thickest part of the meat, keeping it away from the bone, as this will give a false reading. It's always a shame to overcook a lovely cut of meat.

Sea Bass with Dill, Mustard and Madras Curry Powder

This marinade would work with any white fish, but it's important not to marinate the fish longer than a couple of hours, as the lime juice will start to cure the fish. Use plenty of dill or substitute fennel or chervil. The cooking time will be quite brief, as it's important to keep the fish moist.

Serves 6

4 sea bass fillets,
  about 120–150g each

salt

FOR THE MARINADE

60ml sunflower oil, plus extra
  for basting

40ml lime juice

3 tbsp chopped dill

1 tbsp wholegrain mustard

2 tsp Madras curry powder
  (or substitute another curry
  powder)

½ tsp ground turmeric

Put all the marinade ingredients in a bowl. Season the fish with salt and add to the marinade. Leave to marinate in the fridge for 1 hour.

To cook, place the fish flesh side down on a hot barbecue. Cook for a few minutes and then turn over onto the skin side for another minute or two. The timing will depend on the thickness of the fish.

Butterflied Leg of Lamb Marinated with Spices

A butterflied leg of lamb is one from which the bone has been removed. Unless you have some serious knives and plenty of experience, this is best left to the butcher. I always marinate the leg at least a day in advance.

It's easy to have high heat on a gas barbecue to seal the meat on either side, but it requires more attention on charcoal. Once the outside has been exposed to a higher heat, the lamb should be moved so that it can continue cooking over less direct heat. The thinner bits can be carved off at an earlier point.

Serves 6–8

1 leg of lamb, butterflied (ask your butcher to prepare it for you)

6 garlic cloves, coarsely chopped

1 medium onion

80g fresh ginger, peeled and coarsely chopped

175ml lemon juice

200ml olive oil

1½ tbsp ground coriander

1½ tbsp ground cumin

1½ tsp salt

1 tsp garam masala

1 tsp ground turmeric

½–1 tsp cayenne pepper (optional – use less if you like, or none)

½ tsp ground cinnamon

¼ tsp freshly ground black pepper

Using the point of a boning knife or a utility knife, remove the surface skin from the leg and any excess fat or sinew.

Put the garlic, onion, ginger and lemon juice in an electric blender and whizz to a smooth paste. Choose a bowl that will be large enough to hold the leg of lamb. Pour the paste from the blender and all the other ingredients into the bowl. Mix well. Add the lamb and make sure that the paste gets rubbed thoroughly into the meat. Cover and refrigerate for 24–48 hours. Turn the meat at least twice during this period.

Cooking the lamb on the barbecue

Lift the meat from the bowl, reserving the marinade. Place on a hot barbecue grid and sear for about 10 minutes on either side. If using gas, turn the heat down to medium; on charcoal, move the lamb onto a less direct heat. The meat will take a total of 40–50 minutes, but the exact timing will depend on the heat of the barbecue and how you like it cooked. Allow to rest for about 15 minutes before serving.

Marinated Chicken Skewers

These are very simple chicken kebabs. This is not an easy marinade to identify.

Serves 6

6 large chicken breasts

2 garlic cloves, crushed

125ml lime juice

60ml light soy sauce

60ml dark soy sauce, such as Kikkoman

2 tbsp peanut butter

1 tbsp dark brown sugar

1 tbsp Sharwoods medium curry powder

zest of 1 lime

pinch of chilli powder (optional)

oil, for brushing

Chop the chicken into large bite-sized chunks. Place all the ingredients in a dish that will neatly hold the chicken. Break up the peanut butter with a whisk as best you can. Put the chicken in the marinade and leave for about 24 hours. Thread onto skewers and brush with some oil. Place on a hot barbecue and sear on each side until tender, 10–15 minutes in total, depending on the thickness of the meat.

NOTE If using wooden skewers, they should be soaked in water for half an hour beforehand.

Butterflied Prawns with Olive Oil, Garlic and Flat-leaf Parsley

I have used both Dublin Bay prawns (if they are large) and black tiger prawns for this recipe. Butterflying prawns means partially cutting through the shell so that the flesh is exposed. The prawns cook nearly the whole way shell side down on the barbecue so that the shells themselves become charred, imparting a lovely flavour to the flesh. Scooping the meat out and licking your fingers is a messy pleasure.

Serves 6

1kg Dublin Bay prawns or black tiger prawns, shell on

juice of 1 lemon

2 garlic cloves, finely diced

1 large red chilli, deseeded and finely diced

light olive oil, for marinating

sea salt

TO FINISH

12 cherry tomatoes, seeded and diced

½ red onion, finely diced

1 sprig of flat-leaf parsley, chopped

1 lemon

good-quality extra virgin olive oil, for drizzling at the end

If the prawns are complete with head, twist the head and the tail in opposite directions to separate them. Reserve the heads to add to a stock or shellfish sauce (see page 215). Place the prawn tails on a chopping board with their back uppermost. With a serrated knife, cut lengthways down through the shell, being careful not to cut the whole way through. Pick up the prawn and crack the shell just enough to reveal the flesh of the prawn itself but not enough to split it into two halves.

Arrange the prawns on a flat dish in a single layer. Sprinkle with the lemon juice, scatter over the garlic and chilli and drizzle generously with light olive oil. Marinate for up to 2 hours in the fridge.

Season the prawns with sea salt. Place them shell side down over a high heat on the barbecue. Spoon a little marinade over them as they cook. After 2 or 3 minutes, the prawns will start to shrivel, turn pinky-white and juices will collect in the shell. They should continue to cook until only the very centre remains translucent and raw. Quickly turn them over and grill on the flesh side for about 30 seconds for Dublin Bay prawns, 1 minute for tiger prawns. Dublin Bay prawns will cook much faster than tiger prawns, so watch them carefully.

As soon as the prawns are cooked, transfer them to a serving dish. Scatter with the tomatoes, onion and parsley. Add a good squeeze of lemon juice and a very generous drizzle of some good-quality extra virgin olive oil over the prawns. Leave to cool while the flavours blend. Do not refrigerate if serving within a couple of hours.

BARBECUE AT THE COOKERY SCHOOL

Our first barbecue at the school was a memorable affair. There is a yard at the back shared with our neighbours in business. It's a mass of girders, skips full of bits of carpet and pallets of paper (giving some indication of what they do). It's not the prettiest of sights. Faithful Slavik, who can make or adapt anything, had his work cut out for him, but he fashioned a series of poles that could be screwed into the ground and between which rolls of green baize billowed gently. It looked splendid. When we had finished, all you could see was the blue sky, the green surround and the sleek barbecues.

On the appointed night, the wind and rain were of biblical proportions. We could barely open the back door. Within half an hour, the poles unhitched themselves one by one and the green baize was flattened against all the aforementioned skips and pallets. The barbecues stood isolated. There was no choice but to continue. The ever-unflappable Gerry stood outside, and grabbing onto what they could, the group went out to join him. Umbrellas soon went the way of the green baize. I did what any self-respecting chef would do and poured large quantities of alcohol into anyone still able to hold onto a glass. It's still talked about as one of the great evenings. Good food conquers all.

Spiced Hoisin Ribs

Most ribs have so little meat that it can feel like you're just licking the marinade off the bone. The ribs I use come from the pork belly. This is a cut with plenty of meat and enough marbling of fat to keep them moist. Pork belly is a braising cut, so it requires long, slow cooking. My solution is to marinate the ribs overnight, cook them for a few hours in the oven until tender and then to finish them on the barbecue, where the marinade caramelises to a lovely sticky glaze.

Serves 6

pork spare ribs – allow 2 per person

MARINADE FOR 12 SPARE RIBS
280g dark brown sugar
30g fresh ginger, grated
12 garlic cloves, crushed

160ml hoisin sauce
160ml dark soy sauce
80ml medium-dry sherry
1½ tsp Chinese five spice

OVEN *Preheat the oven to 160°C, 140°C Fan, 325°F, Gas 3 after marinating the meat.*

Mix all the ingredients for the marinade together. Place the ribs in the marinade and leave for several hours or overnight.

Place the pork ribs along with the marinade in a deep roasting dish. Cover the dish with tinfoil. Braise the pork ribs in the oven for about 3 hours, or until the ribs are meltingly tender. If the ribs are not fully submerged in the marinade, then turn them over during the cooking. The meat should pull away from the bone easily when cooked. The timing can vary considerably, so check them regularly. The ribs may be prepared up to this point in advance, cooled and then refrigerated.

To cook the ribs on the barbecue, place them directly onto a hot grid. Cook for about 10 minutes on each side, or until the glaze is beginning to caramelise on the bones. Brush with the marinade during the cooking. The glaze can burn if the heat is too high, so a moderate heat works best.

Roast Vegetables with Red Pepper Harissa

While the barbecue is sizzling away, you might roast some vegetables in the oven. Choose a selection of vegetables such as red pepper, aubergine, courgette, red onions, butternut squash, sweet potatoes or new potatoes. Chop the vegetables into rough chunks. Place them on a roasting tray, but keep the vegetables separate, as the cooking times will vary. Drizzle over some olive oil, sprinkle with sprigs of thyme or rosemary and season with salt and pepper. Place in a preheated oven at about 200°C, 180°C Fan, 400°F, Gas 6 and roast until tender. Baby tomatoes can be added towards the end of the cooking.

You can roast the vegetables in advance and then skewer them like vegetable kebabs. About 5 minutes before serving, brush them with olive oil and place on the barbecue to reheat them. The kebabs can be brushed with the red pepper harissa before placing on the barbecue or drizzled with the sauce after cooking. (This red pepper harissa sauce is very different to the harissa recipe with the Turkish pizza on page 105). The preserved lemons (see page 171) can be omitted, though they definitely add another dimension. You can add more chillies to this sauce if you would like it hotter.

3–5 red chillies	60ml white wine vinegar
3 garlic cloves	2 tsp roasted cumin seeds, ground
3–5 roasted red peppers or tinned piquillo peppers (see page 28 on roasting peppers)	2 tsp roasted coriander seeds, ground
50g rind of preserved lemons, chopped (see page 171 for a recipe for preserved lemons)	1 tsp thyme leaves
100ml olive oil	salt and freshly ground black pepper

Chop 3 red chillies and the garlic. Place the chillies, garlic and roasted red peppers in a food processor and blitz until they are chopped finely. Add in the rest of the ingredients and pulse. Taste and add the remaining 1 or 2 chillies if you would like a little more heat. Chillies vary in intensity, so it's best to start with less heat and build it up according to your preference. Taste and add more vinegar if you would like a little more piquancy.

BAKING

My preferred stop in Clifden isn't the supermarket, but The Connemara Hamper, a treasure trove of artisan pâtés, breads and cheeses. Though she doesn't see me for fifty weeks of the year, Eileen always gives me the greeting of the dearest of friends.

On one of my first visits to the shop, I had arrived late and had found the shop closed. I was disappointed. I had ordered salami, which, for reasons that have never been explained to me, the shop staff always refer to as 'the plank'. There was a note that I should go to the pub next door and pay her another time. Not knowing my name, a package had been neatly set aside with a message that 'Mrs Plank' would collect it. The name has stuck.

I can buy plenty for a picnic at Eileen's, but Mrs Plank likes to do her own baking. It's not just the great aromas of fresh baking through the house – I know that the results will lift the day. On top of a mountain with a hot thermos, watching the clouds scud across the sky, or huddled in towels, wondering what possessed us to go for a swim, fresh baking will always make us feel as if the sun has come out.

Chocolate
Oatmeal Cookies
Page 130

Loaf Cake with Orange, Raisins and Sherry

I love to have a cake on a picnic. This is homely on the one hand and yet quite sophisticated on the other. And you thought no cake could be both.

Makes 1 loaf cake

110g raisins

4 tbsp sweet sherry

225g butter, at room temperature

225g caster sugar

4 eggs, beaten

190g plain flour

1 tsp baking powder

Pinch of salt

60g ground almonds

2 tbsp orange juice

Zest of 2 oranges

½ tsp vanilla extract

FOR THE ORANGE GLAZE

50ml orange juice

25g caster sugar

EQUIPMENT *900g loaf tin*
OVEN *Preheat the oven to 180°C,
160° Fan, 350°F, Gas 4.*

Line the loaf tin with some baking parchment.

Put the raisins and the sherry in a small saucepan and bring up to the boil. Remove from the heat and allow to cool.

Cream the butter and sugar together with an electric whisk until light and fluffy. Beat the eggs together in a small bowl and add the eggs to the butter mixture little by little, beating well between each addition. Sieve the flour, baking powder and salt into a bowl and add the ground almonds. Mix the orange juice, grated zest and vanilla extract with the raisins. Fold the dry ingredients and the raisin mixture alternately into the creamed butter mixture. Scoop the cake batter into the loaf tin and spread it out evenly. Bake in a preheated oven for about 55 minutes, or until a skewer inserted into the centre of the cake comes out clean.

Place the orange juice and sugar together in a saucepan and bring up to the boil. Boil for a couple of minutes to thicken the glaze slightly. When the cake comes out of the oven, brush the glaze over the top of the cake. Leave to cool in the tin for about 5 minutes and then remove the cake to a wire rack.

Biscotti with Dried Apricots and Cranberries

Some years ago, I paid a visit to an Italian cookery school counterpart in Milan. I was delighted to find that she had her own pastry shop. Lined up on rows of shelves were huge glass jars of biscotti. There was a great choice (anise, almond, orange, chocolate and so on) and customers would make up a selection, which would be wrapped carefully in shiny brown paper. The rows of jars and the ritual of the assortment brought me back to the sweet shops of my childhood.

Biscotti are not like other biscuits. They are baked twice so that they dry out and are generally dipped into dessert wine, such as the Italian vin santo, or coffee. I love their hard crunch.

The recipe below is my all-time favourite and makes a big batch so you may want to reduce the quantities. Store the biscotti in airtight jars and they'll keep happily for several months. Change the proportions of fruit and nuts as you like.

I'm sure that in the sophisticated shop in Milan, they would find it hard to envisage me savouring my biscotti, my back against a warm Connemara rock, tea in hand, surveying the colours of the sea.

500g plain flour

500g unrefined caster sugar (this is important for the flavour – it's available in most supermarkets)

1 tbsp baking powder

5 eggs, lightly beaten

200g dried apricots, sliced

100g plump sultanas

100g pitted dates, chopped

100g dried cranberries

100g whole blanched almonds chopped in three or whole pistachios

zest of 2 lemons

OVEN *Preheat the oven to 180°C, 160°C Fan, 350°F, Gas 4.*

Mix the flour, sugar and baking powder in a large bowl. Beat the eggs together in a small bowl and add the eggs bit by bit to the flour mixture. You may not need all of the egg, so hold back the last bit. The dough appears very dry at first and then suddenly becomes very soft. Add the fruit, nuts and lemon zest and knead into the mixture.

Turn the dough out onto a heavily floured surface. Divide into 6 and roll into sausage shapes about 3cm in diameter. Place, at least 6cm apart, on baking trays lined with baking parchment or a silicone mat. Very lightly flatten each roll with your hand. Bake until golden brown, 20–30 minutes. Remove from the oven and leave for 10 minutes to cool and firm up. Reduce the oven temperature to 140°C, 120°C Fan, 275°F, Gas 1.

Gently remove the biscotti from the tray and place on a chopping board. With a serrated knife, cut the biscotti into 5mm slices and lay them side by side on the baking tray. Return them to the oven and cook for 12 minutes, then turn the biscotti over and cook for a further 10 minutes, until they are lightly golden. Cool on wire racks and then store in an airtight container. The biscotti will harden when cold.

Chocolate Biscotti

Use the recipe above but replace the fruit and nuts with dark chocolate chips and pistachios. Omit the lemon zest and add vanilla extract to the eggs.

480g dark chocolate chips
160g shelled, unsalted pistachios
2 tsp vanilla extract

SILICONE MATS

Silicone mats are an invaluable piece of baking equipment. No more endless crumpled bits of baking parchment stuffed into the drawer that you plan to reuse but never do. They require no greasing and nothing ever sticks to them. Give them a wipe or wash them down after use, roll them up and pop them neatly back into a drawer. My suggestion is to buy two so that you can bake more at the same time. I would also suggest hunting down baking trays that are large enough to accommodate the mat.

Bran Muffins with Dried Cranberries

I like serious muffins and these bran muffins are my current favourite. Crème fraîche gives a lovely crumbly texture and the best result, but I usually use low-fat natural yoghurt.

Makes 10

100g unsalted butter, at room temperature

75g soft light brown sugar

1 large egg, beaten lightly

240ml crème fraîche or natural yoghurt

3 tbsp treacle or 2 tbsp dark molasses

140g plain flour

100g dried cranberries or raisins

50g bran

1 tsp baking soda

¼ tsp salt

EQUIPMENT *10 muffin cases, a 12 bun muffin tin*
OVEN *Preheat the oven to 200°C, 180°C Fan, 400°F, Gas 6.*

In a large mixing bowl, cream together the butter and brown sugar with an electric whisk until the mixture is light and fluffy, then beat in the egg, crème fraîche and treacle.

In a separate bowl, mix together the flour, cranberries, bran, baking soda and salt. Add the dry mix to the wet and stir the batter until it's just combined. Do not over-mix. Spoon the batter into muffin cases and bake the muffins in the middle of a preheated oven for 20 minutes, or until they are golden brown and springy to the touch. Turn out onto a rack and allow to cool.

Ten seconds in a microwave the following day, and they will taste as if they have just been taken out of the oven.

Biddy's Apple Cake

There are some recipes that you cannot put a value on, but this one you can. It's a €1,000 cake. A friend of old whom I had not seen for some years turned up at the school for a cookery course with a voucher for that amount. She had entered a Bord Bia (Irish Food Board) competition for ways to use Bramley apples (cooking apples) and had walked off with the prize for this simple but gorgeous apple cake. Is it worth that amount? Absolutely.

Serves 6-8

220g caster sugar

110g self-raising flour

110g ground almonds

1 tsp baking powder

3 eggs, beaten

140g butter, melted

2 medium cooking apples, peeled, cored and cut into slices or chunks

flaked almonds, to decorate

EQUIPMENT *20cm springform pan with removable base*

OVEN *Preheat the oven to 160°C, 140°C Fan, 325°F, Gas 3.*

Line the base of the cake tin with a circle of baking parchment. Butter and flour the sides of the cake tin and shake out the excess.

Mix the sugar, flour, ground almonds and baking powder together in a bowl. Add the beaten eggs and melted butter and stir well.

Put one third of the batter into the cake tin. Place a layer of apples over the batter and then spoon the rest of the batter on top. Sprinkle the surface with flaked almonds. Bake in the oven for about 50-55 minutes, or until a skewer inserted into the centre comes out clean.

Cinnamon Pull Apart Bread

There is a protracted ritual about this bread that I like – it really heightens the anticipation. Once the yeast dough has risen, the dough is rolled out and spread with a combination of butter, cinnamon and sugar. The dough is cut into rectangles and they are stacked on top of each other, creating layers that can be peeled off as you eat. I think the bread should always be served warm or reheated in tinfoil. Devour it on the day it's made.

Serves 6-8

FOR THE DOUGH

140ml milk

22g fresh yeast or 2 tsp dried yeast

60g unsalted butter

2 large eggs, at room temperature

1 tsp vanilla extract

400g strong white flour

½ tsp salt

30g granulated sugar

sunflower oil, for greasing the bowl

FOR THE FILLING

150g dark muscovado sugar

2 tsp ground cinnamon

20g unsalted butter

EQUIPMENT *900g loaf tin*

OVEN *Preheat the oven to 180°C, 160°C Fan, 350°F, Gas 4.*

Warm 100ml milk so that it is tepid and add the yeast. Leave for about 5 minutes for the yeast to dissolve. Melt the butter and leave to cool until warm to the touch. Whisk the eggs together in a small bowl and add the vanilla extract. Mix the eggs, melted butter and milk and yeast together.

Place the flour, salt and sugar in a large bowl and gradually mix in the liquid ingredients until the dough comes together and is soft and quite sticky. Add the remaining milk if required.

Grease the inside of a large bowl with 1 or 2 teaspoons sunflower oil and place the dough in the bowl. Cover the bowl with cling film and leave the dough to rest until doubled in size, about 1 hour to 1½ hours.

For the filling, mix together the sugar and cinnamon. Melt the butter and allow it to cool. When the dough has risen, roll the dough out to a 30cm x 50cm rectangle. Spread the melted butter across all of the dough. Sprinkle with the sugar and cinnamon mixture.

Grease the inside of a loaf tin with sunflower oil. Slice the dough vertically into 4 equal-sized strips. Stack the strips on top of one another and slice the stack into 6 equal squares. You should have 6 stacks of 4 layers. Layer the dough squares in the loaf tin like a deck of cards standing up. Place a tea towel over the tin and leave to rest in a warm place for about 30 minutes or until risen to the top of the tin. Bake for 30–35 minutes, until the top is a rich golden colour. Turn the bread out after about 15 minutes and leave to cool on a wire rack.

Chocolate Oatmeal Cookies

The pinhead oatmeal in these biscuits gives them their distinctive crunch. Very thin. Very crispy. Very delicious.

Makes 45 x 7cm cookies

230g soft light brown sugar

150g unsalted butter, at room temperature

1 egg, lightly beaten

2 tsp vanilla extract

125g plain flour

1 tsp baking powder

pinch of salt

240g pinhead oatmeal

175g chocolate chips

OVEN *Preheat the oven to 180°C, 160°C Fan, 350°F, Gas 4.*

Line 3 large baking trays with baking parchment or a silicone mat.

Cream the sugar and butter together in a bowl until fluffy and smooth. Add the egg and vanilla extract and beat until smooth. Sift the flour, baking powder and salt into the bowl and mix lightly. Add the oats and chocolate chips and stir to combine.

Scoop a tablespoon of dough at a time into balls and place on the baking trays. Flatten the balls with a fork dipped in flour. Bake the cookies for 20 minutes until pale golden. Remove from the oven and cool on the trays for 5 minutes before transferring to a wire rack to cool completely.

FREEZING COOKIE DOUGH IN PARCHMENT PAPER

Sometimes you might crave something sweet but not have the inclination to bake. For that reason, it is handy to make more dough than you need so that you have some for that rainy day. Cookie dough can be placed on clingfilm or parchment paper, rolled into a tight cylinder (with a diameter of about 5cm) and the ends twisted like a Christmas cracker.

Store the cookie dough in the freezer and slice off discs as you need them. Allow the dough to defrost for about 5 minutes so they do not crack. Place the discs straight onto a silicone mat or baking parchment and bake as suggested in the recipe. This method works for all sorts of other biscuit recipes.

Chapter Three

BRANCHING OUT

Build on your foundations and branch out in different directions. This chapter will bring you to shelves in the supermarket you never knew existed.

FIND OUT ABOUT THE VERSATILITY OF A FRITTER · HOW TO PRESERVE A LEMON OR STUFF A COURGETTE FLOWER · COOK MUSSELS · MAKE RICE SALAD WITHOUT RICE · PICKLE A CAULIFLOWER · BRAISE DUCK LEGS · MAKE A VELOUTÉ SAUCE · LEARN ABOUT QUINOA, SPELT AND SAFFRON

THE ROUX BROTHERS
AND BOILED CABBAGE

My mother-in-law is not only a wonderfully colourful character, but she has friends who are her match. Though they are in their nineties, they have a remarkable capacity to live in the present. It's not always easy to dig out the details of their fascinating lives. One of them, Hilary, had invited me over, ostensibly to give me some windfalls from her apple trees (a lure for me to do some weeding), when she casually referred to the day she had the Roux brothers to lunch. I nearly fell into the flowerbed.

I thought at first that she must be mistaken. At that time, Albert and Michel Roux had the only Michelin three-star restaurant in these islands and one of very few outside France. The story of how they had come to be eating at her table was one I knew would be highly entertaining – but it would have to wait.

My burning question was what on earth she had given them to eat. She pointed nonchalantly to her cabbages. She could tell from my face that I thought she was joking, so she filled me in on the details: corned beef, cabbage, new potatoes and lashings of parsley sauce. They had written to her the next day to let her know that they had not had a meal like it in years and how much pleasure it had given them. She felt they were being perfectly frank, and as I reflected on it, so did I. Knowing her as I do, I imagine they had a hilarious time and that they could not but have enjoyed such honest food in her company.

When friends are invited, I often think of Hilary. If she can give the Roux brothers her boiled cabbage, I realise that I shouldn't be fretting over what to feed anyone. I still love meat and two veg when someone else is doing all the work, but the fact is that this is not how I cook myself. The Irish food culture has changed more quickly than any I have encountered on my travels. We have surprised ourselves at our openness to influences and ingredients from all around the world. Here are some ideas for branching out.

STARTERS

Leek and Carrot Fritters with Roasted Butternut Squash Wedges and Mint Yoghurt

I have sometimes felt like a football scout trying to find talent before it's more widely recognised. Catch a chef early and you have a friend for life; leave it until he has a TV series and his personal assistant won't even take your calls. I had heard of Yotam Ottolenghi through a colleague in London, but by the time I got around to inviting him to the cookery school, so had half the world. I still send him the odd plaintive invitation. He still replies in person, so maybe I'll lure him yet.

The good news is that two staff who have recently joined our team at the cookery school came directly from working in his restaurants and we are relishing our exposure to Middle Eastern ideas. These fritters are a good example.

Makes 10 x 10cm fritters

FOR THE BASIC MIXTURE

4–6 leeks, white part only and about 3cm of the pale green part (about 450g)

knob of butter

olive oil

3 shallots, finely chopped

salt

200g grated carrots

1 red chilli, deseeded and sliced

1 tsp ground coriander

1 tsp ground cumin

1 tsp caster sugar

¼ tsp ground cinnamon

25g chives, finely chopped

FOR THE BATTER

120g self-raising flour

2 tsp baking powder

1 egg

150ml milk

55g unsalted butter, melted

salt

1 egg white

FOR THE YOGHURT DIP

200g Greek yoghurt

20g fresh mint, chopped

1 garlic clove, crushed

zest of 1 lime

1 tbsp lime juice

1 tbsp good-quality extra virgin olive oil

salt

roasted butternut squash wedges (page 140), to serve

To prepare the basic mixture

Split the leeks in half and wash the leaves under running water to remove any grit. Place the halved leeks on a chopping board and slice finely into rings. Heat a knob of butter and 1 tablespoon of olive oil in a saucepan, and when hot, add the leeks and shallots. Season with salt, cover with a lid and cook slowly for about 5 minutes. Add the carrots and chilli and cook again, until the leeks and carrots are softened, about 10 minutes. Add in the coriander, cumin, sugar and cinnamon and cook for 2–3 minutes to incorporate the flavours. Mix in the chives, taste for seasoning and adjust as necessary. Leave to cool. The leek mixture may be made in advance up to this point.

To make the batter

Place the flour in a bowl along with the baking powder and make a well in the centre. Mix the egg and milk together, then pour them into the middle. Using a hand whisk, gradually draw the flour in from the sides until all the flour has been incorporated. Add in the melted butter and season with salt. Pour the batter over the leeks and carrots and stir to combine. Finally, using a hand whisk or electric beater, whip up the egg white until stiff and fold it in with a spatula.

To make the yoghurt dip

Mix the yoghurt and all the other ingredients in a bowl. Do not overmix. Season with salt. Refrigerate until ready to use.

To cook the fritters

Heat 2 tablespoons of olive oil in a frying pan over a medium heat. When hot, spoon a heaped tablespoon of the batter into the pan to create a fritter about 10cm in diameter. The exact size of each fritter isn't important. Cook on a medium heat until the fritters are golden on the bottom. Turn over and cook on the other side. Transfer the fritters to a baking tray. Cover with foil and keep warm in a low oven. Alternatively, the fritters can be made in advance, left to cool and reheated in tinfoil. Serve with the yoghurt dip and roasted butternut squash wedges.

Roasted Butternut Squash Wedges

Serves 6–8

2 butternut squash

4 tbsp olive oil

sea salt and freshly ground
  black pepper

OVEN *Preheat the oven to 220°C,*
  200°C Fan, 400°F, Gas 6.

With a large knife, top and tail the butternut squash and then peel with a
vegetable peeler. Cut in half across the middle. Stand the top piece on its end
and cut it down through the centre, then cut each half into 2 or 3 wedges,
depending on the size of the squash. It's important to cut into even-sized pieces
so they cook evenly. (The wedges should be about 2cm at their widest part.)
Slice the bottom of the squash in half and scoop out the seeds. Cut into similar-
sized wedges.

Place the wedges in a large bowl and drizzle with the olive oil. Season well. Toss
and then place onto a baking tray lined with parchment. Spread out the slices so
that they have plenty of room to roast.

Roast in the oven for 20–25 minutes. They should have taken on plenty of
colour and be tender when pierced with a small knife. Remove from the oven
and allow to cool a little before handling and serving.

Roasted Nectarines with Buffalo Mozarella, Walnut Pesto and Rocket

Pomegranate molasses is made by boiling down the juice of a tart variety of pomegranate to a thick syrup. It's an extraordinary ingredient, rich and luscious, tart and sweet all at the same time. It can be used as a marinade for meats or drizzled over roasted veggies. It adds an extra dimension to this salad, creating a balance between the milky mozzarella and the warm nectarines. Serve either on individual plates or on a platter on a sunny summer's evening.

Serves 6

6 ripe nectarines (or peaches)

sea salt

3 tbsp extra virgin olive oil

2 tbsp pomegranate molasses, plus extra for drizzling

120g rocket

3 x 125g balls of buffalo mozzarella

FOR THE WALNUT PESTO

110g walnuts, roughly chopped

75g freshly grated Parmesan

120ml good-quality extra virgin olive oil

OVEN *Preheat the oven to 180°C, 160°C Fan, 350°F, Gas 4.*

Split the nectarines in half, remove the stones and place on a baking tray lined with baking parchment. Rub all over with olive oil and sprinkle with a little sea salt. Roast in the oven for 15 minutes.

Meanwhile, to make the walnut pesto, place the walnuts on a baking tray and toast in the oven for 5–8 minutes. Set aside and leave to cool. Chop the nuts finely. Mix the Parmesan, walnuts and olive oil in a bowl.

Make the dressing by whisking together the olive oil, pomegranate molasses and sea salt. Place the rocket in a bowl. Just before serving, pour some dressing over the leaves just to coat.

To serve, place a bed of rocket salad on each plate and sit 2 roasted nectarine halves on top. Break up the mozzarella into chunks and place it around the leaves. Spoon over some walnut pesto and then drizzle with some pomegranate molasses.

NOTE An alternative way to prepare the nectarines is to griddle them. Preheat the griddle until smoking. Rub the nectarines with olive oil. Place flesh side down on the hot griddle for 2–3 minutes. Remove from the griddle and continue as above. See page 42 for tips on griddling.

Courgette Flowers with Goat's Cheese in Tempura Batter

When I worked in restaurants with their own kitchen garden, it was a joy to go and cut the male courgette flowers, which grow on their own stem. They are not just spectacular in colour, but they have a wonderfully subtle flavour. The female courgette flowers are much smaller but are equally prized and are generally sold attached to the courgette itself.

The last time I bought courgette flowers at a market, the grower told me that she picked them in the morning because the flowers would be open at that time and so much easier to stuff. By evening, they would be tightly closed and harder to handle.

I love to serve courgette flowers deep-fried with tempura batter. If the courgettes are not much bigger than a thick pencil, I deep-fry them with the flowers attached. If the courgettes are much larger, I cut off the courgettes and pan-fry them separately. A large variety of vegetables, such as cauliflower, aubergine, carrot and sweet potato (thinly sliced), also work well in tempura batter.

Makes about 8 flowers,
  depending on their size

200g soft goat's cheese, such as
  Fivemiletown or St Tola

40g Greek yoghurt

20g chives, finely chopped

zest of 1 lemon

8 courgette flowers

tomato chutney with star anise and
  cinnamon (page 148), to serve

FOR THE BATTER

100g plain flour

100g cornflour

100ml sparkling water

salt

sunflower oil, for deep-frying

EQUIPMENT *1 small plastic piping bag
  (or see the note on page 146).*

To prepare the filling

Place the goat's cheese and Greek yoghurt in a bowl. Beat with an electric or hand whisk for a few minutes to aerate the mixture. Mix in the chives and lemon zest and fill into a piping bag.

Carefully remove the stamens from the centre of the courgette flowers. Pipe some of the goat's cheese mixture into the centre of each flower, being careful not to overfill them. Twist the ends of the flowers gently. The flowers may be stuffed a few hours in advance.

To prepare the batter

Mix the plain flour and cornflour in a bowl. Whisk in the sparkling water and season with salt.

To cook the flowers

Line a tray with kitchen paper. Pour the sunflower oil into a wok (or saucepan) to a depth of about 6cm (or use a deep-fat fryer if you have one). Heat the oil to 180°C or 350°F. If you don't have a thermometer, test the temperature by dropping a small piece of bread into the oil. The bread should turn golden in 10–15 seconds. If the oil starts to smoke, turn down the heat and delay the cooking until it has cooled a little.

Dip the courgette flowers into the batter one by one and drop them straight into the hot oil. Cook only a few at a time. Deep-fry until the batter goes crispy. This particular batter stays quite pale even when fully cooked. If there are small courgettes attached to the flowers, it's best to deep-fry them both for a few minutes longer until the courgettes are tender but still with a bite. Remove the flowers (and courgettes) with a slotted spoon and drain on the kitchen paper. Serve immediately with the chutney.

A QUICK PIPING BAG

If you don't have any piping bags, use a ziplock plastic bag instead and snip off a corner with a scissors to create a 'nozzle'.

Tomato Chutney with Star Anise and Cinnamon

I love to serve this chutney warm. It's a perfect match for the gentle flavour of the courgette flowers and the crispy batter on page 145.

2 tbsp sunflower oil

1 onion, finely chopped

salt

2 garlic cloves, crushed

1 red chilli, seeds removed and finely diced

15g fresh ginger, grated

150g caster sugar

200ml white wine

200ml white wine vinegar

3 star anise

2 cinnamon sticks

650g cherry tomatoes

Heat the oil in a medium saucepan and add the onion. Season with salt, stir and then cover with a lid. Turn down the heat to low and cook until the onion has softened, about 10 minutes. Remove the lid and add the crushed garlic, chilli and ginger. Cook for another minute or two and then add the sugar, white wine, white wine vinegar, star anise and cinnamon sticks. Bring up to the boil and add the cherry tomatoes. Reduce the heat and simmer for about 20 minutes, until the tomatoes have softened and the liquid has thickened considerably. The skins of the tomatoes often become separated from the tomatoes themselves, so these can be removed if you wish. Taste to check the balance of sweet and sour. As vinegars will vary, you may need to readjust the seasoning, adding a little more sugar if it's too tart, a little more vinegar if it's too sweet.

Store the chutney in a sterilised jar. It will keep for a couple of weeks in the fridge.

SUPPER DISHES

Onion, Parma Ham and Taleggio Tart

In any field, some skills become redundant. I used to pride myself on my ability to make puff pastry, but there isn't much call for it now. In big kitchens they have huge rollers doing the job of my rolling pin, and in smaller kitchens they are likely to buy in high-quality ready-made puff pastry.

Classic puff pastry is made from just flour and butter, so check the ingredients before you purchase. Puff pastry is a great standby in the freezer, as you can rustle up a tart with all sorts of toppings in no time at all. Always keep the pastry well chilled, work quickly and return it to the fridge before cooking so that the butter does not soften. If you leave out the Parma ham, this is an easy way to make a quick vegetarian tart.

Serves 4–6

375g all-butter puff pastry

1 egg yolk

1 tsp cream

3 tbsp olive oil

3 medium onions, finely sliced

salt

2 tsp fresh thyme leaves (or lemon thyme if you have it)

150g Taleggio cheese (or use an Irish cheese such as Durrus)

85g Parma ham

fresh thyme sprigs, to garnish

tossed salad, to serve

OVEN *Preheat the oven to 220°C, 200°Fan, 425°F, Gas 7.*

If you have a pizza stone, place it in the oven and preheat it 30 minutes in advance.

Roll out the pastry into a 30cm x 25cm rectangle and place on a sheet of parchment paper. Draw a line with a knife to create a border about 2cm wide and score the border lightly in a criss-cross pattern. Prick the inner rectangle with a fork. In a small bowl, mix the egg yolk and cream together. Using a pastry brush, paint the edges of the tart with a little of the egg wash. Lift the parchment paper onto a tray and chill the pastry for 30 minutes in the fridge (or in the freezer for about 15 minutes).

Heat the oil in a heavy-based saucepan and add the sliced onions. Season with salt, cover and turn down the heat. Cook with the lid on for about 30 minutes, stirring occasionally, until the onions are completely softened. Mix in the thyme, then remove from the heat and allow to cool.

If you're not using a pizza stone, preheat a baking tray in the oven for about 10 minutes. Remove the tart from the fridge/freezer. Brush the edges of the tart with another layer of egg wash. Spread the onions over the base of the tart. Leaving it on the baking parchment, transfer the tart onto the preheated tray or pizza stone. Cook in the oven for about 15 minutes, until the edges of the pastry and the base are golden.

Meanwhile, remove the rind from the cheese and cut into slices. Remove any excess fat from the Parma ham and slice it into strips about 2cm wide. Remove the tart from the oven and drape the Parma loosely over the onions, followed by the strips of cheese. Return to the oven for another 5 minutes, until the cheese has melted. Garnish with sprigs of fresh thyme and serve immediately with a tossed salad.

PROSCIUTTO

Italian prosciutto is ham that has been dry aged for a period of nine months or up to two years. The two most famous types of prosciutto are prosciutto di Parma (hence Parma ham) and prosciutto di San Daniele. Prosciutto di Parma comes from the same region as Parmigiano-Reggiano, the most famous Parmesan cheese. The whey that is left over from making the Parmesan is sometimes fed to the pigs, which also contributes to the ham's distinctive flavour.

Pan-seared Sea Bass Fillet with Chorizo and Rocket and Pistachio Pesto

Sea bass have a skin, when cooked, that is beautifully crispy and this contrasts with the softness of the flesh. Be sure, however, that the skin has been descaled before cooking, or ideally, ask your fishmonger to do this for you.

The sea bass fillets that are readily available tend to be small. If you are lucky enough to find a larger wild sea bass, the fillets may be pan-fried initially and then transferred to a hot oven. This dish is simple, quick and very tasty.

Serves 4

4 x 150g fillets of fresh sea bass (fillet sizes will vary)

olive oil, for pan-frying

140g chorizo, cut into small chunks

24 cherry tomatoes, cut in half

salt and freshly ground black pepper

120g rocket leaves

30g pitted black olives (optional)

4 tbsp rocket and pistachio pesto (page 154) (or simply use a classic basil pesto instead)

EQUIPMENT *Non-stick frying pan for cooking the fish*

Remove the pin bones from the sea bass with a fish tweezers. Cut the sea bass fillets in half at an angle. Turn the fish over so that the flesh side is on the board. With a small sharp knife, cut 2–3cm gashes crossways on the skin of the fish, trying not to cut too deeply through the flesh. Set the fish aside until ready to use or refrigerate if preparing in advance.

Heat a frying pan and add a tiny dash of oil. Add the diced chorizo and cherry tomatoes. Turn down the heat to medium and cook until the fat has rendered out of the chorizo and the tomatoes have just begun to soften. Pull the pan off the heat.

Season the fish on both sides. Heat a non-stick frying pan until very hot. Add a dash of oil to the pan and as soon as it's hot, add the fish, skin side down. If the fish doesn't sizzle when it hits the pan, the oil isn't hot enough. Cook the fish over a medium heat, without moving it, until the edges of the skin start to go golden. This will probably take about 2 minutes. Peek at the underside of the fish when the edges start turning colour. Leave for another 30 seconds or longer, if necessary. Turn the fish over and cook briefly on the second side, about 30 seconds or so. It's important to keep the fish moist, so don't leave it in the pan longer than necessary. Remove to a warm plate, skin side up.

Meanwhile, quickly reheat the chorizo and tomatoes. Add in the rocket and the olives (if using). Toss and remove from the heat. Spoon some chorizo, tomato,

rocket and olives onto the centre of each plate. Top with 2 fillets of sea bass, one flesh side up and the other skin side up. Drizzle some of the rocket and pistachio pesto over the fish and around the plate. Serve immediately.

Rocket and Pistachio Pesto

When I worked in Liguria, one of my tasks was to pound the basil in a giant marble pestle and mortar to make the pesto. Making pesto by hand is more aromatic than that made in a food processor, so the extra effort is worthwhile.

Pesto originates from this area and the cultivation of basil from around Genoa is a source of intense pride. Commercial producers have even been awarded an appellation for their distinctive basil.

The classic version of pesto is made with basil, pine nuts, garlic, Ligurian olive oil, Parmesan and sometimes Pecorino Romano, an Italian sheep's cheese from Sardinia. You can ring the changes by substituting the basil with rocket, another herb or even wild garlic when in season. The pine nuts may also be replaced with other nuts, such as walnuts, pistachios, cashews or almonds.

For the fish dish on page 152, I like quite a dry pesto. If I'm using pesto with pasta, I prefer to add the larger quantity of olive oil.

Makes 375ml

2 garlic cloves

salt

60g shelled pistachios (about 100g unshelled)

60g rocket

40g freshly grated Parmesan cheese

200–250ml good-quality extra virgin olive oil

Crush the garlic finely with a little salt. Put the nuts in a blender and pulse until coarsely ground. Add the rocket and continue to pulse until you have a coarse paste. Scrape this out into a bowl, then stir in the garlic, Parmesan and oil. Taste for seasoning.

Pesto may be stored in a sterilised jar in the fridge covered with a film of olive oil for a couple of weeks.

Spanish Chicken with Rice, Saffron and Smoked Paprika

This is a one-pot chicken dish that uses of some favourite Spanish ingredients: paella rice, paprika and saffron. For a summer version, add some seasonal vegetables, such as asparagus or broad beans (blanched and added at the end), or for a vegetarian version, include some finely chopped leeks in the early stages. The amount of saffron and smoked paprika added to the dish will define the balance at the end, so trust your own taste.

Serves 4

olive oil

8 chicken legs or thighs, skin on

salt and freshly ground black pepper

1 large Spanish onion, finely chopped

1 red pepper, halved, deseeded and cut into strips

1 green pepper, halved, deseeded and cut into strips

3 garlic cloves, finely chopped

120g chorizo, sliced

250g Sollana or Bomba rice (see the box page 158)

¼ tsp fennel seeds (optional)

100ml Fino sherry or white wine

800ml chicken stock (page 30) or vegetable stock (page 32)

½ tsp smoked Spanish paprika

½ tsp saffron threads

Heat a wide frying pan and add 2 tablespoons of oil. Season the chicken with salt and pepper and place in the hot pan, skin side down. Cook over a medium heat until the chicken turns golden on the underside. Turn over and brown on the other side. Cook the chicken for about 20 minutes in the pan, keeping the heat at low to medium. (Alternatively, place the chicken pieces in an oven preheated to 180°C, 160°C Fan, 350°F, Gas 4 for about 15 minutes after browning.) Remove to a plate while you attend to the rice.

Add 4 tablespoons of olive oil to the pan and when hot, add the chopped onion. Season with salt and pepper and cook with a lid on for about 10 minutes, or until totally softened. Add the peppers, garlic and chorizo and cook for a further 5 minutes. Add the rice and fennel seeds (if using) to the pan and stir for a minute to coat with the vegetables and oil. Pour in the sherry or white wine and boil for a minute or two. (The rice will take approximately 20 minutes to cook from the moment that you add the liquid.) Add the stock and the smoked paprika.

Crush the saffron in a pestle and mortar and add a few tablespoons of hot stock or just pour the stock over the saffron. Pour the saffron and its liquid into the rice. Return the chicken to the pan and simmer gently for 15 minutes. Taste

the rice. It should not be fully tender yet, but this is the point to assess flavour. Consider adding a little more saffron (diluted with a few tablespoons of water) or another touch of smoked paprika. Cook for another few minutes, until the rice is tender but still with a bite. Serve immediately.

To use chicken breasts instead of legs and thighs

Chicken breasts cook much faster than chicken thighs and legs, so allow for a total of 15 minutes cooking time if they are large, less if they are small. The breasts may be cut into 2 or 3 pieces crosswise, seared off in the pan with a bit of olive oil until golden on the skin side and then removed and set aside. They should be added back into the rice about 10 minutes before the end of the cooking.

A LITTLE TASTE OF SPAIN

Premium rice

The very best rice in Spain is cultivated near the coast in Valencia or just further south. The two most interesting strains – Sollana and Bomba – almost died out, as they were slow growing and low yielding. They are now fully appreciated for their capacity to absorb liquid: the grains increase in size by almost 50% during cooking. The rice is sometimes packed by place name (such as Calasparra) and sometimes by the name of a family business (such as Sivaris) and this can get confusing. It's often easier to look out for the distinctive cloth sacks they are sold in.

Paprika and smoked paprika

Paprika is a spice made from ground pepper, chilli pepper or a combination of the two. There are many different types of paprika, each with their own flavour, some of which are more intense, more smoky or more fiery than others. I use a Spanish variety (which comes in distinctive red tins), Pimenton de la Vera. It comes in three varieties: *dulce* (mild and sweet), *agridulce* (moderately spicy) and *picante* (very spicy). This Spanish paprika has a distinctly smoked flavour and aroma, as it's smoke dried over oak wood. Note that Hungarian paprika is more intense, so much less would be required.

Saffron

Saffron comes from the stigma of a particular type of crocus. There are only three to each flower, which is why, by weight, it's the most expensive spice of all. However, only a tiny amount is required.

Saffron is produced in many of the Mediterranean countries. It is easily adulterated (particularly powdered saffron). You need to find a reliable source and develop a sense of how much (which, in fact, is how little) it takes to make all the difference. And remember, if you find cheap saffron, then it probably isn't saffron.

SIVARIS

DETAIL

ARROZ

Roast Chicken Breasts with Peas and Salsa Verde

As so many supermarkets these days sell skinless chicken breasts, it's often a revelation to taste chicken breast cooked with a lovely crispy skin. The skin keeps the chicken moist and adds enormous flavour and texture. Serve this dish in wide, deep soup bowls and a spoon on the side so that you get the last drop of the broth.

The salsa verde here is a variant of the salsa verde on page 51 – with the addition of mint and extra capers.

Serves 6

500g baby potatoes

sunflower oil

200g bacon lardons

400ml chicken stock (page 30)

6 chicken breasts, skin on (thick breasts about 220g in weight if available)

salt and freshly ground black pepper

3–4 sprigs of thyme

10g butter

220g frozen peas

FOR THE SALSA VERDE

15g mint leaves

15g chives

15g basil leaves

15g parsley, leaves only

1 garlic clove

3 tbsp capers, rinsed and dried

150ml extra virgin olive oil

1 tbsp lemon juice, or a little more if required

OVEN *Preheat the oven to 200°C, 180°Fan, 400°F, Gas 6.*

With the skin on, boil the potatoes until just tender but still firm. Drain and slice the potatoes into halves or quarters. Set aside until ready to use.

For the salsa verde, whizz the herbs and garlic in a food processor until finely chopped. Add the capers and whizz again. Finally, add the olive oil and lemon juice. Taste and season if required. With this many capers, salt probably won't be necessary.

Heat a pan and add 2 teaspoons of sunflower oil. Sauté the lardons until most of the fat has rendered out and the lardons are golden in colour. Drain on kitchen paper to remove the excess oil. Return to the pan, add the chicken stock and reduce by half. Set aside.

Season the chicken with salt and pepper. Heat 1 tablespoon of oil in an ovenproof pan and when hot, add the chicken, skin side down. Brown the chicken over a medium heat for 5–10 minutes, until the skin is a deep, rich golden brown all over. Add the sprigs of thyme during the cooking.

Add the butter to the pan and transfer the frying pan to the oven (or move the chicken to a baking tray or ovenproof dish if necessary). Cook in the oven for 6–8 minutes, depending on the thickness of the chicken. Remove and leave to rest for about 5 minutes. Reheat the broth, then add the peas and the baby potatoes. Simmer for a couple of minutes, draw off the heat and add a few tablespoons of the salsa verde.

Arrange the potatoes in the centre of a wide soup bowl and pour the pea broth around. Slice the chicken in half and place in the centre of the plate on top of the potatoes.

CHICKEN SUPREME

If you want a more stylish presentation, you can ask the butcher for a chicken supreme. This is the chicken breast with the wing tip attached. In restaurants, they cut off any of the meat attached to the wing bone, which gives the bone a clean look.

MOROCCAN

Tagine of Lamb with Raisins and Almonds

The word "tagine" refers both to the North African recipe and the conical-lidded pot in which it is cooked. In a traditional tagine, the meat or slower-cooking vegetables cook over the direct heat and the circulating hot air cooks the softer vegetables, which are piled on the top, allowing for all the ingredients to be ready at the same time. I am not presuming that you have such a piece of equipment to hand.

Moroccan tagines are not generally heavily spiced or particularly hot. They commonly include fruit, both fresh and dried, adding a natural sweetness that I love. In this instance, it is the raisins that add a fruity sweetness and take on the flavours from the meat and the sauce.

Serves 6–8

30g unsalted butter, melted

2 tbsp light olive oil

300g Spanish onions, chopped

salt

3 garlic cloves, finely chopped

1 tbsp finely chopped fresh ginger

1 tsp ground turmeric

1.3–1.6kg lamb shoulder, cut into 3cm chunks

2 whole tinned tomatoes, chopped

350ml chicken stock (page 30) or vegetable stock (page 32)

170g raisins

1 tbsp honey, or more to taste

TOASTED ALMONDS

2 tsp sunflower oil

70g whole blanched almonds

OVEN *Preheat the oven to 180°C, 160°C Fan, 350°F, Gas 4.*

Heat the butter and olive oil in a casserole pot and add the chopped onions. Season with salt, cover the pot with a lid and cook for about 10 minutes over a medium heat. Remove the lid and add the garlic, ginger and turmeric. Continue cooking for another few minutes and add the meat. Season the lamb and toss over a high heat until the lamb changes colour. Add the chopped tomatoes and the stock, adding a little extra if necessary so as to barely cover the meat. Bring up to the boil, place a lid on the pot and then transfer to the preheated oven. Cook the lamb for 45 minutes. Remove the lid and add the raisins. If the meat is looking a little dry, add in some extra stock. Return the pot to the oven and continue cooking for a further 30–45 minutes, until the lamb is tender.

Mix the honey into the sauce. Taste and add more seasoning if required and another drizzle of honey if you would like some extra sweetness. The tagine may be cooked in advance and served the next day. The almonds should only be added just before serving, otherwise they would lose their crunch.

To toast the almonds

Heat a frying pan. Add the sunflower oil, followed by the almonds. Toss for a few minutes, until the almonds become very lightly toasted. Scatter over the tagine just before serving.

Grilled Moroccan Aubergine with Honey and Harissa

The harissa you buy in tubes is largely chilli paste and is good for a burst of heat. The harissa that you make yourself will add many more shades of subtle flavour. With either, this is a glorious dish. The honey and lemon provide the sweet and sour elements and the sauce is heightened by the addition of freshly ground cumin.

Serves 4–6

2 aubergines

olive oil

salt

2–3 garlic cloves, crushed

40ml lemon juice

5cm piece of fresh root ginger, peeled and grated

4 tbsp clear honey

1 tsp freshly ground cumin

1 tsp harissa if bought or 1 tbsp if homemade (page 103 and 117), or to taste

Cut the aubergines in half and then cut each half lengthways into about 3 wedges, depending on the size of the aubergine. Keep the wedges a similar size. Heat a griddle pan until smoking. Using a pastry brush, paint both sides of the aubergine with olive oil, season with salt and place on the hot griddle. Cook until lightly browned on each side and then remove.

Alternatively, if you don't have a griddle, heat some olive in a frying pan and brown both sides of the aubergine wedges until golden. Remove from the pan and set aside.

In a clean frying pan, heat 2 tablespoons of olive oil and add the garlic. Cook for a few seconds and then stir in the lemon juice, ginger, honey, cumin and harissa. Lay the aubergines in the pan in a single layer and add enough water to cover the base. Cook the aubergines gently for 10–15 minutes, turning them over halfway through the cooking. By the end of the cooking, the aubergines must be totally tender. Test with the point of a sharp knife – there should be no resistance. If the liquid evaporates before the aubergines are ready, add another dash of water. At the end, you should be left with a thick glaze. If the liquid is too runny, reduce by boiling it for a few minutes. There should be a balance of sweet and sour as well as a kick from the harissa. Taste and adjust as necessary with more honey, lemon juice and/or harissa.

Fluffy Couscous

I have only once had a truly authentic Moroccan meal. What lingers with me is the intimacy of eating with my hands (just my right hand, as it turns out) from the shared pot.

Couscous can be prepared quickly, but it benefits hugely from a little more care. Allowing time for the grains to swell makes it much lighter. I always use the steaming method to accompany a tagine, but the quick method (see page 170) also works well.

Serves 6

450g couscous
sunflower oil
250ml water
1 tsp salt

30g butter, melted (optional)
2 ladlefuls of broth (chicken, lamb, beef) or water
sprinkling of chopped fresh coriander or parsley, to garnish

Rinse the couscous in a sieve under running water until completely moistened. Spread it on a flat dish and let it sit until the grains swell, 5–10 minutes. Break up any lumps by rubbing the couscous through your fingers.

Lightly oil the inside of the perforated bottom of a steamer and sit it on top of a saucepan filled with boiling water. When the steam is rising through the perforated holes, pile the couscous into the colander. (The rising steam will prevent the couscous from falling through the holes.) Cover and steam the couscous for 20 minutes.

Transfer the steamed couscous to a shallow, wide dish and sprinkle with the water and salt, forking it through as you pour. When it is cold enough to handle, oil your fingers lightly and run the couscous through your hands again. Cover with a damp tea towel. The couscous may be prepared to this point up to 3 hours in advance.

Before serving, steam the couscous for a further 25 minutes or so or, better still, steam the couscous over the pot of stew as it's simmering. Tip into a wide serving dish, add the melted butter (if using) and fluff the couscous with a fork. Moisten with 2 ladlefuls of broth and toss lightly. Sprinkle with some chopped coriander or parsley if desired.

Optional additions at the end

Add 1 teaspoon of harissa to 250ml of broth, a squeeze of lemon juice and a good pinch of cumin or coriander. Pour into a jug and serve separately.

Quick Couscous

This is a quick cook method for couscous.

Serves 6

450g couscous

1½ tbsp olive oil

820ml vegetable stock (page 32)
  or water

Place the couscous in a wide bowl and drizzle with the olive oil. Rub the oil through the grains with your hands so that they are lightly coated. In a saucepan, bring the stock to the boil and as soon as it boils, pour it over the couscous. Mix through quickly with a fork, cover with clingfilm and set aside for 10 minutes. Remove the clingfilm and use a fork to fluff up the couscous. Serve warm.

Chicken Tagine with Caramelised Apricots and Preserved Lemons

I went to a restaurant in San Francisco called Bar Tartine earlier in the year. Lined up on shelves beside our table were stacks of jars full of preserved lemons and pickled vegetables. When a chef takes the time to prepare such ingredients with care, it's generally a clear indication that you are going to eat well. The meal more than lived up to such expectation.

Preserved lemons are not an essential ingredient in this dish, but they are a great ingredient to experiment with and are available in specialty shops (or they can be made at home – see the next page). The tagine also includes apricots. Unsulphured dried apricots are worth buying if you see them in health food shops.

Serves 4

1 tsp ground cumin

1 tsp ground coriander

1 tsp dried chilli, chopped or crushed

8 chicken thighs (or use a combination
  of thighs and legs)

salt

30ml vegetable oil

1–2 onions, finely chopped

2 garlic cloves, finely chopped

20g fresh ginger, peeled and finely
  chopped

1 x 5cm cinnamon stick

1 preserved lemon, rind only, finely
  diced

1 x 400g tin whole tomatoes

100g dried apricots

150g green olives (optional)

fresh chopped coriander, to garnish

CARAMELISED APRICOTS

15g unsalted butter

1 tbsp honey

100g dried apricots

Mix the cumin, coriander and chilli together. Rub half of this mixture over the chicken thighs, season with salt and leave to sit for 15 minutes or longer.

Heat the oil in a pan and add the chicken pieces, skin side down first. (Brown in batches if necessary.) Cook for about 5 minutes, until the skin becomes coloured, then turn over and cook on the other side for a further 5 minutes. Remove the chicken from the pan. Add the onions, season with salt and cook for about 10 minutes to soften. Add the garlic and ginger, the remaining spice mix and the cinnamon stick. Stir to mix and cook for a few more minutes.

Return the chicken to the pot and add half of the preserved lemon along with the tomatoes, apricots and enough water just to cover the chicken. Bring up to the boil and then turn down the heat to a simmer. Cook with the lid off until the chicken is tender, about 30 minutes. Towards the end of the cooking, add in the green olives (if using) and the remaining preserved lemon. If the sauce is too runny, remove the chicken thighs and boil until it has a thicker consistency.

For the caramelised apricots

The apricots should be prepared at the last minute. Heat the butter and honey in a saucepan. Add the apricots and toss. Simmer for 5 minutes at a gentle heat, until the apricots are glossy and have absorbed the honey and butter. Scatter the apricots over the top of the tagine just before serving and garnish with the chopped coriander.

Preserved Lemons

You can buy preserved lemons to give an authentic taste of Moroccan cooking, but you can also preserve your own. It does require a little forethought though, as the lemons need to marinate for a month before use. In North Africa, they are widely used not just in tagines, but also in salads, where their saltiness and citrusy acidity are an extraordinary addition.

Makes a 1 litre jar

6 small lemons (preferably unwaxed) or 4 large lemons, for pickling

85–100g Maldon sea salt

6–10 lemons, for juicing

EQUIPMENT *1 litre preserving jar*

Scrub the 6 small (or 4 large) lemons with a brush under running water and dry thoroughly. Standing the lemons on a chopping board, quarter them from the centre top to within 1cm of the bottom.

Pour the salt into a large bowl. Holding one lemon at a time over the bowl, pick up some salt and push it into the quartered lemon. Don't be afraid of adding too much. You will end up having about 2 tablespoons of salt in each lemon. Push each lemon into the jar, pressing them down a little to release the juice. Repeat the process with the other lemons, pressing them down forcefully so that they will fit snugly together. Leave the jar covered overnight. Salt draws out moisture, so the lemons will soften a little. This may allow you to push another lemon into the jar the next day. The jar should be packed to the brim.

Juice the remaining lemons (you may need more or less) and pour the juice into the preserving jar until the lemons are completely submerged. Seal the jar. Keep the lemons in a dark place and shake every day for the first week to redistribute the salt that sinks to the bottom.

The lemons will be ready to use in a month and will keep for a year. Top up the lemon juice as required so that the lemons continue to be submerged. If you see a little bubbling on the side of the jar, this is part of the natural fermentation process. Before use, rinse the lemons under running water.

Salting will remove all or most of the bitterness, but this depends on the lemons. If there is a predominant bitterness when you bite into the rind, then remove the pith with a sharp knife. (Cut the lemon into quarters and sit the quarter on the board with the skin side down. Slide the knife under the pith or scrape it away with a teaspoon.)

It is generally the rind of the preserved lemon that is used and the pulp is discarded. However, you can use the whole lemon if you wish. If adding preserved lemons to slow-braising dishes like tagines, the longer the dish is braised with the preserved lemon, the more pronounced the lemon flavour will be. Depending on the dish, you may choose the timing of when to add it.

SIDES AND SALADS

Mixed Beetroot Salad with Pomegranate Molasses Yoghurt Dressing and Spicy Pecans

If you can find different colours of beetroot, they would add to the presentation here. But even with the regular red beetroot, this is an extraordinary salad. The real star of this dish is the dressing, which could be used in many other ways.

Serves 6–8

2.25kg beetroot, in a mix of red, yellow and candied, if available (or 1.5kg cooked beetroot)

20g chervil, roughly chopped

FOR THE BEETROOT MARINADE

120ml olive oil

120ml cider vinegar

50ml maple syrup or honey

salt

FOR THE SPICY PECANS

25ml olive oil

1 tbsp dark muscovado sugar

1 tsp ground allspice

1 tsp ground cinnamon

salt

120g pecans

FOR THE YOGHURT DRESSING

350g Greek yoghurt

1 small garlic clove, crushed

2 tbsp pomegranate molasses

1 tsp maple syrup

salt

OVEN *Preheat the oven to 200°C, 180°C Fan, 400°F, Gas 6.*

To prepare the beetroot

Wash the beetroot, place in a roasting tin and half fill with boiling water. Cover with a double layer of tinfoil (or a tight-fitting lid). If using 2 or 3 different coloured beetroot varieties, cook them in separate roasting tins or the colours will bleed into each other. Cook for 70–90 minutes, until tender. To test, pierce the beetroot with the point of a knife. Leave to cool slightly, then remove the skins while still warm. Slice into wedges of a similar size.

To make the marinade for the beetroot, combine the olive oil with the cider vinegar and maple syrup in a bowl and whisk to combine. Season well. Keeping the beetroots in separate bowls, pour some of the dressing over each. Leave to marinate to allow the flavours to develop.

To make the spicy pecans

Reduce the oven temperature to 160°C, 140°C Fan, 325°F, Gas 3. Combine the olive oil, sugar and spices in a bowl and season well. Mix through the pecans. Spread onto a baking tray and roast for 8–10 minutes. Remove from the oven and leave to cool fully on the tray. Roughly chop and set aside.

To finish the salad

To make the yoghurt dressing, stir all the ingredients together gently. Don't overmix, as the yoghurt should remain thick.

To assemble, keep all the beetroots in their separate bowls. Check the seasoning and mix some chopped chervil into each bowl. Carefully layer the beetroots on a platter, scattering over the chopped spiced nuts and large spoonfuls of the yoghurt dressing. Serve at room temperature.

Spelt and Quinoa Salad with Roasted Butternut Squash, Feta and Pomegranate Seeds

Grains such as spelt and quinoa have become trendy in recent times due to their health properties. Spelt is a nutty grain with a texture similar to shortgrain brown rice. Quinoa, on the other hand, is grown mainly for its seeds, which bring a light touch to any salad. In this recipe, the grains are brought together to form a base for a variety of vegetables and seeds. The lemony dressing adds to the flavour and freshness.

Serves 6–8

60g pumpkin seeds

60g sunflower seeds

250g spelt

250g quinoa

150g green beans

1 butternut squash

3–4 tbsp olive oil

sea salt and freshly ground black pepper

1 pomegranate

juice of 1½ lemons

zest of 1 lemon

150g feta, crumbled

FOR THE HERB OIL

50g basil leaves

50g rocket

20g parsley

3 garlic cloves

100ml extra virgin olive oil

salt and freshly ground black pepper

OVEN *Preheat the oven to 160°C, 140°C Fan, 325°F, Gas 3.*

Place the pumpkin seeds and sunflower seeds on a baking tray, keeping them separate. Roast the sunflower seeds for about 6 minutes and the pumpkin seeds for about 8 minutes.

Place the spelt in a large pot of cold water. Bring to the boil, then reduce the heat and simmer for 35–45 minutes, until the grains are tender. For a salad like this, the grains should be barely cooked so that they retain their texture and firmness. Make sure to have plenty of boiling water ready to top up the pot during the cooking process. Drain immediately in a colander in the sink and refresh by running under cold water until all the grains are cold to the touch. Tip onto a tray or plate lined with absorbent paper and leave to dry.

For the quinoa, bring a large pot of water to the boil. Add the quinoa and boil for 9 minutes. Drain, refresh and dry in the exact same way as for the spelt.

Top and tail the green beans. Bring a pot of salted water to the boil, add the green beans and cook until tender, about 2 minutes. Drain immediately, refresh under cold water and pat dry with kitchen paper.

Turn the oven temperature up to 220°C, 200°C Fan, 425°F, Gas 7.

Peel the butternut squash. Slice in half across the middle. Standing each piece on its end, cut in half vertically. Scoop out the seeds with a spoon. Cut into small wedges, each one about 1½cm at its widest. It's important that the pieces are of a similar size so that they cook in the same time.

Place the pieces in a bowl and drizzle with the olive oil, sea salt and black pepper. Place on a baking tray, spaced slightly apart from each other, and roast for 20–25 minutes, until all the pieces are cooked through. They should be tender when tested with a small knife. Remove from the oven and set aside to cool.

Slice the pomegranate in half crossways. Hold half of the pomegranate in one hand, with the cut side facing down over a wide bowl, and smack the pomegranate with the back of a wooden spoon. The seeds and some of the pith will fall into the bowl through your fingers. Repeat with the other half and then remove any bits of pith that have fallen into the bowl and discard. Set the seeds aside.

To make the herb oil, blend the herbs in a food processor with the garlic, olive oil and seasoning.

In a large mixing bowl, combine the spelt and quinoa with the herb oil, lemon juice and zest, mixing until all the grains are well coated. Check for seasoning and balance. If it looks dry, add a little more olive oil. Mix in the green beans, butternut squash, pumpkin and sunflower seeds and butternut squash pieces. Serve on a large plate, layering through the crumbled feta and pomegranate seeds as you go and scattering some of both on top.

As an alternative, leave the cooked squash on a separate plate and serve with the mint yoghurt prepared for the leek and carrot fritters on page 136. Serve the spelt and quinoa salad alongside for a full vegetarian meal.

Tender Stem Broccoli with Chilli and Garlic Oil

For its short season, it's worth celebrating tender stem (or purple sprouting) broccoli, which is so much more delicate than its ever-present cousin.

Serves 6

1kg tender stem broccoli
2 long red chillies
olive oil
3 large garlic cloves, finely sliced
salt and freshly ground black pepper

If using purple sprouting or tender stem broccoli, trim off any coarse-looking leaves or tough ends of the stalk. If using regular broccoli, cut it into florets.

Bring a large saucepan of salted water to the boil. Add the broccoli and cook until just tender, about 2 minutes – no more. Remove and plunge into a bowl of ice-cold water. Drain well and place on a tray or plate lined with absorbent paper and refrigerate until ready to use.

Cut the chillies in half lengthwise and finely slice into thin strips. Add enough olive oil to cover the base of a frying pan in a thin layer. Add the chillies and their seeds to the frying pan, along with the garlic. Heat gently for about 3 minutes, until the garlic has started to colour and the oil is flavoured. Raise the heat to medium and add the broccoli, tossing with the chilli and garlic until well coated in the oil. Season with salt and pepper if necessary. Transfer to a hot dish, leaving behind any surplus oil.

Wild Rice and Orzo with Crème Fraîche and Herbs

Both of the components of this dish look like rice, yet neither is. Firstly, there is orzo (called risoni in some parts of Italy), which is a pasta shaped like a grain of rice. Secondly, there is wild rice, which is in fact an aquatic grass native to North America.

Wild rice was traditionally harvested by the native tribes in North America who passed through the reeds in their canoes and gathered the rice by knocking the seeds into the base of their canoes with poles. By law, Minnesota wild rice must still be harvested by the traditional methods and only by designated groups so that local tribes do not lose this part of their heritage. Most wild rice is collected by mechanical threshers and this is what is usually available to us.

When buying wild rice, look for long, slender, unbroken grains, as there are lower grades sometimes on offer. Never buy wild rice mixed in with other types of rice, as the cooking times vary.

Serve this wild rice and orzo as a simple side dish to fish, meat and vegetarian dishes. As an alternative way of using wild rice and orzo, dress them with a vinaigrette and add other ingredients for texture and interest.

Serves 4

100g wild rice

pinch of salt

250g risoni/orzo

40g butter

40g crème fraîche

bunch of chopped herbs, such as dill, basil, fennel or chervil – whatever complements the dish best

NOTE The proportion of wild rice to orzo does not need to be exact.

To prepare the wild rice

Wash the wild rice in a big bowl of cold water and place it in a measuring jug to check the volume. Transfer to a heavy-based saucepan. Measure 3 times the volume of boiling water and pour over the rice. Cover with a lid, add a pinch of salt and simmer until all the water has been absorbed. This takes about 40 minutes. (If the rice is not quite cooked, just add a little more boiling water and cook for a little longer.) The grains of rice will burst when the rice is tender, but the rice should still have a nice bite to it.

To prepare the orzo

The exact cooking time of the orzo may vary slightly, so check the back of the packet for instructions. About 10 minutes before the wild rice is ready, start cooking the orzo. Place the orzo in a pot of boiling salted water (add about 1 tablespoon of salt to 4 litres of water) and simmer for the required time, 8–11 minutes. Remove from the heat and drain through a sieve, reserving some of the pasta water.

Mix the orzo and the wild rice together. Heat the butter and crème fraîche and add in the bunch of chopped herbs. Pour this over the wild rice and orzo and add a good dash or two of pasta water. Check the seasoning and serve.

THE VERSATILITY OF SAUCES – WITH MEAT

When it comes to branching out, how high do you want to climb? A vital element of elevating your cooking is confidence with sauces. Those chosen here can translate beyond the recipes themselves and provide strong building blocks for much wider use. While you may be happy just to get supper on the table most nights of the week, there may be times when you want to take your cooking up a notch.

In Chapter 1 (page 29) there are instructions on how to make your own stock cubes using reduced chicken stock (with the vegetarian alternative of Marigold bouillon). These can form the base of a great sauce. You may push the boat out further and have the additional option of richer meat stocks, such as veal or beef. These stocks are becoming much more widely available in good food shops and some supermarkets. They can be reduced and frozen in the same way as the chicken stock cubes so that they are to hand whenever you need them.

With stock in hand, I find it helpful to think of meat sauces as falling into two main categories. The first is a reduction sauce, which is particularly suitable for tender cuts of meat (or roasts). There are a few steps involved.

The meat is seared over a high heat until the surface is caramelised. (At this point, the meat exits stage right to the oven so that we can keep focused on the sauce.) The pan is deglazed with alcohol, such as red wine, sherry, Madeira or cider. Deglazing involves scraping up all those lovely crusty bits that remain in the pan from browning the meat. The alcohol is then reduced by at least a half (sometime even almost to a glaze) by boiling in the open pan. Then stock is added and this is reduced further. Finally, the sauce can be finished with some herbs, some meat juices or even a knob of butter to give it a sheen as well as some richness. If you have the stock, this sauce can be made easily and will be ready long before the meat is cooked.

The second category of sauce comes from less tender cuts of meat that are cooked slowly, or braised. The long, slow cooking in the oven produces the base of the sauce. This can be augmented with vegetables (onions, celery, carrots, fennel and leeks are commonly used), herbs, liquid (stock, wine or other alcohol), tomatoes (tinned or fresh) or vinegar (balsamic or an aged sherry vinegar). At the end of the cooking, the sauce may well need to be degreased. Skim the fat off the top. Then it may or may not be reduced until it's the consistency you are seeking. Finally, this sort of slow sauce benefits from being refrigerated overnight. The time allows the flavours to develop and the fat to come to the surface, making it easier to remove. If you have a sense of these two sauces, it will be easier to follow what is happening in the recipes below.

SALTING MEAT IN ADVANCE

Salt enhances flavour – dramatically. If you cook a piece of meat without salt and then sprinkle it on at the end, the meat will never have the same flavour. It is worth salting meat before cooking, or in the case of large joints of meat, they would benefit from being salted many hours in advance or even overnight.

A Wild Mushroom Sauce for Chicken

One of my favourite sauces for chicken is made with either wild mushrooms (such as chanterelles on a good day) or the farmed shitake mushrooms, which are always readily available (button mushrooms don't count!).

Slice the mushrooms, sauté them in a pan with a tablespoon of oil and toss over a high heat until they begin to wilt. Add in a sliver of crushed garlic and a scattering of chopped thyme leaves, deglaze the pan with a dash of Madeira or sherry, boil for 20 seconds and add a little cream or cream and chicken stock. Simmer for a minute or two and serve with a pan-fried or roasted chicken breast (see page 161 for details on roasting a chicken breast).

Fillet Steak with Red Wine Jus and Potato Gratin

The red wine jus is a classic meat sauce. I often serve steak with the red wine jus and salsa verde (page 51), which cuts through the richness of the meat. The salsa can be spooned over the steak or over a selection of fresh vegetables.

Serves 6

6 x 170g thick fillet steaks, ideally centre cut

salt and freshly ground black pepper

sunflower oil, to pan-fry the steaks

salsa verde (page 51), to serve

potato gratin (page 188), to serve

FOR THE RED WINE JUS

15g butter

2 shallots, finely chopped

50g shitake mushrooms or button mushrooms, finely chopped

300ml Cabernet Sauvignon red wine (or a Cabernet and Merlot blend)

3 black peppercorns, crushed lightly

2 sprigs of fresh thyme

1 bay leaf

300ml rich golden veal, beef or reduced chicken stock

salt

OVEN *Preheat the oven to 200°C, 180° Fan, 400°F, Gas 6.*

To make the red wine jus

In a medium saucepan, melt the butter and sauté the shallots and mushrooms until light golden. Deglaze the saucepan with the red wine, then add the peppercorns, thyme and bay leaf. Bring to the boil and reduce the wine by about three-quarters, then add the stock. Simmer and reduce again until the stock has reduced by about half. Judge the consistency by eye. (If you feel it has reduced too much, just add a dash of water.) Taste and season as required. If the sauce is a little bitter, add a good pinch or two of sugar. The acidity can vary depending on the red wine that has been used. Pass the sauce through a strainer, discarding the solids. The sauce can be made up to this point in advance.

To cook the steaks

Remove the steaks from the fridge well ahead of time to allow them to come to room temperature.

Choose a frying pan large enough to fit the steaks comfortably. Season the steaks with salt and pepper. Heat the pan with a dash of sunflower oil until very hot. Place the steaks in the pan, being careful not to overcrowd them. You may need to sear them in two batches. Cook over a high heat for about 2 minutes

on each side, until a nice golden crust forms on the outside, then transfer the steaks to a baking tray. Place the baking tray in the oven and cook the steaks for a few more minutes – the exact length of time required to cook the steaks will depend on their thickness. Allow the steaks to rest for 5–10 minutes before serving. If you wish to hold them for longer, keep them covered with tinfoil to retain the heat. If there are any residual juices from the meat after resting, add these to the sauce.

Serve the steaks with a spoonful or two of red wine jus and some salsa verde on the side. Accompany with crunchy vegetables, potato gratin or mashed potato.

Potato Gratin

Serves 4–6

butter, for greasing the dish

900g potatoes, peeled (such as Kerr Pinks or Roosters)

1 large or 2 small garlic cloves, finely chopped

salt

375ml boiling milk

200ml cream

EQUIPMENT *Gratin dish approx. 23cm x 20cm and 5cm deep, or its equivalent*

OVEN *Preheat the oven to 200°C, 180°C Fan, 400°F, Gas 6.*

Butter the gratin dish generously. Cut the potatoes into slices about 3mm thick. Layer the potatoes with the chopped garlic, slightly overlapping the slices. Season each layer with salt. Do not scatter garlic over the last layer. Pour over the boiling milk and the cream. The liquid should just barely come up to the level of the potatoes. If this is not the case, add a bit more milk and cream. Cook for about 50 minutes, until the top is golden and most of the liquid has evaporated.

The gratin may be prepared in advance and reheated.

NEVEN MAGUIRE COOKING IN MY KITCHEN

When I returned to Dublin after my cooking travels, I ran classes twice a week from my home kitchen. While I loved teaching, I missed the buzz of working in kitchens and so decided to invite guest chefs. The prospect of spending time in a rearranged home kitchen would not have been a great lure for the top chefs in the city. I knew that to get the ball rolling, I would have to get someone very talented, but someone not at all well known. Word had reached me of a chef who was causing a sensation in Co. Cavan, but I had no idea what it meant to be making waves in Blacklion. I took the bull by the horns and made the invitation. When he arrived, I was worried by the fact that he appeared so youthful (how could he have learned enough to impress a pile of Dublin foodies at the age of 22?). Moreover, he seemed naïve to have shut his restaurant on a Friday evening to do the demo.

He arrived only shortly before the 24 punters, who found themselves carrying in plates and ingredients and some pre-prepared tasters. I need not have worried. While it may have looked casual, he was hugely prepared. His menus were brilliantly chosen to show off his technique and to stretch those who would recreate what he had produced. Perhaps most impressive of all, he had an intuitive sense of theatre. He showed me that a cookery demonstration isn't just about food; it's also entertainment. I had never seen anyone work a group like that before. They were entranced. They raucously applauded each presentation plate. I would not have anticipated it (although he clearly had), but most made the journey to MacNean restaurant over the following months. He was building his Dublin clientele and I was building the base for my cookery school. Five books and four TV series later, it's no surprise to me that Neven Maguire has the longest waiting list anywhere in the country. What is a surprise (a gratifying one) is that he still carves out time to come and teach at Dublin Cookery School.

Pan-fried Duck Breast with Madeira Sauce and Balsamic Lentils

Every chef has their own way of making a sauce. They may use similar ingredients, but they still have their own stamp. Neven Maguire, for example, has his own approach, which he can then tweak in all sorts of ways. If stock is to hand, his sauce can be rustled up in 10 minutes.

Start by choosing a saucepan that is appropriate for the amount of sauce. When the pan is hot, pour in some balsamic or sherry vinegar. Expect a blast of steam, and as the vinegar sizzles, add Madeira, sherry, red wine or port and reduce for a few minutes. Add stock and reduce further. To balance the acidity from the vinegar, add a touch of brown sugar or honey. This basic sauce has very few ingredients relative to the depth it achieves. It's one to master.

This sophisticated sauce can be used with many meats, but here it's paired with duck. There are numerous accompaniments that would work with the duck, but Neven's choice would be balsamic lentils.

Serves 6

6 duck breasts

sea salt

FOR THE MADEIRA SAUCE

1 tbsp balsamic vinegar

4 tbsp Madeira or sherry (medium or medium dry, preferably)

240ml veal, duck or beef stock (or reduced chicken stock)

1 tsp soft light brown sugar (if needed)

Balsamic lentils (page 191), to serve

OVEN *Preheat the oven to 180°C, 160°C Fan, 350°F, Gas 4.*

Score the fat on the duck breasts in a criss-cross pattern and season on both sides. Heat a dry ovenproof pan (or 2 pans) and add the duck breasts, skin side down. Cook over a medium heat until the skin becomes crisp and a rich golden colour. As the duck cooks, pour off the fat that collects in the pan (reserve for another use). Rendering out the fat at a low to medium heat will make a big difference to the final result. Turn the duck breasts over and transfer the pan to the preheated oven, or place them on a baking sheet if your pan isn't ovenproof. Cook the duck breasts for 10–15 minutes – the timing will vary according to the thickness of the meat. When cooked to your liking, remove from the oven and allow to rest in a warm place for about 5 minutes or up to 15 minutes.

To make the sauce, heat a dry saucepan until very hot. Pour in the balsamic vinegar. Allow it to boil for a few seconds and then add the Madeira or sherry. Boil for a minute or so and then add the stock. Simmer the sauce until reduced by about half to two-thirds. Add a pinch of sugar and taste the sauce. If the sauce is a little too bitter, add another pinch of sugar. The sauce may be made in advance and reheated as needed. While the duck is resting, pour any of the juices from the meat into the sauce.

To serve, slice the duck breasts into 3 pieces and spoon some of the sauce over and around the duck. Serve with the balsamic lentils.

Balsamic Lentils

Serves 6

200g Puy lentils or brown lentils

salt

1 tbsp olive oil

2 tbsp finely chopped carrot
  (as fine a dice as possible)

2 tbsp finely chopped onion
  (as fine a dice as possible)

125ml veal, beef, duck or chicken
  stock

1–2 tbsp aged balsamic vinegar or
  sherry vinegar

1 rounded tsp soft brown sugar

¼ tsp tomato purée

Rinse the lentils in cold water and place in a saucepan. Cover generously with water and bring up to the boil. Add salt and simmer the lentils until tender, 15–20 minutes, topping up with more water if necessary. The lentils should be tender but still have a nice bite to them. Drain, rinse the lentils again under running water and set aside.

Heat the olive oil in a medium saucepan and add the chopped carrot and onion. Season, cover with a lid and turn down the heat to low. Cook for a few minutes to soften and then add the lentils, along with the stock, vinegar, sugar and tomato purée. Cook for about 5 minutes to blend the flavours. Season to taste. Set aside until ready to use.

Glazed Baby Carrots with Tarragon

Serves 4

20 baby carrots
15g unsalted butter
pinch of caster sugar
2 small sprigs of tarragon
salt

Peel the carrots. In a large sauté pan, melt the butter with a pinch of sugar, then add the carrots so that they sit in a single layer in the pan. Add just enough cold water to barely cover the carrots in the pan and bring to the boil. Cover with buttered baking parchment (or butter paper) and simmer for about 10 minutes, until tender but still with a bite. Remove the paper and increase the temperature to reduce the liquid until the carrots are glazed. Add the tarragon towards the end of this process. Season with salt. The same method can be used for baby turnips.

Braised Duck Legs with Pomme Purée

Braising is a technique that works particularly well for cuts of meat that would otherwise be tough. Slow-cooking duck legs (or chicken legs) in a broth with vegetables and aromatics makes for a comforting dish that requires nothing other than some mashed potato as an accompaniment. Cabbage is included here, but carrots or baby turnips would also work well. This dish is adapted from a recipe by Alice Waters in her inspiring book *Chez Panisse Cooking*.

Serves 4

4 duck legs and thighs

sea salt and freshly ground black pepper

1½ tsp thyme leaves

2 large red onions, halved and cut into slices crossways

¼ head of Savoy or other white cabbage, shredded

3 tbsp sherry vinegar, preferably aged

450ml full-bodied poultry, veal or beef stock

3 whole tinned tomatoes, quartered

pomme purée (page 195), to serve

OVEN *Preheat the oven to 180°C, 160°C Fan, 350°F, Gas 4.*

Using a boning or chopping knife, separate the leg and the thigh into separate pieces. Trim the excess fat from the duck legs, making sure that the skin covers the meat completely. Skin will always shrink back a little during cooking, so allow for this. Season the duck with sea salt, black pepper and thyme leaves. If time permits, let the duck sit at room temperature for half an hour. Alternatively, season in advance, refrigerate and leave for several hours or overnight.

Heat a wide frying pan and add the duck legs, skin side down. Cook over a medium heat for about 15 minutes, until the skin becomes a rich golden colour. Pour off the excess duck fat and reserve. When the legs are browned, remove from the pan.

Pour a couple of tablespoons of duck fat back into the pan and add the red onions. Season with salt and cook slowly for 10–15 minutes. Add the shredded cabbage and cook for about 5 minutes, tossing regularly. Deglaze the pan with the sherry vinegar, boil for about 10 seconds and then add the stock. Transfer the vegetables and the broth to an ovenproof dish and sit the duck legs on top. Scatter the quartered tomatoes around the duck.

Transfer the dish to the oven and cook for about 1½ hours, until the duck legs are meltingly tender. If you pull a piece of meat off the bone, it should come away really easily, otherwise return it to the oven to continue cooking. Always check during the cooking time that there is still sufficient broth in the dish. Remove from the oven and allow to settle. Spoon off any excess fat that rises to the surface. If the broth is too runny, you may strain it off the duck legs and vegetables and reduce it in a separate pot by boiling.

To serve, place a good spoonful of pomme purée in the centre of wide soup bowls. Spoon the sauce and vegetables around the potato and sit a duck leg on top. Serve immediately.

Pomme Purée

Serves 6

900g potatoes

110g butter

200ml milk or a combination of milk
  and cream

salt

Peel the potatoes and steam until completely tender. While still hot, pass them through a potato ricer back into the saucepan (or use a potato masher).

Put the butter and milk (or milk and cream) in a saucepan and bring up to the boil. Place the potatoes over a low flame and begin adding the warm milk mixture. Season the potatoes and keep adding the liquid until the potato is a creamy consistency. The amount of liquid will vary each time and also depends on the type of potatoes, so add it gradually. Adjust the seasoning.

HOW TO AVOID LUMPY MASHED POTATO

Always make sure that both the potato and the liquid are hot. If the potato has gone cold, you can either reheat it carefully in the saucepan, or better still, reheat it in a microwave before adding the hot liquid.

Roast Belly of Pork with Beetroot Tzatziki and Rocket

On every full-time three-month course at the cookery school, we all head off for a trip together. The favoured destination is Paul Flynn's restaurant, The Tannery, in Dungarvan. I love his restaurant and how he and Maire have developed quirky luxury accommodation as well as a spectacular kitchen garden.

I see Paul as the chef's chef. There is no one I know who is more knowledgeable. If I'm curious about anything, I put it on my 'want' list for our next trip down to him, knowing he will respond to my question, effortlessly weaving in stories and recipes.

On our last visit, I asked him to cook a belly of pork. I was also interested to see what sauce he would choose as an accompaniment. When he had finished and I enquired about the sauce, he pointed at the beetroot tzatziki. "That's it," he said, and if Paul Flynn says that this is a sauce, then this is a sauce.

Serves 4

1 large onion, sliced into rings

4 garlic cloves, finely chopped

1 bunch fresh sage, chopped

300ml chicken stock (page 30)

1.5kg pork belly, rind removed

sea salt and cracked black pepper

150ml dry cider

8 whole cloves

1¼ tsp allspice

1¼ tsp ground cinnamon

75g Demerara sugar

2 handfuls of rocket

2 tbsp olive oil

1 tbsp red wine vinegar

FOR THE BEETROOT TZATZIKI

3 cooked beetroot, peeled and grated

2 garlic cloves, crushed

1 Granny Smith apple, peeled, cored and grated

200ml Greek yoghurt

3 tbsp red wine vinegar

1 tbsp olive oil

1 tsp freshly grated horseradish or 1½ tsp creamed horseradish

Maldon sea salt and cracked black pepper

OVEN *Preheat the oven to 150°C, 130°C Fan, 300°F, Gas 2.*

To prepare the pork belly

Place the onion rings in a single layer in the bottom of a roasting tin. Sprinkle over the garlic and half of the sage, then pour in the stock. Season the pork belly with sea salt and black pepper and sit on top of the onion rings. Splash over the cider. Scatter over the remaining sage along with the cloves, allspice and cinnamon. Season to taste and cover with foil. Cook for 3 hours, until the pork is completely tender and pulls away from the bone easily. (However, the cooking time could be much longer, maybe 4 hours – judge by the tenderness of the meat.) Baste occasionally during the cooking.

Remove the foil and sprinkle the Demerara sugar on top. Increase the oven temperature to 200°C, 180°C Fan, 400°F, Gas 6. Return the pork to the oven for 20 minutes, until it's glazed and golden. Remove the pork to a warm plate and set aside to rest for at least 20 minutes. The pork may be prepared in advance and reheated with a little stock in the bottom of the roasting pan.

To make the tzatziki

Place the beetroot in a bowl with the garlic, apple, Greek yoghurt, red wine vinegar, olive oil and horseradish. Season to taste. Mix well to combine, then cover with cling film and chill until needed. This will keep for up to 24 hours.

To serve

Place the rocket in a bowl and season to taste, then dress with the olive oil and red wine vinegar. Mix lightly to combine. Carve the rested pork into thick slices. Serve with some of the roasted onion rings, beetroot tzatziki and rocket salad.

THE VERSATILITY OF SAUCES – WITH FISH

When I'm choosing a fish dish in a restaurant, my selection is often more influenced by the sauce than the fish. The sauce is the defining element. Five very different examples are presented here to give a sense of the range of possibilities. Don't shy away from trying out a fish stock. It's the most straightforward of all the stocks and also the quickest.

Fish Stock

Fish stock is easy to make. Your fishmonger will give you the bones for free and will tell you which ones work well (turbot makes the best stock, but most white fish bones, such as brill, cod, sole, haddock or hake, are good options) and which ones don't (such as mackerel or salmon). It will take just 20 minutes to extract the flavour, and indeed, it is only likely to get more bitter after that. Although a recipe for fish stock is given here, see this only as a very rough guideline.

Makes 1.2 litres

1 large onion
1 large leek, white part only
1 large carrot
1 celery stalk

1kg white fish bones
1 bay leaf
a few sprigs of thyme
a few parsley stalks
2.25 litres water or enough water
    to cover the bones

Chop the vegetables roughly into small pieces. The stock takes only 20 minutes to cook, so the vegetables must be cut small to extract the maximum flavour in so short a cooking time. Place the vegetables in a large saucepan and put the fish trimmings on top, along with the bay leaf, thyme and parsley. Pour over the water and bring to the boil. Remove the scum that rises to the top (keep a bowl beside the stockpot, as you will skim the stock a number of times throughout the cooking). Turn down the heat to a gentle simmer and simmer for 20 minutes. Turn off the heat and allow to cool. Strain and use as required.

I generally use fish stock within a day, certainly within two. I like it to taste fresh. If there is stock left over, I generally reduce it down to concentrate the flavour, allow it to cool and then pour it into small containers for freezing.

Pan-fried Scallops with Pink Grapefruit, Mustard and Dill Beurre Blanc

Brian Miller was the first American chef to cook in the school. He loved to teach the students how to master sauces. He would often take a classic sauce and then add a twist so that they could see its possibilities.

The classic beurre blanc is made from a reduction of white wine, white wine vinegar and shallots and then the addition of unsalted butter. When I saw the other ingredients Brian proposed to add – dry vermouth, wholegrain mustard, dill and pink grapefruit – some doubt did begin to creep in. I wondered if it was a step too far. Definitely not, as it turned out. There are tastes that stop you in your tracks. This is one of them.

Serves 6

18 scallops

olive oil

salt

FOR THE BEURRE BLANC REDUCTION

120ml ruby red grapefruit juice, strained

60ml Noilly Prat (or other dry vermouth)

60ml fish stock (page 199) (or simply omit entirely if you do not have fresh fish stock)

3 tbsp very finely chopped shallots

2 white peppercorns

a few stalks of fresh dill

225g unsalted butter, at room temperature

salt

1 tbsp chopped fresh dill leaves

2 level tsp wholegrain mustard, at room temperature

2 grapefruit segments, without pith, chopped into very tiny dice and drained of their juice

To make the beurre blanc

Using a medium saucepan, combine the grapefruit juice, Noilly Prat, stock, shallots, peppercorns and dill and reduce over a medium heat until about 4 tablespoons of reduction remains. Remove the peppercorns and dill stalks. Then, over a very low heat and using a hand whisk, incorporate the butter a knob at a time. It's important to be aware of the temperature of the sauce – if it gets too hot, it will split. You may need to remove the saucepan from the heat every so often if the temperature is getting too high. When you have added all the butter, there should be an emulsified sauce that looks smooth and creamy. Season with salt, add the chopped dill and wholegrain mustard and whisk to combine. Taste and season as necessary. Consider adding a teaspoon or two of grapefruit juice at the end, a bit more dill or a bit more mustard. The sauce can hold for about half an hour if kept warm in a bain marie (a water bath of tepid water). Do not leave the sauce over the heat. Seconds before serving, add in the finely diced grapefruit.

To cook the scallops

Remove the coral and the little piece of muscle on the side of the scallop and discard. Dry the scallops on kitchen paper.

Heat a non-stick pan and add a small dash of olive oil. When the pan is very hot, put the scallops on the pan in a single layer, not too close together. If cooking all the scallops, you will probably need to cook them in 2 batches or in 2 pans. Season the scallops individually with salt. Cook on a high heat on the first side until caramelised, about 1 minute or so, depending on the thickness. Turn over and cook on the other side for about 30 seconds. Serve immediately with the sauce.

Pan-fried John Dory with Sauce Vierge and Basil Mash

A classic French way of serving fish is to pair it with a vinaigrette – in this case, a very lemony vinaigrette. Soft, fluffy mash infused with basil sits under the fish and gives a contrasting texture to the crispy skin of the fish.

Serves 4

4 x 170g John Dory fillets

sea salt and freshly ground black pepper

1 tbsp olive oil

knob of butter

basil mash (page 204), to serve

2 tomatoes, skinned, seeded and diced, to garnish

FOR THE SAUCE VIERGE

85ml good-quality extra virgin olive oil

25ml lemon juice

1 tsp coriander seeds, lightly crushed

a few basil leaves, cut into thin strips

salt

Firstly, prepare the basil mash on page 204.

To make the sauce vierge

Place the olive oil in a small saucepan and heat gently just to warm through. (If you overheat the oil, you will lose a lot of flavour.) Remove from the heat and add the lemon juice and crushed coriander seeds. Leave to infuse. When cold, add the basil and season before serving.

To cook the John Dory

Season the fish. Heat a non-stick frying pan and when hot, add the oil. Place the fish in the pan, skin side down. Cook for a few minutes (without moving the fish) until the skin crisps and becomes golden at the edges. Turn over onto the flesh side, add a knob of butter to the pan (this will give both colour and flavour) and cook for another minute or so, until tender – the exact timing will depend on the thickness of the fish.

To serve

Reheat the mashed potato and add in the basil. Mix, taste and recheck the seasoning. Place a large scoop of mash in the centre of each plate. Place the John Dory on top of the mash. Drizzle some sauce vierge over the fish and around the outside of the plate and scatter over some of the tomato dice.

Basil Mash

Serves 6–8

900g potatoes

110g butter

200ml milk (or a combination of
  milk and cream)

salt and freshly ground black
  pepper

bunch of basil leaves, finely
  chopped

Peel the potatoes and steam until cooked. Pass them through a food mill or ricer back into the saucepan (or use a potato masher).

Put the butter and milk in another saucepan and heat until the butter has melted. Place the potatoes over a low flame and begin adding the warm milk mixture. Season the potatoes and keep adding the liquid until the potato is a creamy consistency. The amount of liquid will vary and also depends on the type of potatoes. Mix the basil into the potatoes just before serving. Taste and season as necessary.

NOTE You can make the mashed potato in advance and then zap it in the microwave just before serving. In this case, leave out the basil when preparing the potato earlier in the day and only add it just before serving.

Roast Monkfish Bourguignon

John and Sandy Wyer have been tutors at the cookery school for the last two years. They wanted a base while they hatched their plans to open their own restaurant, Forest Avenue. They have both served their time in the very top European kitchens and there is no substitute for that experience when it comes to teaching.

One of John's favourite days is when he brings the students down to the pier to buy fresh fish and then challenges each pair to produce a dish from a diminishing store of ingredients. He goes around like one of those chess masters playing multiple speed matches at once, exhorting, explaining, challenging, suggesting, tasting.

A couple of students are inevitably left with red wine and a beef jus to accompany a piece of fish and feel that they have drawn the short straw. John explains that many fish are robust enough to stand up to a rich red wine sauce. He encourages them to think in terms of a classic beef bourguignon, the braised meat dish cooked with button onions, lardons of bacon, mushrooms, red wine and veal stock. He gets them to see that this deeply flavoured red wine jus can complement certain fish as well as chicken or red meat. The accompanying pickled baby onions would be sufficiently versatile to be used with many other dishes.

Serves 6

1 tbsp sunflower oil

6 x 140g portions of monkfish, skinned

salt and freshly ground black pepper

knob of butter

pomme purée (page 195), to serve

FOR THE BOURGUIGNON SAUCE

sunflower oil, for frying

60g smoked bacon, diced

150g button mushrooms, quartered

2 garlic cloves, finely diced

4 sprigs of thyme

30ml brandy

100ml red wine

300ml veal or beef stock

1 tbsp chopped flat-leaf parsley

FOR THE RED WINE BABY ONIONS

1 tbsp sunflower oil

18 pearl onions, peeled

10g butter

10g caster sugar

2 sprigs of thyme

150ml red wine

Preheat the oven to 200°C, 180°C Fan, 400°F, Gas 6.

To make the red wine baby onions

Heat the sunflower oil in a medium saucepan. Add the pearl onions and the butter and cook until the pearl onions are lightly coloured. Add the sugar and thyme and continue to caramelise for a minute. Add the red wine and simmer, with a lid on, until the onions are tender, about 6 minutes. Remove the onions and reduce the red wine to a syrup if necessary and pour over the onions. Taste and add a little more sugar if the red wine is too acidic.

For the bourguignon sauce

Heat a dash of sunflower oil in a saucepan and sauté the bacon. When browned, drain the bacon and add the mushrooms. Sauté until golden brown. Add the garlic and thyme, then deglaze with the brandy and boil to reduce by half. Add the red wine and reduce by three-quarters. Add the red wine baby onions and the beef or veal stock. Bring to the boil and simmer until it reduces to a sauce consistency. Just before serving, add in the chopped parsley. The bourguignon sauce can be prepared in advance and refrigerated.

For the monkfish

Heat an ovenproof frying pan and add the oil. Pat the monkfish dry with kitchen paper. Season all over and add to the hot pan. Brown the fish on both sides, then add a knob of butter to the pan and place the pan in the preheated oven (or transfer to a baking tray). Roast for 4–6 minutes, until the fish is cooked (the timing will vary according to the thickness of the fish). Remove from the oven and leave to rest for 2 minutes.

Serve the monkfish with the pomme purée and the bourguignon sauce.

Cod with Cauliflower Purée, Griddled Leeks, Pickled Cauliflower and Fish Velouté

Fish velouté is a classic French white wine and cream sauce to which fish stock is added. The other aromatics added during the cooking – in this case, onion, celery and fennel – are added for flavour and then strained off. This basic fish sauce can be flavoured with herbs such as chervil, dill, fennel or tarragon, all of which have a particular affinity with fish.

In the cookery school, the three-month students run regular pop-up restaurant nights. This dish was chosen by tutor John Wyer for one such evening and included cauliflower purée and cauliflower pickle as an accompaniment – both very simple techniques that elevate the dish.

Serves 6

sunflower oil, for frying

6 x 170g cod fillets

salt and freshly ground black
  pepper

10g butter

200ml fish velouté (page 208),
  to serve

FOR THE CAULIFLOWER PURÉE

½ head of cauliflower

20g butter

1 tbsp sunflower oil

1 shallot, diced

salt

milk, to cover

FOR THE PICKLED CAULIFLOWER

60g caster sugar

100ml white wine vinegar

½ head of cauliflower

FOR THE GRIDDLED LEEKS

2 leeks

olive oil

sea salt

*Preheat the oven to 200°C, 180°C Fan,
  400°F, Gas 6.*

First prepare the fish velouté (see page 208) and set aside.

For the cauliflower purée

Divide the cauliflower into florets and slice thinly. Heat a saucepan and add the butter and sunflower oil. Add the shallots and cauliflower, season with salt and sweat over a gentle heat for 3–4 minutes, until beginning to soften. Add just enough milk to cover the cauliflower, then bring to the boil, reduce the heat and simmer until the cauliflower is tender. Blend until smooth. Check the seasoning.

For the pickle

Heat the sugar and vinegar over a high heat to dissolve the sugar. Slice the cauliflower as thinly as possible, keeping each slice attached to the stalk. The cauliflower is best sliced on a mandoline if you have one. Blanch the cauliflower in boiling water for 10 seconds. Refresh in cold water, drain and add to the pickling liquid. Allow to sit. The pickle may be prepared in advance and will last several days.

For the leeks

Remove the dark green part of the leek and discard. Slice the remaining leek in half. Wash the leek under cold running water. Slice each half leek into 3 lengths, keeping the root of the leek attached so that it will hold together. Blanch the leeks in boiling salted water for 2–3 minutes, then refresh in ice-cold water. Dry on a tea towel.

Heat a griddle pan until hot. Brush the leek with olive oil and season with sea salt. Place the strips of leek on the griddle and cook until chargrill marks appear on the surface. Griddle on the second side and remove. Keep warm if you are serving straight away. The leeks may be prepared in advance, placed on a tray and reheated in a hot oven.

To cook the cod

Heat a non-stick, ovenproof pan and add a dash of sunflower oil. Dry the cod on kitchen paper, season on both sides and add to the pan, skin side down. Brown the skin (5 minutes) and then add the butter. Place the cod in the oven for about 3 minutes, still on the skin side. Turn the cod over and continue to cook for 1 more minute. Remove from the pan and leave to rest for 2 minutes.

To serve

Reheat the cauliflower purée and the fish velouté. Place a swirl of cauliflower purée on the plate, followed by the roasted cod. Scatter a few pieces of the cauliflower pickle around the plate and spoon over the velouté sauce. Garnish with 2 pieces of griddled leek.

Fish Velouté Sauce

Serves 6

20g butter

2 shallots, sliced

1 celery stalk, finely chopped

1 garlic clove, minced

½ fennel bulb, finely chopped

100ml white wine

200ml fish stock (page 199)

150ml cream

Heat the butter in a saucepan and add the shallots, celery, garlic and fennel. Sweat slowly, without colouring, for 3–4 minutes. Deglaze with the white wine and reduce to a syrup. Add the fish stock, bring to the boil and reduce by about half. Add the cream, bring to the boil and simmer to a light sauce consistency. Pass through a fine sieve, discarding the solids. Return to the saucepan and check the seasoning.

Linguine with Shellfish Sauce, Pan-fried Lobster and Dublin Bay Prawns

The most ambitious has been kept to last. This is a sophisticated sauce that takes time, but is always worth the effort. Apart from not wishing to waste lobster, prawn heads or crab shells, they can be used to make the most extraordinary broth. The broth can be used as a shellfish soup or to make a shellfish risotto. Reduced further, it becomes a sauce to serve with white fish or, as in this recipe, as a memorable pasta sauce. The pasta may be accompanied by chunks of lobster, or alternatively, some Dublin Bay prawns pan-fried with a touch of garlic.

Serves 4

lobster meat from 1 medium cooked lobster (see page 79)

clarified butter (see page 81)

sea salt

320g linguine

50g rocket

FOR THE DUBLIN BAY PRAWNS (OPTIONAL)

16 Dublin Bay prawn tails

1 garlic clove

2 tbsp olive oil

salt

SHELLFISH SAUCE

1–1½ litres shellfish stock (page 213)

200ml double cream

pinch of cayenne pepper

few drops of lemon juice

To make the shellfish sauce

Place the langoustine stock in a saucepan and bring to the boil. Boil to reduce the broth to about 250ml. How much you reduce the liquid should be determined by taste towards the end – you are looking for an intense shellfish flavour. (If I feel the flavour isn't deep enough after reducing, I might sometimes add a teaspoon of tomato purée.) Add the cream to the reduced stock and a pinch of cayenne and simmer for 5 minutes to blend the flavours. Finish with a few drops of lemon juice. The sauce may be made up to this point in advance and refrigerated when cold.

To pan-fry the lobster

Chop the lobster into 2.5cm pieces. Heat a couple of tablespoons of clarified butter in the pan and when hot, add the lobster meat. Season with sea salt. Toss over the heat for a few minutes, just until the lobster is warmed through.

To prepare the Dublin Bay prawns

If you are serving Dublin Bay prawns with the pasta dish, the prawns themselves can be parboiled and then refrigerated. They should be pan-fried just before serving.

Take the middle part of the tail fin and twist it back and forth. Slowly pull the fin away from the rest of the tail. The intestinal tract should come out with it, but if it doesn't, you can remove it later with a knife.

Bring a large pot of salted water to the boil. Cook the prawn tails for about 45 seconds. The prawns should not be fully cooked through, as they will be pan-fried later. Refresh in cold water and then drain immediately. Pat dry on kitchen paper. To peel the prawns, turn them over on their backs. With your thumb and first finger, gently press the two sides of the shell towards one another so that the shell cracks. Pull the opposite sides of the shell away from one another and remove the prawn meat from the shell itself. Refrigerate, covered, until ready to use.

Just before serving, slice the clove of garlic lengthways into fine shavings. Lay the slices flat on the chopping board and cut into very thin, long strips. Heat a non-stick frying pan and add the olive oil. When hot, add the prawns to the pan, being careful not to overcrowd them. (You may have to cook them in 2 batches.) Season with salt. Cook for about 20 seconds on each side, then add the slivers of garlic. Remove the prawns from the pan as soon as they are heated through and serve immediately.

To prepare the pasta

Bring a large pot of salted water to the boil (about 1 tablespoon of salt to 4 litres of water). Boil the pasta until tender but still al dente. Drain, reserving a little of the pasta water, and return the pasta to the saucepan. Reheat the lobster sauce and pour it over the pasta, reserving about 100ml. Toss the pasta and add in a dash of pasta water if necessary to loosen the sauce. Add in the rocket and mix gently.

For each serving, twist the pasta around a long meat fork and slide it onto the centre of the plate. Arrange the pan-fried lobster and prawns (if using) over the pasta. Using a hand blender, whizz the remaining sauce until it's light and frothy. Spoon it over the pasta and shellfish and serve immediately.

Shellfish Stock

Makes 1¼–1½ litres

1kg lobster shells, prawn heads or shells

75ml olive oil

50g unsalted butter

3 celery stalks, cut into 2cm cubes

2 carrots, cut into 2cm cubes

1 onion, cut into 2 cm cubes

3 star anise

1 tsp fennel seeds

1 tsp coriander seeds

200ml white wine

1 garlic bulb

2 tomatoes, quartered

1 tbsp tomato purée

2 litres fish stock (page 199)

3 sprigs of tarragon

Break up the lobster and prawn shells into rough-sized pieces. Heat the oil in a large, heavy casserole or frying pan. When the oil is hot, add some of the prawn heads and shells and sauté for 4–5 minutes on a very high heat, until they become caramelised from the roasting. Remove from the pot and roast the remaining shells in batches. Set the shells aside.

Add the butter, followed by the celery, carrots and onion and sauté for 3–4 minutes. Add the star anise, fennel seeds and coriander seeds. Deglaze the pan with the white wine and reduce to a glaze. Return the roasted shells to the pot and crush them up with a pestle or the end of rolling pin. Slice the bulb of garlic in half and add to the pot, along with the quartered tomatoes and the tomato purée.

If you have been using a frying pan to sauté the shells and vegetables, then transfer all the contents of the pan to a deep saucepan. Add enough fish stock to cover the shells (top up with water if you don't have sufficient stock). Bring to the boil and remove any scum that rises to the surface. Turn down the heat and simmer for 1 hour. Remove from the heat and sit the tarragon sprigs on the top. Leave to infuse for 1 hour before straining (if time allows). Strain in a colander, pressing down the shells and vegetables to extract any further broth. Pass the liquid through a fine sieve to remove any particles of shell. The broth, when cooled, will keep in the fridge for 2–3 days. It will keep in the freezer for 2–3 months.

Chapter Four

GOING EAST

Shop with confidence in an Asian market.
Crack open a coconut.

WHAT ARE NIGELLA SEEDS? · HOW DO YOU
MAKE HUNG CURD OR TAMARIND JUICE?
· HOW CAN YOU BEST HARMONISE HOT,
SOUR, SWEET AND SALTY? · WHAT DOES *TADKA*
ACTUALLY MEAN? · HOW TO MAKE TANDOORI
CHICKEN WITHOUT A TANDOOR OVEN

THE ASIAN MARKET

I have never set foot in either Thailand or India. Actually, I have never even been to Asia. The closest I have got is my local Asian food market. This might not mark me out as the obvious candidate to write a chapter on Thai and Indian food. I didn't discover Asian ingredients until well into my adulthood. I can say, without fear of contradiction, that galangal and tamarind were not part of the Roscommon I grew up in.

When I decided it was time to understand Thai cooking, I set off to the Asian food market full of determination, but was utterly disoriented in no time at all. I used to walk around, staring vacantly at the unfamiliar produce. There were only a few other non-Asians present and it was clear that they were in the same position, peering at shelves, stuttering the odd lame question and taking hours to work their way around. They too were startled by the bags of frozen chicken feet every time they passed the freezer. It had all seemed so simple arriving in with my list of ten ingredients, but it turned out to be a minefield of confusion. I might have been looking for a soy sauce under an Indonesian brand, whereas the same sauce might be bottled in Thailand under an entirely different name. My endless questions were met with limited patience from staff who didn't have time to give me a crash course in Asian ingredients. And only I could work out certain problems, such as how to get an enormous pestle and mortar back to the car.

Once I unloaded my purchases, it didn't necessarily get any easier. I would hold my tamarind and wonder how I transformed something that felt like a slab of pitted dates into what the recipe required, which was tamarind juice. The unfamiliarity got more intense because I wasn't really sure what I was aiming for. It may have tasted good to my palate, but I was unsure of the ideal end result.

When people think of the advantages of having a cookery school, they tend to think of how amazing it would be to have all your shopping dropped to your door. It actually gets better: you can have your chef delivered to your door. I had been carrying around David Thompson's inspiring, scholarly and incomparable tome on Thai cooking, *Thai Food*, dipping into it again and again. I still had many questions, so I phoned him and invited him to come over to give a course. He not only came in person, but he brought a chef central to his operation, Tanongsak Yordwai, and later sent his head chef, Matthew Albert, who has become a regular visitor. He offered to bring over ingredients but I played my first card and told him that I had everything he was likely to need. This actually meant that I doubted very much that I had half the things he would need, but I wanted to corner him into using only what was regularly available to me. I would take him to my humble shopping haunts and watch him like a hawk.

The trip around the Asian market was encouraging. There were some ingredients that he was unable to find, but he was quite happy with what was available. It was a quick trip, partly because he knew what he wanted. It was also helped by the fact that the staff responded to his speaking Thai with enthusiasm, no matter how far it was from their Chinese Mandarin. The usually glowering matriarch came out from behind the stacks of gleaming woks to ensure that all his needs were met and I tried to stay as close as I could, hoping that some of the association might rub off on me.

Back in the kitchen there was calm. Even pounding my pestle and mortar seemed violent in comparison. For these chefs, the weight of the pestle was sufficient. There was a smooth action of lifting and lowering, very different from my hammering. And there was care, too, in the handling of the ingredients and in the order in which everything was added. Most tellingly, there was a great deal of adjustment at the point I might have considered the dish finished. Here, they were harmonising between any combination of hot, sour, salty and sweet, sometimes all at once. I was amazed that even to the most tutored palate, this takes great time and attention. The result was quite literally breathtaking.

After all the phoney Thai tastes I had been exposed to, an authentic green curry has a depth that makes me appreciate that this is one of the great cuisines of the world. My master tutors know that an understanding usually comes from visiting the country, but that will inevitably happen. I am now irresistibly drawn. They would be quite happy however I choose to do things. The great Thai sense of acceptance has rubbed off on them.

THAI RED
CHILLIES

GINGER

THAI RED SHALLOTS

KAFFIR LIME
LEAVES

LEMONGRASS

COCONUT

RED TURMERIC

PEA
AUBERGINES

THAI GREEN
CHILLIES

GALANGAL

PALM
SUGAR

TAMARIND

SHRIMP PASTE
(GAPI)

GRACHAI

REGULAR RED
CHILLIES

PANDANUS
LEAVES

INGREDIENTS

CHILLIES

The variety that is most common in Asian markets is the very small bird's eye chillies. I'm moving up the heat tolerance chain but am not yet ready for these. David Thompson calls them scuds. They are green, tiny and harmless looking. Even David says that they are 'viciously hot', but he waxes lyrical about a wonderfully floral aftertaste. When I have risked them, I have usually been left scrambling around looking for yoghurt or alcohol or yelping in the back yard and the aftertaste has been the furthest thing from my mind. I'm getting more used to heat, but for the moment, I'll continue looking for the slightly longer chillies in the Asian market – they measure about 5cm length – and discarding the seeds and membrane (which are the hottest part of the chilli). I never want the heat to overpower my enjoyment of the food.

COCONUTS

I start with a clean slate with most of these ingredients. Coconuts are different. We have a history. I have not had an easy relationship with fresh coconuts. I used to feel that a coconut would look at me stubbornly, daring me. I would hit it around a bit with the blunt end of my cleaver. Then I might head to the garden, put it on a rock and attack it with a variety of instruments. Then it was back into the kitchen for the final coup de grace. I imagined it was a bit akin to a bullfight – there were a series of rituals and the odd occasion when the matador came off worse. Once I had it split in half and could smell the sweetness, I thought it was worthwhile. Until then, I did wonder whether it was all too much trouble – and this is not a thought that commonly occurs to me. Preparing for my first weekend of intensive courses with David Thompson, he said that we would need 75 coconuts and I nearly wept. However, watching Tanongsak work through a sack of coconuts was a revelation. He was like an experienced safe breaker. He charmed them open. I have since put away my axes and rocks and now try to mirror the way he taps around their equator. It's becoming easier, although the debris from my work still seems to spread over an awfully wide area.

Unlike Thai chefs, who would only rarely used tinned coconut milk, it's only on a more special occasion that I would opt for fresh coconut cream or milk (see page 248). For my everyday needs, tinned coconut milk does nicely.

CORIANDER

Coriander is the most widely used herb in the world. The leaves look quite like flat-leaf parsley, but that's where the similarity ends. In Asian markets, coriander stems are often available with the root attached because the root (scraped and washed well) as well as the stem are used regularly in Thai dishes as a base for salads, curries and stir-fries. If the roots have been removed, simply use a portion of the stems.

FISH SAUCE

The idea of fish sauce does not necessarily set the taste buds racing. Small fish are fermented with salt and the liquid is left for several months before being strained and left in the sun, effectively pasteurising it. Watching my Thai chefs, I notice that it is the fish sauce that they most commonly reach for as they make their final adjustments. I am still in awe that an ingredient that is so pungent when tasted alone often retreats into the background when combined with other ingredients. It is the great balancer, with the modesty to support other flavours rather than seek its own limelight.

GALANGAL

Galangal is a kind of first cousin of ginger. They both grow horizontally underground and galangal is more commonly used than ginger in Thai curries. As it matures, the colour changes to a musty gold or red, at which point it's ideal for curry pastes. When you buy it fresh, there is generally a woody stem attached to each piece. This can be used as a flavouring if you are planning to strain and remove the slices. However, if you are pounding the galangal for a curry paste or other dishes, use the main part only. If galangal is unavailable, use ginger instead. Galangal is best stored in the fridge.

GRACHAI (SOMETIMES CALLED KACHAI)

This is sometimes known as wild ginger, but it's an even more distant relation in the ginger family. It yields a peppery flavour that is a good counterbalance to oily ingredients.

KAFFIR LIME LEAVES

It's not often that you come across kaffir limes. They are a knobbly version of the regular lime, but with a slightly darker green skin and an incredibly fragrant zest.

Kaffir lime leaves are much easier to find. I can sometimes find fresh leaves, and if not, frozen lime leaves are readily available in Asian markets and can be kept in the freezer to use when needed (I never use the dried leaves). The leaves can be added whole to sauces, soups and curries. They are often shredded finely with a knife – the central vein can be removed before chopping, but this is not essential.

LEMONGRASS

Lemongrass is perhaps the most widely available of all Thai ingredients. It used to be a rare sighting, but now there are lovely fresh bunches appearing in many supermarkets. Unlike an onion, for example, lemongrass is very fibrous and does not break down in the cooking. The two outer sheaths need to be removed as well as the top third of the stalk and about 1cm from the root end. Then, using a sharp knife, cut it ever so thinly (think tissue paper thin). Even if making a paste in a pestle and mortar, cutting it finely before pounding is essential to avoid being left chewing on little bits of lemongrass. Alternatively, if it's to be used in a dish, the whole stalk may be pounded lightly with a pestle or crushed with the flat of a knife and added whole. The lemongrass stick can then be easily removed before serving. If necessary, lemongrass can be frozen and is easily defrosted under a hot tap.

PALM SUGAR

Palm sugar comes from the sap of the Palmyra palm or the sugar palm. The sap is boiled and reduced to a more concentrated form. The colour depends on many factors, but the one I seek out is like a light fudge or caramel. My guest chefs bring over palm sugar that has a smooth texture, but the sugar most readily available to me is harder and crystallised because it has been mixed with white cane sugar. I buy it in small blocks and shave off what I need with a sharp chopping knife. It is also available in a plastic jar, which generally has a layer of wax at the top. Since I have seen students dig merrily into the wax, I feel it is worth saying that this must be removed first.

PANDANUS LEAF

Pandanus has a long, blade-like leaf. Pandanus leaves are commonly added to stocks and rice dishes. They release their perfumed flavour when they are warm. They are usually knotted to make them easier to remove.

PEA AUBERGINE

These are pea-sized berries that grow in clusters. They are almost worth including in a curry just for their shock value. The name suggests something vaguely familiar, but this is a foreign and very, very bitter taste. It is a good counter to a very sweet ingredient.

RED THAI SHALLOTS

Red Thai shallots (perhaps nearer pink in colour) are used in Thai curry pastes, stir-fries, salads and soups. If they are unavailable, our own shallots make a very good substitute. Deep-fried shallots (see page 233) are used in salads and stir-fries or as a base for pastes in dressings and sauces. The oil left over after deep-frying the shallots can be used as perfumed oil for frying.

RED TURMERIC

Turmeric is a thin rhizome related to ginger and used in similar ways: chopped, pounded or grated. Red turmeric is popular in the south of Thailand, where its extraordinary orangey-red colour gives vibrancy to curry pastes. You have to be a bit careful because this stunning colour also rubs off on anything else it comes in contact with. Ideally, wear a pair of thin plastic gloves when peeling and chopping, and wash knives and chopping boards in hot soapy water straight after use. Since it will stain clothes all too easily, dress with that in mind. If unavailable, substitute yellow turmeric powder but use half the amount.

SHRIMP PASTE

Shrimp paste, called gapi in Thailand, is very pungent and is an essential ingredient in many curry pastes. It's made from fermented shrimp that have been allowed to dry in the sun for up to a year. It should be refrigerated once opened and lasts indefinitely.

SOY SAUCE

Soy sauce is the fermented juice of soy beans. Light soy sauce is mainly used in Thai cooking.

TAMARIND PULP

Tamarind is the main souring ingredient in Thai cooking and is the fruit of a tall tree. The tamarind pods are peeled, seeded, semi-dried and then compacted into blocks. In the shops, they look very similar to a pack of dates. To make tamarind water, break off a bit of the pulp and cover it with a similar amount of warm water. Mash the pulp with the back of a spoon until it begins to dissolve or simply leave it for 15 minutes or longer to soften. Strain the pulp, reserving the pulpy water, and discard the fibres and seeds. It's best to make the tamarind water quite thick. It's easy to dilute it in the recipe if you need to add extra water. Tamarind water will keep refrigerated for about a week. If you pour boiling water over the tamarind initially rather than warm water, the fruit may start to ferment more quickly, which will reduce the shelf life.

THAI BASIL

In Thailand they use holy basil, lemon basil and Thai basil. Thai basil is the one most commonly available here, with its striking purple stems and aniseed flavour. When a Thai curry or stir-fry lists Thai basil among the ingredients, it is definitely worth the effort to seek it out (it will hold for three or four days if bought in good condition), as it can transform a dish, giving an extraordinary depth of flavour. If I can't find Thai basil, Italian basil is not a substitute, and I would probably opt for coriander as an alternative herb. Thai basil is also commonly used in salads.

SOUPS

For those not used to Thai ingredients, a soup is a great place to start. These are not the traditional Thai soups, but use Thai ingredients. Both soups have coconut milk and stock but have very distinct results.

Butternut Squash and Sweet Potato Soup with Lemongrass

Serves 4

25g butter

1 medium onion, diced

salt

1 lemongrass stalk

2 garlic cloves, finely chopped

1 red chilli, split in half and finely chopped (seeds left in if you want a bit of kick)

1 tbsp finely grated root ginger

2 tsp tomato purée

1 tsp Madras curry powder

450g sweet potatoes, peeled and cut into cubes

450g butternut squash, peeled, seeds removed and cut into cubes

1 litre chicken stock (page 30) or vegetable stock (page 32), or more as required

1 x 400ml tin of coconut milk

coriander leaves, to garnish

Melt the butter in a large, heavy-based saucepan and add the chopped onion. Stir, season with salt and cover the saucepan with a lid. Turn down the heat to low and cook gently, stirring regularly, until the onion has softened, about 10 minutes.

Split the lemongrass stalk in half lengthways and bash lightly with the flat of a chopping knife to release the flavours. Add the lemongrass, garlic, chilli, ginger, tomato purée and curry powder to the pot and cook gently for another few minutes with the lid on. Now add the cubes of sweet potato and butternut squash, the stock and the coconut milk and bring to the boil. Season with salt and simmer gently until the vegetables are tender when pierced with a knife. Remove the stalk of lemongrass and discard.

Whizz the soup in a blender or food processor until completely smooth. If the soup is too thick, thin it out with some extra stock or water. Taste, check the seasoning and adjust as required. Sprinkle a few coriander leaves over each serving.

Coconut Laksa with Poached Hake, Salmon and Mussels

A laksa is a coconut-based curry broth, often served with noodles. Laksa is associated more with Malaysia than Thailand, but there are many similar Thai variants. I like to make it a substantial meal by adding chunks of fish. A wide selection of fish, such as salmon, sea bass, scallops and prawns, would be suitable, either on their own or in combination. Instead of mussels, I might add crab-filled wontons (see page 230). Wonton wrappers are available in the freezer section of all Asian markets or stores. For a vegetarian version, use pak choy, slivers of ginger, sliced mushrooms or bean sprouts.

Serves 4–6

1 x 130g fish per person (hake and salmon), skinned

FOR THE PASTE

4 garlic cloves, peeled

1 red chilli

6cm piece of ginger, peeled and roughly chopped

1 tsp finely ground coriander seeds

½ cup fresh coriander, roots, stems and leaves

FOR THE LAKSA

1 tbsp sunflower oil

2 tsp sesame oil

600ml coconut milk

400ml fish stock (page 199), or chicken stock (page 30), plus extra as required

1–2 tbsp Asian fish sauce, or to taste

500g mussels, or 4–6 mussels per person

70ml white wine

bunch of coriander, chopped

Remove all the bones from the fish and then divide the fillets into portions about 4cm wide. Refrigerate until ready to serve.

Put the garlic, chilli, ginger, ground coriander seeds and fresh coriander into a food processor and purée to a coarse paste. Heat a large pot and add the sunflower oil and sesame oil. When hot, add the paste and fry for 1 minute, stirring all the time. Add the coconut milk and stock and bring to the boil. Simmer for 10 minutes, then add the fish sauce to taste. It is imperative that you taste and season until you get the balance right. The laksa may be made up to this point in advance.

Wash the mussels thoroughly. Knock off any barnacles with a knife and pull off any beards. Discard any mussels that are open and don't close when given a good tap. Place the mussels in a large saucepan and add the white wine. Cover tightly and cook over a high heat for about 5 minutes, shaking the pan frequently. Remove the shells one by one as they open. (The mussels may also be cooked in advance and refrigerated until ready to use.) I prefer to leave the mussels in their shells, but you could remove the mussel meat.

To finish the laksa, reheat the broth and add the fish. It may be more practical to put the laksa in a deep, wide frying pan or pot so that the fish will be easy to remove without falling apart. Simmer the broth and the fish for about 5 minutes. Towards the end of the cooking, add in the cooked mussels just to reheat them. Lastly, add in some chopped coriander and serve immediately.

Crab Wontons

These crab wontons could be added to the broth instead of the mussels. Serve about 3 wontons per person.

160g crab meat, drained of excess water (reserve this for the soup)

1 red chilli, seeds removed and very finely diced

1 tbsp very finely diced spring onion

2 tsp fish sauce

20–26 wonton wrappers

Mix the crab, chilli, spring onion and fish sauce together. Lay out the wonton wrappers on the counter, with a corner facing you. Put a teaspoon of the crab filling into the centre. Moisten the edges of the wonton pastry with water, then fold over the corner nearest to you to meet the opposite corner, making a triangle. Press down to seal the two open edges of the triangle. Repeat with the rest of the wontons. Store on a tray covered with cling film. You can refrigerate these for a few hours if you want to make them in advance. Poach in the broth for 2–3 minutes just before serving.

THAI STIR-FRIES

Stir-fried Beef with Chilli and Cumin Paste and Deep-fried Shallots

The first time Matthew Albert (formerly head chef at London's Michelin-starred Thai restaurant, Nahm) made this stir-fry at the school, we were all stunned (in some cases, numbed) by the intense heat, yet I still thought it was one of the most extraordinary stir-fries I had ever eaten. I have reduced the quantity of chillies by half (sorry, Matthew) but you might be braver. It is hauntingly good. Make sure you have a big bowl of rice to accompany it.

This stir-fry is based on making a paste from chilli, garlic and cumin that is fried off in the wok before the beef is added. The wok should be at a good medium heat. If it were searingly hot, the chilli paste might burn, whereas it needs to be cooked at a more moderate heat and allowed to start caramelising. This stir-fry is meant to be rich, oily and slightly sour – the sourness comes from the tamarind. The surprise element is the addition of wedges of raw onion that are added only at the end and cooked so briefly that they don't have time to wilt. They add a crunch that adds a texture to this dish.

Serves 4

320g beef sirloin

1½ tsp freshly roasted and ground cumin seeds, plus an extra pinch

pinch of salt

pinch of caster sugar

½ small onion, peeled, with the root end intact

3 tbsp sunflower oil (or use the oil from deep-frying the shallots)

pinch of ground cumin

drizzle of fish sauce

a few teaspoons tamarind water (see page 225)

a few drops of rice vinegar

2 tbsp deep-fried shallots (page 233), plus extra for garnish

6 coriander stalks, chopped into 2cm lengths

Thai rice (page 236), to serve

FOR THE CHILLI AND CUMIN PASTE

¼ cup dried long red chillies, deseeded

pinch of sea salt

¼ cup finely chopped Thai red shallots (or use ordinary shallots if red shallots are unavailable)

¼ cup garlic, peeled

½ tsp roasted ground cumin

To make the paste

Soak the chillies in cold water overnight, or if using on the day, soak in warm water for at least half an hour. When softened, squeeze out the excess water and pat dry on kitchen paper.

Pound the chillies with a pinch of sea salt in a large pestle and mortar. Add the shallots and garlic in turn and continue pounding to a rough paste. Mix in the roasted ground cumin. The paste can be prepared in advance, packed into a sterilised jar, covered with cling film or wax paper and then sealed. The amount of paste you need for the stir-fry will vary according to your heat threshold. For the quantity of meat in this recipe, 2–3 tablespoons works well.

To prepare the stir-fry

Trim the excess fat from the beef and slice into 3–5cm strips across the grain. (Do not cut the slices too thinly or the beef could become overcooked.) Dry the beef on kitchen paper and place in a bowl. Add the ground cumin, salt and sugar. Leave to sit for 5 minutes or longer.

Stand the onion on the chopping board and cut into 2cm wedges, keeping each piece attached to some of the root end. Have all the other ingredients set out beside the hob.

Heat the wok until it begins to smoke. Add the oil and lift up the wok to swirl the oil around the sides. Add the marinated beef. Spread the beef out around the base and the sides, using all the hot areas of the wok. (If you leave all the meat in a pile, it will stew rather than sear.) Cook the beef over a high heat, tossing every so often, until it's beginning to colour.

Turn the heat down to medium, push the beef off centre and add 2–3 tablespoons of the chilli paste. Break it up with the back of a metal spoon and cook it in the base of the wok initially, stirring it so that it doesn't scorch. Then mix it with the strips of beef and continue cooking until the paste becomes slightly caramelised. Add in another good pinch of ground cumin. The paste will begin to smell sweeter as the shallots and garlic in the paste cook out. You can add a little water to loosen the paste if the beef looks too dry. Add another pinch of sugar, a dash of fish sauce, the tamarind water and a touch of vinegar. When the paste has cooked out (this may take about 5 minutes), add the onion wedges and 2 tablespoons of deep-fried shallots. Toss with the beef and cook for a further 2–3 minutes. Sprinkle in the coriander stems and mix through. Taste and add another dash of fish sauce or tamarind, as required. Remove to a serving dish and scatter over a few tablespoons of deep fried shallots. Servce with Thai rice.

DEEP-FRIED SHALLOTS

Traditionally, deep-fried shallots are cooked in a big wok. If it's more convenient, you can cook the shallots in a deep-sided saucepan. These shallots are quite hard to resist, so it's always better to make plenty. Thai shallots are an important garnish in Thai cooking and are a component in salads, stir-fries and curries. They can be stored in an airtight container for 2 days. The perfumed oil can be kept for general cooking.

As a general rule, 1 cup of sliced shallots will make half that amount when deep-fried. As Thai shallots are very tiny, I'm inclined to use the normal brown shallots for deep-frying. It saves a lot of peeling.

TO PREPARE DEEP-FRIED SHALLOTS

Line a tray with kitchen paper. Peel the shallots and slice them very thinly lengthwise. It's important to keep them an even thickness so as to control the cooking. Fill a wok or a saucepan with sunflower oil to a depth of 6cm or more. Heat the oil until hot and then add the shallots. They will sizzle as you add them. Using a metal spoon, keep moving the shallots so that they cook evenly. The oil should be kept moderately high, but not so high that the shallots will go golden within the first minute – they generally take about 5 minutes, but judge by the colour, not the length of time.

Keep tossing the shallots until they go golden. They will continue to cook a little from the residual heat after removing them from the wok, so don't let them become too dark in colour.

Remove and place directly on kitchen paper. Fluff them up with two forks just to separate them and leave to cool. When cold, store in an airtight container.

TO DEEP-FRY GARLIC

Peel and slice the garlic thinly lengthways, taking care to slice evenly. Add the garlic to the hot oil and toss continuously with a metal spoon until the garlic turns a pale golden. (Always test the temperature with one piece of garlic before adding all the slices.) Remove and place on kitchen paper to drain. Store in an airtight container for up to 2 days.

Garlic slices should always be deep-fried after shallots, as they will flavour the oil. They will also turn the oil a slightly richer colour. This oil can be used for general cooking as well as Thai stir-fries.

David Thompson's Stir-fried Prawns with Curry Powder and Cucumber Relish

The cucumber relish and the stir-fried prawns create such a perfect balance that it's best to consider the two as inseparable. The stir-fry has the interesting technique of adding eggs that coat the prawns and in turn develop a wonderful flavour from the ginger, garlic and curry powder.

Serves 2–3

2 eggs

vegetable oil

16 large black tiger prawns, peeled and deveined

1 rounded tbsp curry powder

2 tbsp coconut cream

2 tsp fish sauce

1 tsp rice vinegar

small pinch of caster sugar

1 small bunch of spring onions, cut into 2cm lengths

bunch of coriander leaves

cucumber relish (page 235), to serve

Thai rice (page 236), to serve

FOR THE PASTE

3 large garlic cloves, peeled

an equivalent amount of peeled ginger

roots from 2 coriander stems (or else use the ends from a few stems)

pinch of sea salt

To make the paste

Using a pestle and mortar, pound the garlic, ginger, coriander roots and salt into a rather coarse paste.

To make the stir-fry

Break the eggs into a small bowl. Have all the other ingredients to hand.

Heat a wok and when it begins to smoke, add 2 tablespoons of oil. Lift up the wok and swirl the oil to coat the sides. Add in the paste and toss quickly for a few seconds before adding the prawns. Spread the prawns out a little around the wok, as this will allow them to start to colour. Toss regularly but not continuously, as you want the prawns to char a little. After a minute or two, sprinkle in the curry powder. Continue to cook the prawns for a few moments, tossing regularly, then push the prawns over to one side and add another tablespoon of oil to the bottom of the wok.

Pour in the eggs and the coconut cream. Allow the eggs to cook for a few seconds, then break up the yolks with a metal spoon. Continue to break up the eggs until they are beginning to set a little, then mix them in with all the prawns. Season with the fish sauce, vinegar and a small pinch of sugar. Mix in the spring onions and sprinkle with the coriander leaves. Serve with the cucumber relish and Thai rice.

Cucumber Relish

The cucumber relish is also fabulous with curries.

Serves 6

120g caster sugar

150ml water

120ml rice vinegar

4 Thai red shallots, finely sliced (or small brown shallots)

1 long red chilli, cut into thin strips or rounds (the seeds and membrane can be removed for less heat)

4cm piece of fresh root ginger, cut into matchstick strips

1 cucumber

20g coriander leaves

20g mint leaves

Combine the sugar, water and vinegar in a small saucepan and bring to the boil. Remove from the heat when the sugar dissolves and allow to cool. It should taste both sour and sweet. This can be prepared in advance and kept in the fridge.

Place the shallots, chilli and ginger in a bowl. Leaving the skin on the cucumber, slice it lengthways into quarters. Remove the seeds from the centre. Slice the cucumber at an angle into thin strips about 5cm long and mix with the shallots, chilli and ginger. Add in the coriander and mint leaves. Pour over the vinegar/ sugar liquid. Mix and serve at room temperature. The relish should be put together at the last minute so that it stays fresh and crisp.

Thai Jasmine Rice

Start by rinsing the rice in several changes of water, very gently rubbing the grains together to remove the excess starch. Drain and repeat the process a number of times until the water becomes clear.

Choose an appropriate size pot for the amount of rice you want to cook – a small, deep pot for small quantities and a wider pot for larger quantities. It's best not to cook too much in one pot. As a general guideline, 2½ cups of rice will be sufficient for 4–6 people. For this quantity, you will need to add about 3½ cups of water. If you have a pandanus leaf (the Thai equivalent of our bay leaf), then knot one or two leaves and place them in the pot to cook along with the rice. If adding salt, allow about 1 teaspoon salt to 2½ cups rice.

Bring the rice up to the boil, turn down the heat to its lowest setting, cover with a lid and allow to cook undisturbed for 10–15 minutes. It's important not to stir during this time or the rice may become too starchy. Towards the end of the cooking time, check the rice. If the grains on the top look a little dry, then sprinkle with a few tablespoons of water, return the lid and continue cooking on a low heat for a few more minutes. When cooked, leave the rice to sit for at least a further 10 minutes before serving.

REHEATING RICE

Care should be taken when you are using rice. There are food risks involved, but these are easily eliminated if these principles are followed:

Serve rice as soon as it's cooked. If that isn't possible, then cool the rice as quickly as possible – ideally within an hour. The best way is to spread it out on a flat tray to cool quickly.

Do not keep rice in the fridge for more than one day.

Do not reheat rice more than once.

When reheating rice, always check that it's steaming hot the whole way through.

THAI SALADS AND DRESSINGS

Spicy Beef Salad with Thai Chilli Dressing

The dressing is the key to this salad. It has all four of the primary tastes of Thai cooking: hot, sweet, sour, salty. Balancing the dressing often comes down to a personal preference – I definitely prefer my dressings to have a hint of sweetness and others prefer the lip-puckering sourness to sing through. Thai salads can be eaten alone, with rice or as one element of a Thai meal.

Serves 8 as a light lunch or starter

100g unsalted peanuts

12 spring onions

½ cucumber

1 red pepper, deseeded and cut into thin strips

½ red onion, thinly sliced

24 cherry tomatoes, quartered

2 handfuls fresh mint leaves

2 handfuls fresh coriander leaves

4 x 170g thick fillet steaks

1 tbsp olive oil

salt and freshly ground black pepper

FOR THE DRESSING

2 garlic cloves, crushed

1 small regular red chilli, deseeded and roughly chopped

25g palm sugar or soft brown sugar

2 tbsp light soy sauce

2 tbsp freshly squeezed lime juice

1 tbsp fish sauce

OVEN *Preheat the oven to 200°C, 180°C Fan, 350°F, Gas 6.*

To roast the peanuts

Place the peanuts on a baking tray and toast in the oven for about 5 minutes. Leave to cool.

To make the dressing

Whizz all the dressing ingredients together with a hand blender. Alternatively, pound the garlic and chilli in a pestle and mortar, then add the remaining ingredients. Mix well until the sugar is dissolved. Taste the dressing and correct the balance, if necessary.

To prepare the salad

Slice the green and white parts of the spring onions into 1cm strips. Peel the cucumber and shave into long, thin slices with a vegetable peeler. Place in a bowl and add the strips of pepper, red onion, cherry tomatoes, peanuts, mint and coriander leaves. Cover and set aside until the steaks are ready.

To cook the steaks

Remove the steaks from the fridge well ahead of time to allow them to come to room temperature.

Heat the oil in a frying pan until very hot. Season the steaks with salt and pepper. Place the steaks in the pan and cook over a high heat for a few minutes, until the steaks have caramelised on the surface. Turn over and repeat on the other side. Remove the steaks from the pan and transfer to a baking sheet. Place the steaks in the preheated oven and cook for 3–4 minutes, depending on the thickness of the steaks, making sure that the steaks remain rare. Remove from the oven and allow to rest on a plate for about 5 minutes before serving. Slice the beef thinly and add to the ingredients in the bowl. Spoon the dressing over the salad and toss to mix. Serve immediately.

Scallop Salad with Peanut Brittle and Peanut Jim Dressing

This is an extraordinary salad, so different to what we are used to. Once again, there is much balance to be found in the Thai dressing. In addition, there is a peanut praline to add both sweetness and texture. Even the scallops are approached differently – lightly poached so that the strength of the dressing still shines through. The salad needs to be prepared as close as possible to serving.

Serves 4

1 x 4cm piece of fresh root ginger

1 green bird's eye chilli (about 5cm in length)

20 scallops

deep-fried garlic (page 233)

up to 1 tbsp fish sauce

pinch of caster sugar

pinch of chilli powder

2 tbsp fresh lime juice

1 tbsp mandarin juice

2 Thai red shallots, finely sliced

1 stalk regular or Asian celery, finely sliced

2 tbsp very finely sliced lemongrass (see page 224)

2 large handfuls of Thai basil leaves

FOR THE PEANUT BRITTLE

120g toasted peanuts

120g caster sugar

100ml water

1 tbsp palm sugar or soft brown sugar

FOR THE PEANUT JIM DRESSING

8 coriander roots, cleaned (or use a few ends of coriander stems instead)

12 very thin slices of galangal (replace with ginger if unavailable)

2 tbsp chopped garlic

pinch of sea salt

1–2 Thai green chillies (about 5cm in length), deseeded

8 tbsp freshly squeezed lime juice

6 tbsp palm sugar or soft brown sugar

about 2 tbsp fish sauce

squeeze of mandarin juice

OVEN *Preheat the oven to 180°C, 160°C Fan, 350°F, Gas 4.*

To make the peanut brittle

Start by preparing the peanut brittle. Line a baking sheet with a silicone mat or a piece of baking parchment. Place the peanuts on a baking tray and toast in the oven for about 5 minutes. Allow to cool.

Place the sugar and water in a saucepan. Heat to dissolve the sugar, stirring once or twice. Bring up to the boil and continue cooking the syrup. Do not stir at any point while the syrup is boiling. As soon as you see the edges of the caramel turn a pale golden colour, it's important to be vigilant. The caramel will probably cook unevenly, so give the saucepan a swirl as the colour changes to encourage even colouring. Once the caramel is golden all over, add the peanuts and the

palm sugar. Stir to dissolve the palm sugar and to allow the nuts to become coated evenly. Pour immediately onto the lined tray. Allow to cool before handling. The peanut brittle can be stored in an airtight container and will keep for several days.

To make the peanut jim dressing

In a pestle and mortar, pound the coriander roots with the sliced galangal, garlic and salt to a fine paste. Add the chilli and pound slightly just to bruise. Add the lime juice, palm sugar and fish sauce and pound everything together. Using the pestle, break off a few chunks of the peanut brittle and pound once or twice to create several smallish chunks (rather than crumbs), then add to the dressing. Taste the dressing – it should be hot, sweet, sour and salty. It's important to get a balance and this can only be achieved by taste alone, so adjust as necessary. Finish with a squeeze of mandarin juice.

To prepare the salad

Slice the ginger as finely as possible. Stack the slices and cut into very thin matchstick strips. Split the chilli in half and remove the seeds. Slice into very fine matchstick strips.

To prepare the scallops, remove the roe and the muscle that is attached to the side of the scallops and discard. Divide the scallops in half, cutting horizontally. Bring a pot of salted water to the boil. Blanch the scallops for about 1½–2 minutes, depending on size. Remove with a slotted spoon, pat dry and allow to cool. Place the scallops in a bowl and add the deep-fried garlic, fish sauce, sugar and chilli powder. Add a squeeze of lime and mandarin juice. Add the ginger, shallots, celery, chilli, lemongrass and Thai basil to the bowl. Toss with enough dressing to coat the ingredients generously. Pile onto a plate and scatter over some more chunky pieces of the peanut brittle. Serve immediately.

NOTE It's important to dress the salad at the last minute.

THAI CURRY

Thai Green Curry with Chicken

There are many ways to achieve wonderful results with Thai ingredients in a short space of time. Curries, however, are an ambitious challenge, not for the faint-hearted or for those looking to rustle up a quick supper. If the chicken is poached and the paste made the day before, it lightens the workload dramatically. It also means that there is some lovely chicken broth to add to the curry.

The steps involved bring you to the heart of Thai cooking. This is also an opportunity to make fresh coconut milk (see page 248). The ingredients are brought together in ways that are far from familiar to a Western cook. And then there are the series of final adjustments – perhaps a little more fish sauce, Thai basil, some wild ginger. Relish this last stage, building experience and using your developing intuition to achieve a remarkable depth of flavour.

Serves 6

FOR THE GREEN CURRY PASTE

20g scraped and chopped coriander root (or if unavailable, use chopped coriander stems instead)

35g lemongrass, very finely chopped (tender part only, see page 224) – about 4 lemongrass stalks

25 Thai green chillies (about 5cm in length), deseeded and chopped (see note on chillies on page 247)

5 long green chillies (regular size), deseeded and chopped

15g finely chopped galangal (or ginger if galangal is unavailable)

½ tsp finely chopped kaffir lime zest (if unavailable, simply omit)

50g chopped Thai red shallots (about 4 red shallots), or substitute the equivalent amount of small brown shallots

20g chopped garlic (about 3 large garlic cloves)

½ tsp chopped red turmeric, peeled (or substitute ¼ tsp yellow turmeric powder)

1 tsp coriander seeds, roasted and ground

¼ tsp cumin seeds, roasted and ground

10 white peppercorns

1 level tsp shrimp paste (gapi)

FOR THE CHICKEN

1 whole free-range chicken

4–5 shallots

1 pandanus leaf (optional)

FOR THE CURRY SAUCE

450ml coconut cream

2 tbsp fish sauce, or to taste

450ml coconut milk (fresh or tinned)

250ml chicken stock (page 30), or more if required

TO GARNISH

2 green chillies

4 or 5 sticks of grachai (wild ginger), if available

2 large handfuls Thai basil leaves

3 kaffir lime leaves

To make the paste

Before pounding the ingredients in the pestle and mortar, have each ingredient set out on your chopping board in small piles. Pound the ingredients in the order given here.

With a Thai paste, always start by pounding the most fibrous ingredients first and then work your way down the list. It's important to pound each ingredient thoroughly, reducing it to a fine paste, before adding the next. You can add a little sea salt to the mortar at the beginning, which will help break down the most fibrous ingredients.

When the paste is finished, it can be used immediately or stored in the refrigerator for about a week. If the paste is to be kept, pack it tightly into a sterilised jar and press cling film or parchment paper onto the surface of the paste to prevent it from oxidising. Put a tight-fitting lid on the jar and refrigerate.

To poach the chicken

For this Thai green curry, a whole chicken is used. Poaching the chicken keeps it moist.

Place the chicken in a large, deep pot and cover with cold water. Bruise the shallots with the pestle and add them to the pot along with the pandanus leaf (if using). Bring up to the boil, skim off any scum and discard. Simmer until the chicken is tender. A smallish chicken may take about 40 minutes, while a large chicken will take about 1 hour. Allow the chicken to cool in the water for about 20 minutes.

Remove the chicken from the water and allow to drain. Reserve the broth. Remove the skin from the chicken and, with a knife, remove the breasts in one piece. Pull off thick strips of meat with your fingers. Repeat with the legs and thighs, discarding the skin. Set aside, or refrigerate when cold until ready to use.

To cook the paste and make the sauce

The next phase is fascinating. The initial task is to 'crack' the coconut cream. This means that the cream is simmered until the coconut oil separates from the solids. To start the process, place the coconut cream in a saucepan and bring up to the boil. Reduce the heat and let it simmer, stirring regularly, to prevent the paste from catching on the bottom of the saucepan. After several minutes, the coconut oil will start coming to the surface. Keep simmering until there is a clear film of oil on the surface.

Add the curry paste to the 'cracked' coconut cream. Fry over a medium heat, stirring regularly to prevent the paste from burning. As the paste continues to cook, you can smell the changes taking place. At first the raw shallots and garlic predominate. As it cooks further and the water evaporates, the aromas of the lemongrass and galangal will come through more strongly. As a very rough guideline, it will take about 5 minutes to cook out a paste made with fresh chillies and perhaps twice that time for a paste made from dried chillies. As the paste is cooked out, the colour deepens. The oil will separate and return to the surface and the fried paste will develop a scrambled appearance. When the paste starts to smell fragrant and loses the rawness of the shallots and garlic, it is time to moisten the paste with coconut milk.

At this point, season the curry with a little fish sauce and add the coconut milk and some chicken broth. Continue cooking the curry for 10 minutes, or longer. If the curry seems rather thick, thin out with a ladle of chicken stock. Traditionally, green curry is a thin curry. Taste and add some more fish sauce, if necessary. The amount of fish sauce required will vary each time and will add great depth of flavour to the curry. However, add the fish sauce by degrees. The curry may be prepared up to this point in advance. Refrigerate when cold, if necessary.

Just before serving

Slice the chillies in half, deseed and cut into strips. Peel the grachai (wild ginger) and cut into fine matchstick strips. Reheat the sauce and add the chicken. Simmer the curry for a few minutes to reheat the chicken and to bring out the flavours. When hot, finish with the green chilli, the strips of shredded grachai (if using) and the Thai basil leaves. Crush the lime leaves in your hand and add to the sauce. This is the ideal opportunity to experiment – adding, tasting, adjusting and learning the impact of each ingredient.

At what point is it ready? If it tastes only very, very good, then there is still some adjusting to do. When it has the depth you are aiming for, you will feel your knees trembling and you may need to sit down. Hopefully you will have sufficient energy to contact those dear to you. Tell them to drop whatever they are doing and come immediately.

NOTE Pea aubergines can be added for a little surprising bitterness. Add about 2 tablespoons of pea aubergines into the curry about 5 minutes before the end of the cooking.

THAI BIRD'S EYE CHILLIES

Thai bird's eye chillies are considerably hotter than the slightly larger Thai green chillies which measure about 5cm in length. If using bird's eye, adjust the quantity radically.

Fresh Coconut Milk and Cream

Fresh and tinned coconut milk are interchangeable. At some point, it's worth trying to make your own fresh coconut milk and cream.

Coconut milk can be extracted a day in advance, and this is often a good option. In the cookery school, if we have large numbers, we would often break open the coconuts into chunks the night before. Covered with plenty of cold water and refrigerated, they keep well and indeed could last another day if the water was changed after 24 hours. They lie there ready to be scooped and whizzed as we need them.

A general rule of thumb is to allow one coconut per person for a curry. When choosing coconuts, check that there are no cracks on the shell and give them a good shake to make sure that there is still some water inside. If you hear nothing sloshing around, it means that the water has dried up, which makes it much more likely that there will be mould on the surface of the coconut flesh when you open it up. Mould around the eyes of the coconut is another sign of likely spoilage.

To start, heat some water in a saucepan. Ideally bring the water up to the boil and then let it cool to lukewarm, as this sterilises the water and helps keep the coconut milk/cream for longer. If you are planning to use the milk within 24 hours, it can be brought to this temperature without boiling.

You will then need the following:

1 or 2 tea towels

large chopping knife/cleaver

1 oyster shucker
  (this is a tool for opening oysters)

1 large bowl

food processor or blender

plastic or glass bowl, for storing the
  coconut milk/cream

large piece of muslin

Now arm yourself with a tea towel – fold it a few times and lay it on the palm of your hand. Sit the coconut on the folded cloth. Place a large bowl underneath your hand. Take a knife or cleaver and using the blunt side at a point near the handle, strike the coconut around its middle, turning it around a little after each blow. The aim is not to split the coconut open with a single blow, but to develop hairline cracks that shimmy their way around the surface. It's easier to remove the flesh if the coconut breaks into a number of pieces rather than simply in half.

The water that comes out of the coconut can be discarded.

To remove the flesh I start, as a right-hander, by wrapping the tea towel fully around my left hand. Then I prise the flesh out of the coconut using the point of an oyster shucker (I would never use a knife, since the tip is so easily damaged in this sort of task). After removing all the flesh, rinse it in a large bowl of water. This is an important step that prevents the coconut flesh from souring as well as removing any last pieces of husk.

Chop up the flesh into small chunks and then add in batches to your food processor or blender. Whizz until the coconut is fairly fine and then add a little warm water as you blend. The warm water will help release the oils and the cream from the coconut, giving a much better yield.

Place a sieve over a bowl and line it with a double layer of muslin. Put a good ladleful of coconut and liquid from the processor/blender into the muslin, gather up the edges and twist tightly, squeezing out as much liquid as you can into a plastic or glass bowl. Repeat with the remaining coconut. Leave the coconut milk and cream to sit at room temperature for 1–1½ hours to separate. Refrigerate.

If you want to use the coconut cream and milk separately, then spoon the coconut cream off the top, leaving the thinner milk underneath. Both the coconut milk and cream will last for about 2 days in the fridge.

Hake with Thai Flavours Wrapped in a Banana Leaf

Using banana leaves to wrap fish is a simple way of cooking and allows for a dramatic presentation. I buy a regular jar of curry paste from the supermarket for these parcels (homemade red curry paste needs to be cooked out) and add Thai ingredients such as lemongrass, lime leaves and, if available, my favourite of all, Thai basil leaves. I have barbecued a whole halibut in banana leaves, but I usually make individual servings. The parcels are opened at table, allowing you to inhale the aromas as you unwrap the fish and to mop up all the juices.

Serves 6

6 large sheets of banana leaves

6 kaffir lime leaves

4 tbsp red curry paste (2 tsp per parcel)

12 tbsp coconut cream

good handful of Thai basil leaves, if available

6 x 170g pieces of hake fillet (or other thick white fish, such as cod, haddock or halibut), skin removed

salt

2 sticks of lemongrass, halved, bruised with the back of a knife and cut into 6cm lengths

Thai rice (page 236), to serve

EQUIPMENT *Wooden skewers, soaked for about 1 hour in cold water*

Sit a large steamer over a pot of boiling water. Steam the banana leaves for a minute or two so that they will bend more easily. Remove from the steamer and lay them out on the counter. Wipe the leaves clean with a cloth. Remove the central vein from the kaffir lime leaves and shred the leaves as finely as possible with a knife.

Cut out 6 rectangles measuring approx. 25cm x 30cm (exact size is not important), allowing enough leaf to wrap around the fish comfortably (shinier sides outermost). Cut 6 more rectangles, this time slightly smaller than the first. Lay out 6 of the larger banana leaves on the counter and place the 6 smaller leaves on top.

In the centre of each leaf, spoon in 1 teaspoon of red curry paste, 1 tablespoon of coconut cream, some of the shredded lime leaves and a few Thai basil leaves. Season the fish on both sides and sit in the centre of the leaf. Repeat the same layering of ingredients on top and cap with a piece of bruised lemongrass. Fold the inner banana leaf to cover the fish and then wrap up the outer banana leaf (quite tightly) and seal with some wooden skewers. The parcels may be prepared in advance and refrigerated for several hours.

To cook, place the parcels on a medium-hot barbecue. They will take about 10 minutes, but the timing will depend on the heat of the barbecue and the thickness of the fish. To serve, peel off the outer layer of banana leaf. Serve with some Thai rice.

NOTE Another option is to preheat a griddle until smoking and to cook the parcels initially on the griddle and then to transfer them to an oven at 200°C, 180°C Fan, 400°F, Gas 6.

NO BANANA LEAVES? A SIMPLE SOLUTION

As an alternative to banana leaves, the fish can be cooked in a sealed parcel made from baking parchment. Fold a sheet of baking parchment in half and cut out a semicircle approximately 18cm in radius. When the double sheet is opened out, the circle will then be 36cm in diameter. If you have a long roll of baking parchment, you can fold the paper back and forth, each time approximately 18cm in depth, in order to cut out all the semicircles together.

Spread out each sheet of paper on the countertop. Layer the fish and all the other ingredients on one half of the paper, adding the ingredients in the same order as the recipe above. Fold over the free half of each paper so that both ends meet and fold the edges in twice to seal them, creasing as you go. The parcels can be cooked in the oven at 200°C, 180°C Fan, 400°F, Gas 6 for 12–15 minutes, depending on the thickness of the fish. Open up one of the parcels and peek inside to check if the fish is ready. If not, seal it up again and return to the oven. Remove the parcels from the tray as soon as they come out of the oven.

INDIAN
STALKING ATUL

Historians are interested to follow the Spice Trail, the old routes along which spices were traditionally transported. My own Spice Trail was to track down Atul Kochhar, the first Indian chef to get a Michelin star.

I was intrigued as to how he had impressed such traditionally conservative critics with his Indian food. When I was in London, I went to hunt him down in person but was unsuccessful. I narrowly missed him twice at Benares, his flagship restaurant in London for the last decade. I can remember the details of both meals vividly, including the fish with the herb and spice crust that's featured in this chapter. Atul was still proving elusive, however. A year later, I found out that he was one of the guest chefs at Taste of Dublin. Purrfect, I thought. I watched him in action at the demo theatre and then bided my time. When the actual moment arrived, I was speechless. Fortunately, he rescued me with great charm and was happy to accept my invitation to come and teach at the cookery school.

Atul is a co-owner of Dublin's best Indian restaurant, Ananda, so he enjoys his trips to the city. Ananda's head chef is Sunil Ghai, who has become a regular tutor at the school. In this section, I share some of the recipes, skills and tricks I have picked up while cooking with my two Indian mentors. My real journey into the world of spices began with them.

INDIAN SPICES

SHOPPING LIST

If you don't have spices in your cupboard, it can be dispiriting to have to go to a specialist shop each time you plan a meal. Buy a range of spices in one visit to an Asian market. If you buy the following, you can cook all the recipes in this section.

black mustard seeds

cardamom pods (green and black)

chaat masala

chilli powder (Deggi Mirch brand)

cloves

cinnamon sticks

cinnamon, ground

coriander seeds

cumin seeds

curry leaves

fennel seeds

fenugreek seeds

garam masala

mustard seeds

onion seeds (sometimes called kalonji or nigella seeds)

paprika

turmeric

BLACK MUSTARD SEEDS

I love these little black seeds (actually, they're often more brown than black) and use them in everything from rice dishes to tadkas (page 259) and vegetable dishes. When added to hot oil, they jump out of the pan (sometimes quite high), which I always find entertaining.

CARDAMOM PODS (GREEN AND BLACK)

Cardamom pods come in two varieties: green and black. The green pods are used whole, as the outer casing itself has a wonderful flavour, but they are not meant to be eaten. Some recipes call for cardamom seeds. These can be removed by breaking open the pods.

Black cardamom pods have thick black outer husks and an extraordinary aroma that's intense and smoky. They need to be used sparingly and are not usually substituted for the green pods, as they impart a completely different flavour. They can be added to rice dishes, lamb curries or as a flavouring when cooking pulses.

CHAAT MASALA

Chaat masala is a combination of spices, typically dried mango powder (amchoor), coriander, dried ginger, asafoetida, black pepper, black salt, cumin and chilli powder. One of the reasons it's the spice of choice for street vendors is that it's reckoned to increase your appetite! It's a mild spice that is sold in powdered form and is often sprinkled on dishes just before serving. In this chapter, it's an important ingredient in the spice paste for the brill and for the chicken tandoori. When seasoning a dish, bear in mind that there is already salt in this mix.

CHILLI POWDER – DEGGI MIRCH BRAND

This is a mild chilli powder that is made exclusively from Kashmiri chillies. It adds flavour, heat and colour. If you want to use another type of chilli powder, it is advisable to consider using less than the recipe states.

CINNAMON OR CASSIA

Cinnamon and cassia come from the same botanical family. Cinnamon bark comes in smoother scrolls, has a more delicate flavour and is more expensive.

CORIANDER SEEDS

There is no waste in Indian cooking. A good example is coriander – roots, stalks, seeds and leaves are all used in different ways. Coriander seeds are round and similar in size to black peppercorns. They have quite a mild flavour. Ideally, they should be ground freshly as needed.

CUMIN

This is my favourite spice. It has a natural affinity with lamb and is added to many rice dishes. It can be used whole, roasted or ground to a powder. Like so many other spices, it's best to buy the seeds whole and grind them as required.

CURRY LEAVES

Curry leaves tend to arrive attached to stalks, so they stand out on the shelves. I scoop them up so that I can keep some for immediate use (or store for a few days in a plastic bag in the fridge) or freeze them. The strength of curry leaves is highly variable. They freeze really well, whereas the dried leaves have little flavour.

FENNEL SEEDS

The greenish-yellow fennel seed comes from the fennel plant. Fennel seeds give a delicious, aniseed-like flavour to meat and vegetables.

FENUGREEK SEEDS

Fenugreek seeds are rectangular and are actually a bean, but because of their bitter taste are used as a spice. They can be whole or powdered.

ONION SEEDS OR NIGELLA SEEDS

Onion seeds have nothing to do with onions at all, but they look like an onion seed and the name has stuck. They go by a range of other names, including nigella seeds and kalonji. They have a sweet taste.

TURMERIC

Turmeric is widely used in Indian food. It has a mild flavour and a great yellow colour. Its woody aroma blends best with onion and tomato sauces. If you are a messy eater, don't put on the white linen tablecloth or the party dress when you are using turmeric – it does stain easily.

SOME TERMS AND TECHNIQUES

STORING SPICES

If you have spices that have been lurking in the cupboard for too long, the only option is to get a fresh supply. Spices lose their intensity over time and should certainly not be kept longer than six months. Buying certain spices whole and grinding them just before use radically improves their flavour. Spices should be stored in a cool, dark place.

Certain spices, such as yellow turmeric, paprika or chaat masala, should be bought in ground form.

GINGER GARLIC PASTE

Ginger garlic paste is a major ingredient used in so many Indian dishes. It's common to make it with 50% garlic and 50% ginger, but some prefer a balance of 60% ginger, 40% garlic. To make the paste, peel both the garlic and ginger and put in a blender with a dash of water and sunflower oil and purée to a paste. Press the paste into a small jar and level the surface. Cover with a thin layer of oil to prevent it from oxidising. The ginger garlic paste will keep for about 3 weeks in the fridge.

GRINDING AND POUNDING

A good pestle and mortar are really useful. A heavy pestle means you don't have to work so hard. Pounding spices gently gets you in the mood as the wonderful aromas are released. However, it's also important to have an electric spice grinder (or coffee grinder), as this means that you can grind spices quickly and to a fine powder.

Coriander and cumin are good examples of spices that I always buy whole and grind in small quantities for immediate use.

HOMEMADE GARAM MASALA

Garam masala is a good example of how grinding your own spices in small quantities will yield a much better result than buying a ready-made pack. Put 1 tablespoon of cardamom seeds, a 5cm stick of cinnamon, 1 teaspoon of black cumin seeds, 1 teaspoon of whole cloves, 1 teaspoon of black peppercorns and a quarter of a nutmeg into a grinder for half a minute and then store in a small jar with a tight-fitting lid. This can be added to many dishes, often towards the end of cooking.

DRY ROASTING

Some recipes call for dry roasting. This involves putting spices into a dry pan, which brings out a more intense flavour. To roast the spices, heat a frying pan until hot and then add a layer of spice. Shake the pan, tossing regularly until the spice goes a slight shade darker and has a nutty aroma. Allow to cool before grinding.

HUNG CURD

Hung curd is yoghurt that is hung for some hours to allow the whey to drain out, resulting in a consistency between yoghurt and cheese. Hung curd is the base for the spicy paste that is rubbed on Atul's tandoori chicken (page 280) as well as various starters and accompaniments suggested in this chapter.

To make hung curd, cut out two squares of muslin and place the Greek yoghurt in the centre. Bring the muslin together and tie it at the top with string. Hang up the muslin bag and allow it to drip into a bowl for a number of hours, preferably overnight.

The overnight version leads to a much thicker curd that holds its shape well and adheres to the chicken during cooking. I remember the day, prior to an Indian class with Sunil, when we had only managed to hang the curd for a few hours beforehand. Sunil enquired how long it had been draining. "Overnight," replied one of the staff with a smile. He flicked the muslin with his index finger as he went past and, just from the touch, he said with a grin, "I think nearer three hours." There isn't much that gets past him.

GHEE

Ghee is a type of clarified butter (see page 81) that is used extensively in Indian cooking. Unlike regular clarified butter, however, the butter is simmered on the cooker to allow all the water to evaporate. The milk solids then develop a nutty flavour, which perfumes the butter itself. Ghee can be made at home or bought in tins in Asian stores. I tend to use the basic clarified butter where ghee is specified.

TADKA (TEMPERING SPICES)

Tempering spices, or tadka, is a process in which different spices/herbs are added to hot ghee or oil. This releases the essential oils and aromas, flavouring the oil and adding depth and an enticing aroma to the finished dish. It is the essential last step in making a dal, but it is a method used in many other dishes.

The process of making a tadka only takes seconds, so it is vital to have all the spices ready beside you. When whole spices are added to hot oil, they will crackle and change colour, so it's imperative to check the temperature of the oil before you begin. Start by adding one or two grains of spice to the oil to check the heat. If they sizzle, you can proceed. If they don't, wait a few more seconds and test again.

Sunil's Potato Cakes with Spiced Peas and Mint Chutney

These small potato cakes, golden and crispy on the outside, have a stuffing of peas, raisins and cumin. Match them with a mint chutney and a spoonful of hung curd (page 259) or Greek yoghurt and they become something quite special.

Makes 12 potato cakes

1kg Rooster potatoes

salt

FOR THE STUFFING

2 tbsp sunflower oil

2 green chillies, deseeded and finely chopped

1 tbsp scraped and minced fresh ginger

180g peas, fresh or frozen

60g golden raisins, chopped

1½ tsp ground roasted cumin seeds (see page 259)

good pinch of red chilli powder, or to taste

salt

gram flour, for dipping the cakes (or use plain flour)

2–3 tbsp ghee or clarified butter (page 81), for pan-frying

TO SERVE

mint chutney (page 263)

hung curd (page 259) or Greek yoghurt

good pinch of roasted cumin

salt

Steam the potatoes in their jackets. Peel while still hot, then pass through a potato ricer or mash with a potato masher. Place in a bowl and season with salt. Set aside to cool.

To make the stuffing, heat the pan and add the oil. Add the green chillies and ginger and sauté for a minute or two. Add the peas and raisins. Mix in the ground cumin seeds and chilli powder and check the seasoning. Continue cooking for another couple of minutes. Allow to cool.

To make the potato cakes, divide the mashed potato into 12 portions. Gently flatten each portion into a round about 1cm thick. Place a portion of stuffing in the centre. Fold the edges over very carefully so that the potato covers the pea mixture. Now very gently flatten it between the palms of your hand into a potato cake about 6cm wide and 3cm deep (the exact size isn't important). Repeat the procedure until all the potato is used up.

Just before cooking, sieve some gram flour onto a plate. Dip the potato cakes in the flour and shake off the excess. Heat 1 or 2 tablespoons of ghee or clarified butter in a non-stick pan. When hot, add the potato cakes and pan-fry on both sides till crisp and golden brown, adding more ghee/clarified butter if required. When the potato cakes are golden on the surface, turn down the heat and

continue to cook slowly. This will make the potato cakes crispier and will heat them all the way through. The potato cakes may be pan-fried in advance and then reheated in the oven just before serving.

To serve, mix the hung curd or Greek yoghurt with a good pinch of roasted cumin and salt. Spread a circle of mint chutney on the plate and then place 2 potato cakes in the centre, the second leaning on the first. Top with a spoonful of hung curd or Greek yoghurt. Serve additional mint chutney on the side.

NOTE The potato cakes can be made in advance and refrigerated for up to a day.

Mint Chutney

This is a chutney that is made in seconds by whizzing everything in a blender. You could serve it with tandoori chicken (page 280), naan bread (page 268) or as a side dish for all sorts of curries. It's best made and eaten on the same day so that you can enjoy the freshness of the herbs. Throwing some ice into the blender is a trick that prevents the motor from heating the herbs and turning them a dull green.

Serves 6–8

75g fresh mint
75g fresh coriander
3 green chillies
1 apple

small piece of fresh ginger
salt
juice of 1 lime
1 tbsp olive oil
1½ tsp caster sugar, or more to taste

Place all the ingredients in a blender along with 4 or 5 ice cubes. Add a dash of water. Whizz until the mixture is blended to a purée.

The mint chutney can also be mixed with Greek yoghurt.

Aubergine Stuffed with Potatoes and Spices, Mustard and Yoghurt Chutney

This is not a traditional dish. There was such a demand for aubergines at Ananda that the team was inspired to come up with this winning combination. There are a few steps involved but the effort is well worth it.

Serves 4

400g aubergine

salt

sunflower oil, for pan-frying

1 tsp cumin seeds

3 garlic cloves, chopped

20g fresh ginger, finely chopped

1 green chilli, deseeded and finely chopped

½ tsp ground turmeric, plus a little extra

¼ tsp red chilli powder, plus a little extra

200g potatoes, boiled, cooled and grated

30g fresh coriander, chopped

semolina or fine polenta, for dipping the aubergine

mustard and yoghurt chutney (page 266), to serve (optional)

chilli oil, to serve (optional)

deep-fried aubergine slices (page 266), to garnish (optional)

Cut 4–5 slices from the widest part of the aubergine, each 2cm thick. Using a cutter if you have one, cut out an inner circle within the round of aubergine, leaving a border of about 7mm. Chop the pulp from the centre into small, even cubes. Sprinkle the aubergine rings and cubes with salt and set aside for 30 minutes or longer. Rinse the aubergine and pat dry.

Meanwhile, make the stuffing. Heat some oil in a frying pan, add the cumin seeds and let them crackle. Add the garlic and toss it around the pan for about 20 seconds, being careful not to let it brown. Add the finely chopped ginger and green chilli and toss again, continuously moving the spices so that they don't brown too much.

Add the cubed aubergine, turmeric and red chilli powder and toss in the pan to cook the aubergine. After a few minutes, add 1 tablespoon of water to help prevent the spices from burning. Continue cooking until the aubergine becomes tender, then add the grated potatoes and season with salt. Toss well to mix all the ingredients.

You're not looking for a purée, but you do want the aubergines and potatoes to be well blended together. Add the chopped coriander and check the seasoning. Turn out onto a plate and leave to cool completely.

In a bowl, toss the aubergine circles with some salt, a pinch of turmeric and a pinch of chilli powder. Place the aubergine slices on a board and spoon the stuffing into the centre. Compact it really well with a spoon so that it's level with the surface of the aubergine rim.

Dip both sides of the aubergine in semolina or fine polenta . Heat the pan, add some oil and once warm, gently fry the aubergine until crisp on both sides. Reduce the heat and continue cooking until the aubergine is tender. Turn several times during the cooking. The aubergine can also be pan-fried on both sides until golden and then transferred to a baking tray and finished off in a hot oven.

Serve warm with mustard and yoghurt chutney, and a drizzle of chilli oil (if using). Garnish with deep-fried aubergine slices (optional).

Mustard and Yoghurt Chutney

This is my favourite chutney. The fresh curry leaves are worth hunting down, as they are the key ingredient. Fresh curry leaves are available in most Asian markets and freeze well.

Serves 6

300g Greek or natural yoghurt
1 tsp salt
2 tbsp sunflower oil
1 tsp mustard seeds

10 fresh or frozen curry leaves
½ tsp ground turmeric
4 tsp lime juice
2–3 tsp honey

Place the yoghurt in a bowl and season with the salt. Heat the oil in a pan and when hot, add the mustard seeds. They should sizzle as soon as they hit the oil and then will start popping and jumping. As soon as they quiet down, add the curry leaves and turmeric. The curry leaves will curl up from the heat of the oil. After about 10 seconds, pour the curried oil, along with all the spices, on top of the yoghurt and stir in. Add the lime juice and honey.

If the yoghurt is a little sour, add more honey (I like it to be on the slightly sweet side). If it's a little too sweet, add more lime juice.

Deep-fried Aubergines Slices

As a garnish, it looks impressive to have a few crispy slices of aubergine that have been deep-fried. These need to be prepared at the last minute.

Heat some vegetable oil until hot. Thinly slice some aubergine and cut each slice in two. Season with salt and deep-fry until golden. Drain on kitchen paper and serve immediately with the stuffed aubergine and mustard and yoghurt chutney.

A drizzle of chilli oil, some quartered cherry tomatoes and micro leaves are a nice addition to the plate (see the photo on page 265).

Chutneys and naan bread from *Ananda*.

Naan

Naan bread is traditionally made in a tandoor oven. As an alternative to the tandoor, naan breads can be cooked on a pizza stone. The intense heat of the stone makes the dough puff up instantly and they are cooked in the space of just 2 to 3 minutes. They can be served with chutneys, as we do in the cookery school, or served alongside almost any Indian meal. Sprinkle them with seeds, such as nigella or cumin seeds, stuff them with an almond filling to make Peschwari naan or press some coriander and garlic on the surface before cooking and you have a range of flavoured naans. Naan breads are usually brushed with melted butter or ghee as soon as they come out of the oven.

There are numerous recipes for naan bread, most made with yeast and often yoghurt and others made with self-raising flour. The naan bread recipe below is made by the latter method.

Serves 6–10

1kg self-raising flour

25g caster sugar

15g salt

1 egg

100ml milk

50ml sunflower oil

400–500ml water

melted butter, for brushing on the naan

Place a pizza stone in the oven 1 hour before cooking. Turn the oven up to its very highest setting – ideally 250ºC, 230ºC Fan, 475ºF, Gas 9. If you don't have a pizza stone, you can cook the naan on a baking tray. In that case, preheat the baking tray in the oven for about 10 minutes.

In a bowl, mix the self-raising flour, sugar and salt. In another bowl, mix together the egg, milk and half the oil. Gradually add this liquid to the dry ingredients and then start drizzling in the water, little by little. Add just enough water to bring the dough together into a softish dough. It should not be sticky. Scoop out onto a lightly floured counter and knead for a minute or two to bring the dough together. Cover the dough with cling film and leave for about 10 minutes. Knead again and incorporate the remaining oil into the dough. Keep kneading until the dough is smooth, about 5 minutes. Brush the inside of the bowl with a touch of sunflower oil and return the dough to the bowl. Cover with cling film, making sure that the bowl is completely sealed. Set the dough aside for at least 2 hours to prove.

Divide the dough into 10 pieces. On an unfloured surface and with unfloured hands, shape each piece of dough into rounds (see box below) about the size of small doughnuts. Dip the rounds in flour and place on a tray lined with cling film. Cover and leave to rest in a warm place for at least 15 minutes before shaping. The dough can be left for several hours in the fridge, provided that it is very well covered.

To cook the naan

There is a skill to stretching the dough by hand that is somewhat mesmerising. I still settle for my rolling pin to do the task.

Roll out each ball into a circle and then pull out one side to make a teardrop shape. You can flavour the naan with a sprinkling of onion seeds (also known as kalonji or nigella seeds), cumin seeds or some finely chopped garlic and chopped coriander leaves. Do not use ground spices, as they burn easily.

Cook on a preheated pizza stone or baking tray in the oven until puffed up and pale golden on the underside. The bread will still be quite pale on the top. The naan will cook in about 4 minutes on a pizza stone or twice as long on a baking tray. Brush with melted butter as soon as they come out of the oven. Serve warm. If you wish to reheat the naan, wrap them in tinfoil and place in a hot oven for about 5 minutes.

SHAPING THE DOUGH INTO ROUNDS

Place one piece of dough on an unfloured counter. Cup one hand over the dough, keeping the thumb resting on the counter. Placing a little bit of pressure on the dough, roll the dough quickly in an anticlockwise movement, using the thumb to keep the dough pressed into a round. Keep rolling the dough in this fashion until it becomes a perfectly smooth ball. You will achieve a much better result if you pre-shape the dough into a round and then allow it to relax for at least 15 minutes.

Sunil's Tomato Chutney

Indian chutneys vary from ones that are cooked over a number of hours to others that are just whizzed in a liquidiser or cooked briefly with fresh ingredients. This chutney fits into the latter category and can be rustled up in under a quarter of an hour. In order to achieve consistent results, I am inclined to use cherry tomatoes, but any good tomatoes with a deep flavour will work well. I pair this chutney with naan (page 268) or tandoori chicken (page 280), among other things. If you want to serve two chutneys with the naan, the mint chutney on page 263 provides a great contrast to this one.

Serves 6

2 tbsp sunflower oil

5 cloves

4 bay leaves

1 tsp onion seeds

100g onions, sliced very thinly

40g fresh ginger, chopped

400g baby vine-ripened tomatoes

2 tbsp white wine vinegar

2 tsp caster sugar

¼–½ tsp Deggi Mirch brand chilli powder (see page 257)

salt

Heat the oil in a pan and add the cloves, bay leaves and onion seeds. Let them crackle, then add the onions and ginger and sauté until the onion becomes translucent. Add the tomatoes, vinegar, sugar, chilli powder and 4 tablespoons of water and cook for a further 10–15 minutes. You may need to add more water if all the liquid evaporates before the tomatoes have softened. The speed of evaporation will depend on the size of the pot and the juiciness of the tomatoes. Taste towards the end of the cooking and balance the sweet and sour element. If the chutney is too tart, add more sugar; not tart enough, add more vinegar. Finally, correct the seasoning.

INDIAN CURRIES, FISH AND MEAT

Most people who wish to get to grips with Indian food want to master a curry. Here are three very different examples. When you have mastered these curries, you will have the confidence to experiment further.

Coconut Milk Curry with Curry Leaves and Crab Claws

It's interesting to talk to Sunil about the sort of food his mother would cook. This is a homely and straightforward curry. It's also very versatile and can be made with a wide range of white fish.

Serves 4

4 tbsp sunflower oil

2 tsp mustard seeds

2 dried red chillies

1 onion, cut in half and sliced thinly

salt

2 green chillies, deseeded and cut into strips

5cm cube of fresh ginger, peeled, sliced thinly and cut into matchstick strips

1 tbsp ginger garlic paste (see page 258)

15 curry leaves

1 x 400ml tin coconut milk

200ml vegetable stock (page 32) or water

½ tsp ground turmeric

16 cooked jumbo crab claws

6 cherry tomatoes, quartered

juice of ½ lime

FOR THE TADKA

2 tbsp sunflower oil

¼ tsp mustard seeds

10 curry leaves

good pinch of chilli powder (ideally Deggi Mirch brand; see page 257)

To make the curry

Heat the sunflower oil in a frying pan. When the oil is hot, add the mustard seeds. They will splutter and pop. After about 10 seconds, the popping will subside. Add the dried red chillies, followed by the sliced onion. Season with salt and continue cooking, stirring regularly, for 3–4 minutes. Add the green chillies, thinly sliced ginger and ginger garlic paste. Cook for another minute and add the curry leaves. Continue cooking, stirring regularly, until the onions are tender and translucent. (If the onions don't soften sufficiently at this point, they will be crunchy at the end.) Add in the coconut milk, vegetable stock or water and turmeric. Simmer for few minutes, taste and check the seasoning. The curry may be made up to this point in advance.

Add the crab claws and the cherry tomatoes. Simmer for a few more minutes and taste for seasoning. Add a squeeze of lime juice, then taste and balance as necessary.

To make the tadka

The tadka should be prepared just before serving. Heat the oil in a saucepan and when it's hot, add the mustard seeds. They will sizzle and start jumping. Add the curry leaves and chilli powder and allow them to sizzle for 5–10 seconds. Pour directly onto the hot curry.

Atul's Prawn and Green Mango Curry

This is one of the most extraordinary curries I have ever eaten. The flavour comes not just from the spices, but from the addition of green mangoes. These are Indian mangoes that are firm and have a sour flesh and are readily available in all Asian markets. There are numerous different varieties, depending on where they come from – some are very small, not much bigger than the size of an egg, and some are much larger. Frozen grated mango is also available in Asian markets and is a useful standby.

Serves 4

FOR THE PASTE

2 tbsp coconut or sunflower oil

½ onion, finely chopped

1 tsp fennel seeds

100g fresh coconut, grated or
 puréed in a food processor

FOR THE CURRY

20 large black tiger prawns,
 uncooked

2 tbsp coconut or sunflower oil

1 onion, finely sliced

2 green chillies, chopped

1½ tbsp ginger garlic paste
 (page 258)

1½ tsp ground coriander

½ tsp turmeric

¼ tsp chilli powder

100g green mango, sliced into thin
 strips, plus extra for garnish

salt

1 x 400ml tin coconut milk

pilau rice (page 291), to serve

FOR THE TADKA

1 tbsp coconut or sunflower oil

1½ tsp black mustard seeds

25 curry leaves

¼ tsp fenugreek seeds

Peel and devein the prawns, leaving the tail attached. Rinse and pat dry.

To make the paste

Heat the coconut or sunflower oil in a pan. Add the onion and the fennel seeds and sauté over a medium heat. Mix in the coconut. Stir and cook until the coconut is golden brown. Remove and grind to a smooth paste using a blender, adding a little water as you go.

To make the curry

Heat the coconut or sunflower oil in the pan. Add the sliced onion and fry until translucent. Add the green chillies and the ginger garlic paste and sauté for 2–3 minutes. Stir in the ground spices and half the mango strips. Add the prawns to the pan, season with salt and cook for a few minutes until the prawns are no longer translucent. Stir in the coconut paste, coconut milk and the rest of the mango. Simmer gently for another couple of minutes.

To make the tadka

Just before serving, heat the oil in a separate pan and when hot, add the mustard seeds. When they begin to pop, add the curry leaves and fenugreek seeds. Cook for about 10 seconds and pour immediately over the prawn curry. Serve the prawn curry topped with the extra green mango strips. Accompany with rice.

Lamb Curry with Chickpeas

The wonderful thing about so many curries is that they can be made in advance. Not only that, but they generally improve if left for 24 hours. Black cardamom pods are a feature in this curry. They are totally different to their green cousins and they have an interesting smokiness that goes so well with lamb.

Serves 6

sunflower oil

1.75kg shoulder of lamb, trimmed and cut into large bite-size cubes (1.2kg trimmed weight)

salt

12 cloves

6 black cardamom pods

5 bay leaves

400g white onion, finely chopped

4 tbsp ginger garlic paste (page 258)

4 tsp freshly ground coriander seed

4 tsp ground cumin

½–1 tsp red chilli powder

1 x 400g tin chopped tomatoes

1 x 400g tin chickpeas, drained

chopped coriander leaves, to garnish

OVEN *Preheat the oven to 160°C, 140°C Fan, 325°F, Gas 3.*

Heat a couple tablespoons of sunflower oil in a casserole pot. Add some of the lamb pieces in a single layer, season and brown the meat over a high heat. Remove and set aside. Continue with the rest of the lamb, adding more oil as necessary.

When all the lamb has been browned, add another tablespoon of oil to the pot and when hot, add the cloves, cardamom pods and bay leaves. Sauté for a few seconds, until the spices crackle. Add the onions, season with salt and cook over a medium heat until softened. Stir regularly and scrape up any caramelised bits left on the bottom of the saucepan from browning the meat. Add the ginger garlic paste and cook for a few more minutes.

Return all the lamb to the pot. Add the ground coriander, ground cumin and chilli powder and cook over the heat, stirring, for a few minutes. Add the tomatoes, salt and enough water to just cover the lamb. Bring up to the boil, cover with a lid and then transfer to the preheated oven. Cook for 1¼–1½ hours, until the lamb is tender. During the last 10 minutes of cooking, add the chickpeas.

Before serving, remove the bay leaves and black cardamom seeds. Garnish with freshly chopped coriander.

NOTE When buying lamb shoulder from the butcher, I always request a whole boned shoulder of lamb. This way I can remove any excess fat more easily and chop it into even-sized pieces.

Atul's Tandoori Chicken

Tandoor ovens are an essential piece of equipment in most Indian restaurants and a member of the team will manage the tandoor oven for the whole of service. The tandoor oven is traditionally made from clay and can reach temperatures of 500°C (930°F) and above. However, even without a tandoor oven, you can achieve a very good result.

The hung curd that is used for the marinade isn't essential, but it does result in a thicker paste that adheres to the chicken more easily during cooking.

Serve with mint or tomato chutney.

Serves 4

1 x 1kg chicken, skin removed and jointed into legs, thighs, breasts (reserve wings for another use)

30g butter

2 tbsp vegetable oil

1½ tsp lime juice

1 tsp chaat masala (or mango powder)

chopped fresh coriander, to garnish (optional)

mint chutney (page 263) or tomato chutney (page 271), to serve

FOR THE FIRST MARINADE

2 tbsp lemon juice

1 tbsp ginger garlic paste (page 258)

1 tsp mild red chilli powder (Deggi Mirch brand)

1 tsp salt

FOR THE SECOND MARINADE

250g thick natural yoghurt or hung curd (page 259)

2 tbsp vegetable oil

1½ tsp salt

1 tsp garam masala

½ tsp ground cinnamon

¼ tsp red chilli powder

OVEN *Preheat the oven to 200°C, 180°C Fan, 400°F, Gas 6.*

To make the first marinade, simply mix all the ingredients together.

Make 3 or 4 deep incisions on each piece of chicken (2 breasts and 2 thighs/legs) without cutting the whole way across the flesh. Place the chicken in a bowl, apply the first marinade and set aside for 20–30 minutes. Drain off any excess juices and discard.

Mix all the ingredients for the second marinade together and rub all over the chicken, making sure the marinade gets into all the gashes. Cover and leave to marinate in the fridge for 2 hours or longer.

Place the chicken pieces in one layer in a large roasting pan, quite close to one another, and transfer to the oven. After about 15 minutes, melt the butter and oil together, then use it to baste the chicken. The breasts will be cooked in about 20-30 minutes and the legs/thighs in about 40–45 minutes. Remove from the oven and baste again. Squeeze some lime juice over the chicken and sprinkle with the chaat masala. Garnish with some chopped coriander and serve with mint or tomato chutney.

MADHUR JAFFREY

My introduction to using spices came with a battered copy of *Madhur Jaffrey's Indian Cookery*, published in the 1980s. I met her just once, when she graciously led a tour of food professionals around New York, showing us where she bought ingredients and bringing us for bites in some of her favourite local restaurants. She is an extraordinary raconteur. At one lull in the conversation, I was driven to the typically Irish conversational trick of seeing whether we might by chance know anyone in common. I told her of the only Indian friend I have in Ireland. It was only after I had enquired that I realised how utterly daft it was to think that there could be some connection in a country of over one billion people. To the astonishment of the others on the tour (whom it must be said had been a little sceptical to this point), it turned out that my dear friend Chandana is the daughter of Madhur's cousin. They had never previously come into contact but they have since met in Ireland and discussed all the 'aunties' they have in common.

This is by way of saying that I sometimes get a chance to cook with Chandana (not often enough) and I do sometimes use her recipes. If on occasion they bear a resemblance to those of Madhur Jaffrey, well, now I know why.

Chicken Roasted with Fresh Spices

In this recipe, a whole chicken is coated in a yoghurt marinade, covered with meltingly tender, spicy onions and then roasted in a parcel. The chicken juices mix with some of the paste that falls off during the cooking, leaving a sauce that can be spooned over each serving. Cooking a whole bird on the bone means that you get a lot more flavour (and a much better sauce). For a quick supper, I sometimes use the marinade to coat chicken breasts wrapped in foil.

Serves 4–6

2.5cm piece of fresh ginger, peeled and finely grated

2 large garlic cloves, crushed

6 tbsp natural or Greek yoghurt

1 tsp salt

½ tsp ground turmeric

1 large free range chicken, about 2.2kg

FOR THE ONION SPICE MIXTURE

2 tbsp sunflower oil

2 onions, chopped very finely

salt

4 garlic cloves, crushed

4cm cube of fresh ginger, peeled and finely grated

1 tbsp ground cumin seeds

1 tbsp ground coriander seeds

1 tsp paprika

½ tsp ground turmeric

30g ground almonds

2 tbsp lemon juice

OVEN *Preheat the oven to 200°C, 180°C Fan, 400°F, Gas 6.*

To marinate the chicken

Mix together the ginger, crushed garlic, yoghurt, salt and turmeric. Skin the chicken, except for the wings. Put the chicken, breast side up, on a tray or plate. Rub the marinade all over the chicken. Set aside, unrefrigerated, for 30 minutes or cover and place in the fridge for several hours or overnight.

To roast the chicken

Heat the oil in a frying pan. Add the onions, season with salt and cook for 10 minutes over a medium heat until softened, stirring regularly. Add the crushed garlic, ginger, cumin, coriander, paprika and turmeric and cook for a further 3–4 minutes. Add the ground almonds and lemon juice. Stir and remove from the heat. If you are roasting the chicken straight away, spread this directly over the yoghurt marinade. If you are not cooking the chicken until later, allow the onion mixture to cool.

Cut a piece of aluminium foil large enough to enclose the whole chicken. There should be enough room to allow air space above the chicken. Place the foil in a large roasting tin and put the chicken in the centre. Bring the pieces of foil together and pleat well above the breast bone. Crimp the two ends together so that the package is tightly sealed.

Roast the chicken for 1¼–1½ hours. Exact timing will vary according to the size of the chicken. Carve the chicken and serve with the spice paste and all the juices that have accumulated in the bottom of the dish.

Raita with Cucumber and Mint

A raita is a yoghurt side dish. It adds a freshness to all sorts of Indian dishes and is also like a cool breeze if you have added a bit too much heat. It typically has an addition of vegetables or fruit and spices. This cucumber, mint and roasted cumin raita is a classic.

570ml natural yoghurt

½ cucumber, peeled and coarsely grated

bunch fresh mint leaves, finely chopped

1 tsp salt

½ tsp ground roasted cumin seeds

¼ tsp cayenne pepper

freshly ground black pepper

Put the yoghurt in a bowl. Add all the other ingredients and mix. Cover and refrigerate until ready to eat.

Pan-fried Brill with Green Spice Paste and Oven-Roasted Tomatoes

Atul claims that this recipe evolved by chance. His account is that during service, a bowl of mint and coriander chutney fell on top of the portioned John Dory on the shelf below, resulting in a layer of green paste on the fish. With no time to waste, he decided to dip the fish in gram flour, leaving a thick layer of paste on both sides. He then cooked it in the pan before serving it on a bed of cherry tomatoes sautéed with shallots and spices. Atul has been to Dublin so often that I am no longer sure when he is pulling my leg.

There are two ingredients in the paste that may be unfamiliar. Chaat masala is a combination of eight spices, which can be bought in ground form. This is a very mild spice that has a sweet and sour tang and is traditionally brushed over chicken tandoori or grilled fruit chaat, typical street food. Fenugreek leaves come from the fenugreek plant and are available in dried form. They have a very different flavour to fenugreek seeds, which come from the same plant.

The choice of fish will vary according to availability. Other options to the brill suggested here are John Dory, turbot, halibut or sea bass.

Serves 4

4 x 170g fillets of brill

salt

4 tbsp gram flour (chickpea flour) or plain flour

4 tbsp vegetable oil

fresh coriander sprigs or micro leaves, to garnish

FOR THE GREEN SPICE PASTE

50g fresh mint leaves

50g fresh coriander leaves

20g fresh ginger, peeled and chopped

2 green chillies, deseeded

1 tbsp sunflower oil

2 tsp chaat masala

1½ tsp fenugreek leaf powder

½ tsp salt

squeeze of lemon juice

FOR THE OVEN-ROASTED TOMATOES

1 tbsp vegetable oil

1 tsp cumin seeds

2 shallots, finely chopped

½ tsp finely chopped fresh ginger

½ tsp ground coriander

½ tsp chaat masala

¼ tsp turmeric

sea salt

4 strings of tomatoes on the vine or 20 baby tomatoes

OVEN *Preheat the oven to 200°C, 180°C Fan, 400°F, Gas 6.*

To make the green spice paste

Whizz all the ingredients for the spice paste in a blender.

To make the oven-roasted tomatoes

Heat the oil in an ovenproof pan and when hot, add the cumin seeds. After about 10 seconds, add the chopped shallots and toss them around for a minute or two. Add the ginger and remaining spices to the shallots and toss to mix. Sit the tomatoes on top (keeping them in bunches if they are on the vine). Transfer the pan to the preheated oven and cook until the tomatoes start to wilt, about 5–8 minutes. Keep warm.

To prepare the fish

Pat the fish dry and season. Spread the green spice paste generously over the flesh and skin side of the fish. Leave to marinate in the fridge for about 30 minutes or longer.

Sieve some gram flour onto a plate. Dip both sides of the brill in the flour and shake off the excess.

Heat the oil in a non-stick frying pan. When the oil is hot, place the fish, flesh side down, in the pan. Cook for a few minutes, until the surface turns golden. Turn the fish over onto the skin side and cook for a few more minutes. The exact length of time will depend on the thickness of the fillets. If the fish is quite thick, transfer the fillets to the oven for a few minutes to finish the cooking. Remove and place on a piece of kitchen paper.

To serve, spoon some of the oven-roasted tomatoes and onions into the centre of the plate. Sit the fish on top. Garnish with a sprig of coriander or a few micro leaves and serve.

VEGETABLES AND RICE

Sauté Potatoes with Dill Leaves

What is so unusual about this dish is that the chana dal, which are normally cooked in lots of water till tender, are toasted in the pan and added solely for texture and crunch. It is essential that the potatoes are still quite firm when precooked. The potatoes are then added to the spiced oil and the toasted dal and finished with a handfull of fresh dill.

Serves 4

400g new potatoes
2 tbsp vegetable oil
2 tsp chana dal
½ tsp mustard seeds
½ tsp sesame seeds
1 small onion, chopped

1½ tsp ground coriander
1 tsp chopped fresh ginger
½ tsp ground turmeric
salt
25g dill leaves, chopped
30g butter
squeeze of lime juice

Boil the potatoes until they're tender but still firm, then peel and cut into halves or quarters.

Heat the oil in a pan. Add the chana dal, mustard seeds and sesame seeds and sauté until the mustard seeds splutter and the chana dal and sesame seeds start to colour. Add the chopped onions and sauté until they are pale golden. Mix in the ground coriander, chopped ginger and turmeric. Cook for a few minutes, add the potatoes and season. Continue cooking until the potatoes are heated through. Mix in the dill and toss together. Finally, add the butter and a squeeze of lime juice. Taste and adjust the seasoning. Serve hot.

Green Beans with Black Mustard Seeds

Mustard seeds are a very mild spice, so these green beans can accompany all sorts of dishes, not just Indian ones. Crunchy and fresh tasting.

Serves 4

450g green beans

4 tbsp vegetable oil

1 tbsp whole black mustard seeds

2 garlic cloves, finely chopped

1 dried red chilli, broken slightly so that it releases some of the seeds

1 tsp salt

½ tsp caster sugar

freshly ground black pepper

Blanch the beans in a pot of boiling water for 3–4 minutes, or until they are just tender but still with a nice bite. Drain immediately in a colander. If you are preparing the green beans in advance, plunge them directly into cold water, leave for a few minutes until cold, and then drain. The beans may be blanched ahead of time.

Heat the oil in a large frying pan. When hot, add in the mustard seeds. As soon as the mustard seeds begin to pop, add the garlic and the crushed red chilli. Stir for a few seconds. Put in the green beans, salt and sugar and stir to mix. Turn down the heat to low and cook the beans, stirring regularly, for 7–8 minutes, until they have absorbed the flavour of the spices. Add the black pepper, mix and serve.

Chana Dal

I love to include pulses (dried beans, peas or lentils) when I'm in the mood to cook with Indian ingredients. There are about 50 different types that are commonly used, so shopping in an Asian market presents a dazzling choice. Some are left whole and some are split, which helps them to cook faster. It is the split peas that are called dal. My favourite is chana dal – black chickpeas from which the outer husk has been removed. They look like yellow split peas but are a little sweeter and retain more firmness during cooking. Dal in India has a consistency more like a soup. They are commonly ladled over rice, which allows the rice to absorb some of the flavours.

Serves 6

500g chana dal

2–3 garlic cloves, bruised with the back of a knife

1 tsp ground turmeric

salt

2 tsp coriander seeds

2 whole dried red chillies, broken in half

3 tbsp sunflower oil

1 large onion, chopped

100g tomatoes, chopped

2 green chillies, chopped

1 tbsp chopped fresh ginger

1½ tsp ground coriander

½ tsp turmeric

good pinch of chilli powder

1 tsp garam masala

bunch of fresh coriander leaves

juice of ½ lemon

Wash the dal in a few changes of water. Cover with about 3 times the volume of water. Add the garlic, ½ teaspoon of turmeric and salt. Cook until the dal is tender, about 30 minutes. Set aside.

Heat the oil in a pan and add the whole red chillies and the coriander seeds. When they crackle, add the chopped onion. Sauté the onion until it's golden brown, then add the tomatoes, green chillies, ginger, ground coriander, ½ teaspoon of turmeric, pinch of chilli powder and about 2 tablespoons of water. Cook for another 5 minutes, stirring regularly, until the water evaporates and the oil begins to separate from the basic tomato mixture. This is an indication that the spices have cooked sufficiently. Season with salt. Add the tomato mixture to the cooked lentils, then add the garam masala. Finish with fresh coriander and lemon juice.

NOTE You can replace the coriander seeds with fennel seeds. Try both versions and see which one you prefer.

Pilau Rice with Cinnamon and Cumin

My favourite way to cook rice is by the absorption method, which means that all the water will have evaporated by the time the rice is ready. Soaking the rice in advance for 20 minutes improves the texture (and reduces the cooking time).

This recipe calls for cinnamon and cumin, but you may choose to use other spices, such as cardamom pods (either green or black), coriander seeds, mustard seeds, curry leaves or cinnamon sticks, either on their own or a few together.

Atul always has a clean tea towel to hand. When the water has reduced to just below the surface of the rice, he runs it under a tap, squeezes out the excess water and then spreads it directly on the rice. The tea towel prevents the top layer of rice from drying out.

Serves 6–8

500g basmati rice

3 tbsp sunflower oil

15g cumin seeds, roasted and ground

1 cinnamon stick

100g onion, sliced

1 litre water

1½ tsp salt

a few knobs of butter

Put the rice in a big bowl of water. Rinse the rice, handling the grains gently. The water will become cloudy. Drain through a sieve or a colander and repeat the process. Leave the rice to soak for 20 minutes. If you leave the rice for longer, the cooking time will be shorter, so you will need to adjust the amount of water.

Heat the oil, then sauté the cumin seeds and cinnamon stick. Add the sliced onions, stirring until they are a light golden brown. Stir in the rice and add the water and salt. Boil until the water disappears from the surface. Add a few knobs of butter on top and cover the rice with a damp tea towel. Sit the lid on top and continue to cook on a low heat until the rice is tender, about 10 minutes. When ready to serve, stir the rice

Chapter Five

SWEET ENDINGS

A cake good enough for a film star, glazing a blueberry and blowtorching a passionfruit tart.

HOW TO MAKE A SILKY SMOOTH CUSTARD? · WHAT IS A SABAYON? · HOW DO YOU MAKE THE LIGHTEST LEMON SOUFFLÉ AND THE FLAKIEST PASTRY? · MAKE A CHOCOLATE GANACHE, SUGAR A PECAN, CARAMEL A SAUCE

MEMORIES OF MARCHESI

There are moments from the past that I can conjure up very vividly. Waiting on a bench outside Marchesi's kitchen is one of them. I shudder now at my naiveté. I had gone to Milan without a single contact and I spoke dreadful Italian learned from some ancient cassettes. Nobody seemed to understand a word I said.

I had decided that my Italian strategy would be to start at the top. Marchesi was the most well-known Italian chef of the day and he ran a Michelin three-star restaurant that was redefining Italian food. (In fact, in recent years he has handed back his stars to the Michelin Guide, feeling that Italian chefs should not be marching to a French step.) Who knows what possessed me. I just rolled up on my first day in Milan without an appointment.

I think it hit me, sitting there, that this time I had taken one outrageous step too far. I was never as close to doing a runner as I was when I waited the long minutes for him to appear. He turned out to be extremely warm. He explained, with great courtesy and much shoulder shrugging, that his restaurant was closing for two months and so working there was out of the question. Anyway, he didn't think it would be ideal. Apart from anything else, it would be expensive to live in Milan. He recommended I go to a friend of his who had a Relais & Chateaux country house on the coast, where accommodation would be provided and I would be given a freer hand. In fact, one of his young pastry chefs had already been sent there to keep him out of mischief while the restaurant was being renovated.

And so I found myself in Garlenda on the Italian Riviera. The pastry chef had indeed arrived and had taken over. He didn't share his master's easy manner and refused outright to allow me to scribble down recipes and make my detailed notes. It put me under pressure when he took a day off.

On one particular day when he had left me in charge, I had my head down and was too focused to grasp why there was such commotion as lunchtime approached. I couldn't think who must be arriving as we all put on clean starched whites and were lined up like a football team. My heart lifted when I saw it was none other than Marchesi himself, arriving to dine with his friend for lunch. He came down the line shaking hands with great seriousness. When he recognised me, his face lit up as if we were the closest of long-lost friends and there was much kissing of cheeks and enquiring after my welfare. I could feel my stock soaring.

A week later, the young pastry chef disappeared up the hills with one of the waitresses. There was consternation as to what should be done until they remembered the young Irish girl. Was she not a Marchesi protégée? The "young" Irish girl, disguising her terror, was happy to accept the position and finished out the season.

One of the features of my time there was that I liked a different dessert menu every day, depending on what was available and the mood in the kitchen. It was hard work but far more interesting than churning out favoured staples, as had been their custom.

Deciding what recipes to have in this chapter has been a bit like that. Each time I've written out a list of what to include, I've gone for quite different options. This is today's choice.

FRUIT

Grilled Peaches with Mascarpone

When peaches are in their prime, they can be cut in half, topped with a blob of mascarpone, crème fraîche and a spoonful of brown sugar and placed under the grill. The brown sugar will melt and create a creamy topping to be savoured with each mouthful of fruit.

Serving per person

1 ripe peach
2 tsp crème fraîche
2 tsp mascarpone cheese
1 rounded tsp soft brown sugar

Preheat the grill. Slice the peaches in half and remove the stones. You may need to scoop out a bit of the peach if the hollow isn't deep enough or the creamy mascarpone will simply overflow. (This will happen anyway, but you also want to have some left in the middle.) Place the peach halves, cut side up, on an ovenproof plate or dish.

Mix together the crème fraîche and mascarpone and fill each hollow with some of the mixture, then sprinkle the brown sugar over the top. Place under the grill until the topping is beginning to brown in patches. Serve immediately.

Baked Nectarines with Dessert Wine Sabayon

I love to have a simple and a sophisticated version of a single idea. If the previous recipe is the simplest imaginable, then it can easily be made more elaborate. Here, the baked nectarines (peaches and nectarines are interchangeable in the two recipes) are accompanied by a sabayon. This isn't a dessert that can be made in advance, but it's straightforward and a sabayon is a great technique to master.

Serves 6

6 nectarines, halved and stoned
15g unsalted butter, melted
12 tsp soft brown sugar

FOR THE SABAYON

4 egg yolks
3 tbsp caster sugar
125ml Sauternes, Monbazillac or another white dessert wine

OVEN *Preheat the oven to 180°C, 160°C Fan, 350°F, Gas 4.*

To roast the nectarines

Place the nectarines, skin side down, in an ovenproof dish. Brush the surface of each nectarine with melted butter and then sprinkle 1 teaspoon of soft brown sugar over each half. Roast in the oven for about 15 minutes, until warm and beginning to soften. Exact timing will depend on the ripeness of the nectarines.

To make the sabayon

Place the egg yolks and sugar together in a medium-sized stainless steel bowl. Whisk together with a hand whisk – a balloon whisk is ideal for the job – and add the dessert wine. Heat a saucepan of simmering water and sit the bowl on top. The bowl must not touch the surface of the water. Whisk continuously until the sabayon becomes light and fluffy, triples or quadruples in volume and has a consistency similar to softly whipped cream. There should be no liquid left at the bottom of the bowl. Check the temperature every so often by dipping your finger into the mixture. If it feels very hot, remove the sabayon from the heat and continue whisking off the heat until it cools down a little.

To finish

Five to 10 minutes before you wish to serve the dessert, preheat the grill to high (not necessary if you have a blowtorch).

Sit each baked nectarine on a plate and spoon the sabayon over the fruit. Place the plates one or two at a time under the grill, just until the sabayon is lightly golden. Be extremely vigilant, as the sabayon must not get too brown. If you have a blowtorch, this is a more efficient way of brûléeing the sabayon. Serve immediately.

NOTE The nectarines can be served with ice cream and perhaps some crunchy praline crumbs on top (see page 348).

WHAT IS A SABAYON?

Sabayon is a technique in which egg yolks and liquid are beaten over heat to create lightness and volume. The liquid in a dessert sabayon is generally some form of alcohol, such as white wine, champagne, dessert wine, cider or a liqueur. The most well-known sabayon is the Italian dessert called zabaglione (the Italian version of the French term), which is made with Marsala.

A sabayon may also be served cold. In that case, once it has reached its optimum stage over the heat, the sabayon should be whisked continuously over a bowl of ice until cold. When completely cold, whipped cream may be folded into the mixture.

USING DESSERT WINE

There are many wonderful dessert wines on the market and some of them are quite inexpensive. They should still be chosen with care because a wine that is rich and complex with a good balance of acidity and fruit will make a significant difference. In this chapter, the Sauternes pots de crème recipe (page 309) also requires a dessert wine. Any leftover wine may also be used for this dessert (it doesn't have to be Sauternes). Hopefully there will still be enough left to enjoy an accompanying glass with the dessert.

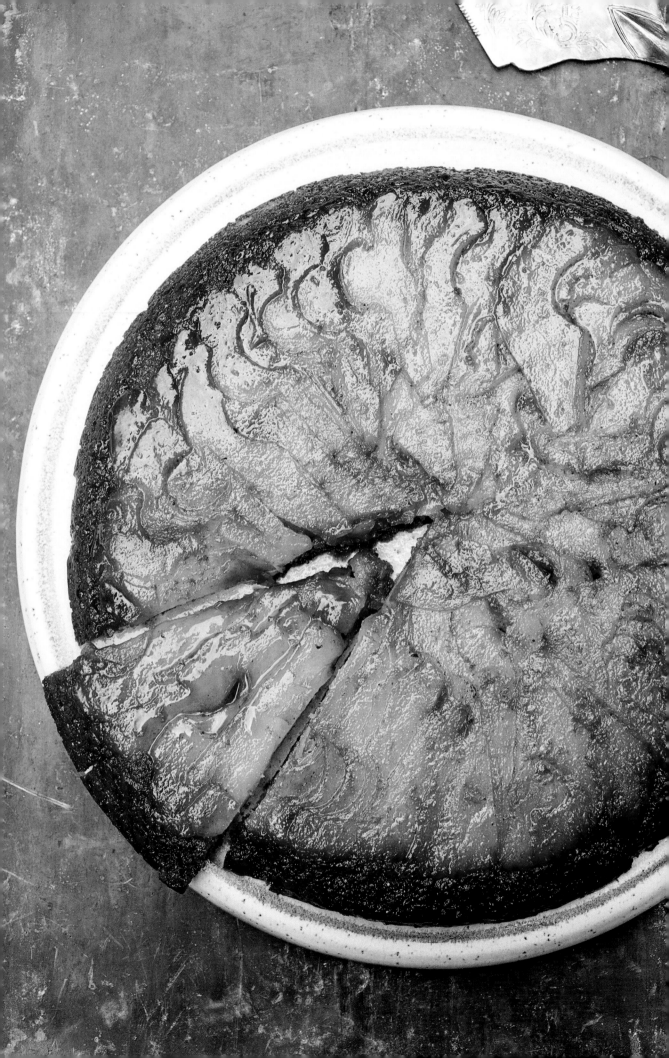

Upside Down Pear and Ginger Cake

This pear and ginger dessert is like a tarte tatin, but with a cake base. When the cake comes out of the oven it is flipped upside down, revealing the pears covered by the caramel and ginger syrup.

Serves 6

FOR THE PEAR TOPPING

3 or 4 large firm pears

squeeze of lemon juice

90g butter

90g caster or granulated sugar

2 tbsp syrup from a jar of preserved ginger (or use 2 tbsp honey plus 1 tsp freshly grated ginger instead)

FOR THE CAKE

125g butter, at room temperature

125g caster sugar

2 large eggs

100g self-raising flour

30g ground almonds

3 tbsp syrup from a jar of preserved ginger (or use 3 tbsp honey plus 2 tsp freshly grated ginger instead)

1 level tsp baking powder

crème fraîche or ice cream, to serve

EQUIPMENT *Ovenproof frying pan, about 28cm across and at least 3.5cm deep, or a tarte tatin tin*

OVEN *Preheat the oven to 180°C, 160°C Fan, 350°F, Gas 4.*

To make the pear topping

Peel, core and thinly slice the pears. Squeeze lemon juice over the slices to prevent them from discolouring. It's important to have the pears ready before preparing the caramel.

Place the ovenproof frying pan over a low heat and add the butter, sugar and the preserved ginger syrup (or honey and grated ginger). Allow the butter and sugar to melt and then turn up the heat. Cook until the mixture turns golden. Don't worry if the butter separates from the sugar, it will all come back together again in the end. Swirl the pan to mix the caramel so that it colours evenly. Remove from the heat as soon as it becomes a rich golden colour. Slide the pear slices immediately into the caramel, spreading them over the base of the frying pan as evenly as possible. Take great care not to cause any splashes with the hot liquid or to touch the caramel.

To make the cake

Using an electric beater, cream the butter and sugar together in a mixing bowl until light and fluffy. Beat the eggs together in a small bowl and add the eggs little by little, beating between each addition. Fold in the flour, ground almonds, ginger syrup (or honey and ginger) and baking powder. Place spoonfuls of the batter at intervals on top of the pears and then spread it out to cover the pears completely.

Place in the oven and bake for about 40 minutes. Test by inserting a skewer into the centre. When the skewer comes out clean, the cake is ready. Remove from the oven and allow to cool for about 5 minutes.

Loosen the sides of the cake with a knife. Place a serving plate (or board), slightly larger than the cake, on top of the pan. Lift the plate and the pan together, holding both tightly, and flip them over sharply (use a cloth to protect your hands from any dribbling juices). Lift off the pan. Serve with some crème fraîche or ice cream.

PRESERVED GINGER

Preserved ginger is fresh ginger that has been blanched in boiling water a number of times and then added to a sugar syrup. It's available in jars in specialist shops and the thick ginger syrup is as wonderful as the preserved ginger itself. Preserved ginger adds another dimension to many cakes, desserts and biscuits. If you are unable to find these jars, then use some freshly grated ginger and honey.

Blackberry and Apple Crisp

When does a crumble become a crisp? I'm not sure. Probably when it's made by Americans. American friends such as Kris and Annie often give me crisps, which usually include nuts (almonds, hazelnuts, pistachios or pecans) and cinnamon. The nuts are chopped finely so that they add texture and flavour. The crisp may be served in a pie dish or, even better, in deep individual ramekins large enough to hold a generous portion of fruit. The bubbling juices of the fruit will then ooze through the crumbly topping, to be savoured with each spoonful.

Serves 6

5 Granny Smith, Cox Pippin or Golden Delicious apples

450g blackberries

80g light brown sugar

2 tbsp plain flour

whipped cream, to serve

FOR THE CRISP TOPPING

130g plain flour

100g butter

90g porridge oats

65g light brown sugar

30g pecans (optional)

½ tsp ground cinnamon

EQUIPMENT *30cm x 20cm ovenproof dish*

OVEN *Preheat the oven to 180°C, 160°C Fan, 350°F, Gas 4.*

To make the topping

Place the flour in a bowl. Chop up the butter very finely and rub it into the flour until it resembles fine crumbs or whizz in a food processor. Add the oats, sugar, pecans and cinnamon. Mix all the ingredients together.

To make the filling

Peel, core and slice the apples. Mix the blackberries, apples, sugar and flour together and put into an ovenproof dish. Sprinkle the crisp on top.

Bake in the oven for 45 minutes to 1 hour, until the fruit is tender, beginning to bubble up and the topping is pale golden. Test the fruit with a skewer or with the point of a knife to see if it's ready. Serve hot with whipped cream.

NOTE The crisp may also be cooked in deep ramekins about 9cm wide x 7cm deep. In this case, chop the apples finely and pack the fruit almost to the top. Sprinkle the crisp on top and bake as above.

Crispy Honey Biscuits with Strawberries and Rhubarb Coulis

This is a dessert that can adapt to different seasons. When forced rhubarb is in season or when the local rhubarb has plenty of vibrant red colour, chunks of rhubarb are sandwiched in between wafer-thin biscuits and served with a rhubarb coulis. As the season moves along, the honey crisps can be filled with strawberries and served with a rhubarb coulis. Rhubarb freezes well when cut into chunks and placed in ziplock bags.

Serves 6

FOR THE HONEY CRISPS

40g icing sugar, sieved, plus extra to serve

30g butter, at room temperature

2 tbsp honey

½ tsp ground ginger

40g plain flour

1 egg white

a few flaked almonds

500g strawberries

225ml cream, whipped

FOR THE RHUBARB COULIS

225g rhubarb, cut into chunks

125ml water

2 tbsp caster sugar

OVEN *Preheat the oven to 180°C, 160°C Fan, 350°F, Gas 4.*

To make the rhubarb coulis

Place the rhubarb in a saucepan with the water and sugar. Cover and cook over a medium heat for about 10 minutes, until the rhubarb is tender. Purée in a food processor or blender. Taste and add more sugar if necessary. Chill in the refrigerator if not using right away.

To make the honey crisps

Cream together the sugar, butter, honey and ginger. Add the flour and egg white and beat until incorporated.

Line 2 baking trays with a silicone mat or baking parchment. Spoon a rounded teaspoon of the batter onto the tray. Using the back of a teaspoon, spread the batter in a circular motion to form a thin circle about 7.5cm in diameter. Continue with the rest of the batter. You will need a total of 18 biscuits (3 per person). Scatter a few flaked almonds on 6 of the biscuits.

Transfer the tray to the oven and bake the biscuits for 5–8 minutes, until they are a rich golden brown colour. Remove from the oven and leave to cool. After about 2 minutes, the biscuits will begin to harden. Peel them off the paper and lay out on a wire rack. When completely cold, store in an airtight container until ready to use.

To serve

Half an hour before serving, slice the strawberries and sprinkle with a little caster sugar.

Just before serving, sprinkle some icing sugar over the 6 biscuits with the almonds. Place a swirl of rhubarb coulis onto each dessert plate. Put the whipped cream in a piping bag with a fluted nozzle. Place a biscuit in the centre of each plate, pipe a circle of cream on each biscuit and spoon over some strawberries. Sit another biscuit on top and repeat. Top with the biscuit coated with icing sugar and serve.

NOTE The biscuits will hold in an airtight container for a number of days. If the biscuits go soft, place them back in the oven at the same temperature until warmed through. Remove to a cooling rack and they will crisp up as they cool.

Sauternes Pots de Crème with Armagnac Prunes

This is a well-travelled recipe, which is always a good sign. I came across it through Martin Webb of Quaglino's in London, but he credits it to a colleague in Sydney, so who knows its precise origin. If the custard is smooth and silky and the taste of the dessert wine shines through, this is a beautifully delicate dessert. Martin was dismayed that customers would only order his accompanying prunes if he calls them "dried plums". Tropical fruit such as mango or papaya would complement the wine, but in my opinion, the 'dried plums' are the best option.

Sauternes is a dessert wine that comes from one of the wine regions in Bordeaux. At its best, it's quite an extraordinary wine but it tends to be expensive. Another dessert wine can easily be substituted.

Serves 6–8

FOR THE CARAMEL

100g caster sugar

2 tbsp water

FOR THE POTS DE CRÈME

4 egg yolks

2 eggs

75g caster sugar (or use vanilla sugar instead of the pod)

350ml cream

180ml Sauternes or other dessert wine

½ vanilla pod

FOR THE PRUNES IN ARMAGNAC

150g caster sugar

400ml water

about 340g prunes, preferably Agen prunes from France

1 cinnamon stick

peel of ½ orange

1 tea bag

2 tbsp Armagnac or brandy, or to taste

EQUIPMENT *6–8 dariole moulds or ramekins*
OVEN *Preheat the oven to 150°C, 130°C Fan, 300°F, Gas 2.*

To prepare the prunes

Bring the sugar and water to the boil. Add the prunes, cinnamon and orange rind and simmer over a low heat for about 20 minutes, until the prunes have swelled and the liquid has reduced substantially. Add the tea bag and remove after 3 minutes. Stir in the Armagnac or brandy. The prunes may be served cold, but are better served warm. They can be reheated in a saucepan or in the microwave.

NOTE If the prunes are quite hard, it's better to soak them overnight in some brewed tea until they swell. The following day, drain them and discard the tea. Continue as above.

To make the caramel

Put the caster sugar and water in a small saucepan. Stir to dissolve the sugar and bring to the boil. Do not stir the syrup after it has started boiling. Cook until the syrup becomes golden all over. Pour the caramel into the dariole moulds or ramekins just to cover the base of each mould. Set aside.

To make the custard

Make the custard by whisking the egg yolks, eggs and sugar together in a large bowl. In 2 separate saucepans, bring the cream and the wine to a simmer. If you are using half a vanilla pod, split the pod in half lengthwise and scoop out the little black seeds. Place the seeds and the pod itself into the cream as you are warming it. Using a hand whisk, whisk the hot wine into the eggs, followed by the cream (remove the vanilla bean). Whisk just enough to mix them together. Pass through a fine sieve into a jug and then pour the custard into the dariole moulds (three-quarters full) or ramekins (almost to the top if they are shallower).

Choose a baking dish large enough to hold all the ramekins or dariole mounds and pour boiling water around them to come about halfway up the sides of the dishes. Bake for 35–40 minutes, until the custard is just set. Always check in advance of the time, however. The silkiness of the custard is dependent on timing. There should still be a slight wobble in the centre when you remove them. Remove the custards from the bain marie and allow to cool. Refrigerate for several hours or overnight.

To serve

Dip the moulds briefly into a jug of very hot water, then run a small knife around the outside. Turn out directly onto the plates. Serve with some of the prunes in their juice.

TARTS

If you are already a master at pastry, or have become a master since reading that section in Chapter 1 (pages 65–68), then here is an opportunity for two rather more sophisticated tarts. The third tart is more rustic and has an interesting, flakier pastry.

Pecan and Coconut Tart

This tart dates back to my time in Vancouver. This was one of the desserts that was dispatched every morning, warm from the oven, to a range of restaurants around the city. It was taken as a good sign that all the restaurants claimed it as their own.

The flaked coconut is now more readily available, but make sure that it's unsweetened. It has a slightly chewy texture, which adds interest to the dessert.

Serves 8

FOR THE PASTRY

170g plain flour

90g chilled unsalted butter

1 tbsp icing sugar, sieved

¼ tsp salt

1 egg, beaten

a little beaten egg, for brushing
  on the pastry base

FOR THE FILLING

110g pecans

55g flaked almonds

25g flaked unsweetened coconut
  (if unavailable, add extra nuts)

85g unsalted butter

85g light brown sugar

3 tbsp honey

3 large egg yolks

3 tbsp cream

1 tsp vanilla extract

crème fraîche, to serve

EQUIPMENT *20cm x 2.75cm quiche tin
  with removable base*

To make the pastry

Place the flour, butter, sugar and salt in a food processor and process until it resembles fine breadcrumbs. While the machine is running, add about three-quarters of the beaten egg and whizz again to mix it to crumbs. Open the lid and feel the consistency of the crumbs. If they feel too dry, add the rest of the beaten egg with the machine running. Whizz the dough quickly to bring it together.

Alternatively, if making the pastry by hand, place the flour, sugar and salt in a bowl. Chop up the butter into small pieces and rub it into the flour mixture until it resembles fine crumbs. Bind with the beaten egg as above.

Turn the dough onto a lightly floured surface and knead it for a few seconds, just to make the underside smooth. Place in a piece of cling film, fold it over and flatten the pastry with your hand to create a disc. Allow it to rest in the fridge for 45 minutes, or overnight if desired.

Preheat the oven to 200°C, 180°C Fan, 400°F, Gas 6.

Roll out the pastry and line the quiche pan (see pages 66–68). Line the pastry with baking parchment and fill with dried beans. Bake the pastry for about 15 minutes, until lightly golden at the edges. Carefully remove the paper and the beans. If the paper appears to be sticking, return the tart to the oven for about 5 more minutes, until the pastry becomes firmer. After removing the beans, brush the base of the tart with a little beaten egg and place back in the oven for a few minutes. Remove and set aside until ready to use.

To make the filling
Turn the oven down to 170°C, 150°C Fan, 325°F, Gas 3.

Put the pecans, flaked almonds and coconut on a baking tray, keeping each item separate, as they will take different times to toast. Place in the preheated oven and toast the coconut for a couple of minutes, until the very outside edges are becoming tinged golden. Remove the coconut and return the tray to the oven to toast the flaked almonds for a couple more minutes. They should still be quite pale when you remove them. The pecans will take a total of about 5 minutes (you don't want them to be too dark). Remove from the tray and allow to cool.

Melt the butter, brown sugar and honey in a saucepan. Stir once or twice to dissolve the sugar. Remove from the heat and whisk in the egg yolks, cream and vanilla. Add the toasted nuts and coconut and stir to mix. Pour into the tart shell. Bake for about 20 minutes, until set and golden brown. Serve with crème fraîche.

Lynda's Passion Fruit Brûlée Tart

This is the only recipe I put my name to. It has been part of my repertoire for as long as I can remember. It has found me employment, averted crises and impressed critics and I have never tired of eating it. It has elements of a crème brûlée but offers so much more. I remember one boss who requested his favourite meal for his birthday and his dessert choice was Lynda's Passion Fruit Brûlée Tart. There was plenty of banter in the kitchen over having my name as the prefix, but it has just stuck. I love to serve it with passion fruit ice cream or the Greek yoghurt and honey ice cream on page 344, with some diced fruits as a garnish.

Serves 8

FOR THE PASTRY

200g plain flour

140g chilled unsalted butter

2 tbsp icing sugar, sieved

pinch of salt

1 egg, beaten

a little beaten egg, for brushing on the pastry base

FOR THE FILLING

150g caster sugar, plus extra to brûlée the tart

175ml passion fruit juice (about 15–20 passion fruit; see page 318)

5 eggs

200ml double cream

Greek yoghurt and honey ice cream (page 344), to serve

EQUIPMENT *25cm x 3.5cm quiche tin with removable base*
A blowtorch, to brûlée the tart

OVEN *Preheat the oven to 200°C, 180°C Fan, 400°F, Gas 6.*

To make the pastry

Place the flour, butter, sugar and a pinch of salt in a food processor and whizz until it resembles fine breadcrumbs. While the machine is running, add about three-quarters of the beaten egg and whizz again to mix to crumbs. Open the lid and feel the consistency of the crumbs. If they feel too dry, add the rest of the beaten egg with the machine running. Whizz the dough quickly to bring it together.

Alternatively, if making the pastry by hand, place the flour, sugar and salt in a bowl. Chop up the butter into small pieces and rub it into the flour mixture until it resembles fine crumbs. Bind with the beaten egg as above.

Turn the dough onto a lightly floured surface and knead it for a few seconds, just to make the underside smooth. Place in a piece of cling film, fold it over and flatten the pastry with your hand to create a disc. Allow to rest in the fridge for 45 minutes, or overnight if desired.

On a lightly floured board, roll the pastry out in a circle large enough to line the bottom and side of the tart dish. The pastry should be about 3–5mm thick. Line the tart tin with the pastry (reserving any extra pastry for patching, if necessary). Place a sheet of baking parchment or greaseproof paper over the pastry, fill with dried pulses and bake in the preheated oven until the paper comes away easily from the base, about 15 minutes. The edges of the tart should be slightly golden but the base will still be pale. Gently remove the sheet of paper and the dried pulses. Brush the base of the tart with a little beaten egg and place the tart back in the oven for about 5 minutes to dry out. Remove from the oven.

Lower the temperature to 180°C, 160°C Fan, 350°F, Gas 4.

To make the filling

Whisk the sugar into the passion fruit juice. In a separate bowl, whisk the eggs and cream together using a hand whisk. Gently whisk the egg and cream into the fruit pulp just until combined. (If you over-whisk, you will create too many air bubbles.) Pour this mixture into the prebaked pastry case and bake for 25–30 minutes. Check the tart towards the end of the cooking by shaking it very slightly – it should be barely set in the centre. Remove from the oven and allow to cool.

If you have a blowtorch, you can caramelise the top of the tart just before serving or up to 30 minutes in advance. Sprinkle a good layer of caster sugar over the top of the tart, leaving a margin of 2.5cm from the rim (this is to prevent the pastry from burning). Caramelise the sugar until it turns golden. It will harden immediately.

NOTE I normally leave the crust on the passion fruit tart. However, sometimes for presentation, I remove the outer edge so that I can brûlée the entire surface of the tart.

TROPICAL FRUIT GARNISH

As an optional garnish for the dessert, you could dice some fruit such as mango, pineapple and/or papaya and add these to a sugar syrup flavoured with passion fruit. If you leave the fruit to marinate for an hour or two, the syrup will pick up the flavour of the fruit.

40g caster sugar · 60ml water · 1 passion fruit
½ mango, papaya or a few slices of pineapple, finely diced

Heat the sugar and water until the sugar has dissolved. Remove from the heat. Cut the passion fruit in half and scoop out the pulp and seeds into the sugar syrup. Leave to cool, then add in the diced fruit. Serve alongside the passion fruit tart.

MAKING PASSION FRUIT JUICE

Passion fruit vary in size, so the yield will vary. When choosing passion fruit, the skin should be wrinkled, not smooth and taut. Choose fruit that feels heavy for its size and looks plump, despite the wrinkles. If smooth, ripen the fruit for a few days at room temperature. Ten passion fruit will yield anything from 80ml to 120ml juice.

To extract the juice from passion fruit, there are two options. The first is to scoop all the passion fruit pulp, seeds and all, into a food processor. Whizz just to release the pulp from the seeds and pass through a sieve, discarding the seeds. The second method is to scoop all the passion fruit pulp, seeds and all, into a saucepan. Heat until the seeds separate from the juice and pass through a sieve.

Fresh passion fruit purée is available in some specialist shops and online and it's worth tracking down. For all desserts that require large quantities of passion fruit juice, this is by far the simplest and the cheapest solution. Passion fruit purée also freezes really well, so if you're buying it a litre at a time, freeze it in 100ml or 200ml batches for easy access.

Rustic Open Apple Tart

This pastry is different from the basic shortcrust pastry used for the other tarts. Rather than rubbing the butter in until it reaches the consistency of fine breadcrumbs, it is cut with knives or a pastry blender to the point that the butter pieces are the size of peas. The morsels of butter help to trap pockets of air in the pastry. The pastry is also given two rollings to create extra layers of flakiness. This is a particular technique that is used when making puff pastry.

This tart can be filled with many different fruits, including nectarines, peaches, apricots, plums or rhubarb. It's best cooked on a pizza stone so that any excess moisture will be absorbed by the porous surface of the stone, leaving the pastry totally crisp on the bottom. Warm out of the oven with its juicy fruit and its flaky pastry, this tart is irresistible.

Makes 1 x 36cm tart / Serves 8

FOR THE FLAKY SHORTCRUST PASTRY

200g plain flour

⅛ tsp salt (or if using salted butter, no salt is required)

175g cold unsalted butter, straight from the fridge

75–100ml iced water, or as required

FOR THE FILLING

8 Granny Smith, Cox Pippin or Golden Delicious apples

45g unsalted butter, melted

60g caster sugar

100g blackberries, fresh or frozen (optional)

whipped cream or crème fraîche, to serve

To make the pastry

Place the flour and salt in a wide bowl. Cut the butter up into 5mm cubes and add to the flour. With a table knife in each hand, cut up the butter using a criss-cross motion, pulling the knives outwards like the radiating spokes of a wheel. Keep gathering the flour back into the centre and continuing the cutting motion until the mixture resembles coarse crumbs – the pieces of butter will be slightly irregular and some of them may be at least as big as a pea. Alternatively, use a pastry blender to get to the same point.

Using a fork, gradually mix in the cold water, stirring rather than mashing, and add just enough water to bring the dough together into a ball. Transfer the dough to a work surface and wrap in cling film. Flatten the dough into a disc with your hand and refrigerate until well chilled, about 1 hour or longer. Alternatively, place in the freezer for 20–30 minutes (set a timer). The pastry can be held in the fridge for 24 hours before going to the next stage.

When the pastry is quite firm (this is very important), roll the dough into a rectangle on a well-floured counter. Roll with short, quick strokes (rather than long, steady ones) and always roll in one direction. Make sure that the ends

are straight. Check regularly to make sure that the pastry isn't sticking to the counter by loosening it with a palette knife.

As you roll, sprinkle more flour evenly over the counter, if needed. When it's rolled to about 40cm long (this is a guideline only), fold the dough in three, as if you were folding a business letter. Fold the bottom third up to past the middle and brush off the excess flour with a pastry brush. Then fold the top third down to cover it so that the edges of the pastry meet. Press down gently on the right edge with the rolling pin, keeping the pin just inside the edge. Seal the other edge in the same way and finish by sealing the edge closest to you. All three edges have now been sealed.

If the butter starts peeping through the pastry, then chill it again until firm. Continue with a second rolling as long as the butter is not starting to leak out and become soft. If this starts to happen, then wrap the pastry in cling film and return to the fridge or freezer to chill again.

For the second rolling, turn the pastry 90° in an anticlockwise fashion. It should be similar to a book, with the spine on the left and the open leaves on the right. Repeat the rolling, following the same method as before and folding the pastry over in the exact same manner. Always roll in one direction only. Wrap the pastry up in cling film and chill until firm and ready to use, at least 1 hour but preferably 2 hours. The pastry may be kept for up to 48 hours in the fridge before using or frozen for later use.

To make the filling
Preheat the oven to 200°C, 180°C Fan, 400°F, Gas 6.

Place a pizza stone on a rack in a cold oven 45 minutes before cooking and bring up to temperature. Alternatively, cook the tart on a baking tray. On a lightly floured surface, roll out the pastry to about 36cm in diameter. Slide the pastry onto baking parchment and place on a tray in the fridge for about 15 minutes. Refrigerating the pastry after rolling will give you the best results.

Peel the apples and cut into slices about 5mm thick. Remove the pastry from the fridge and spread the apples over the pastry base, leaving a border of about 3.5cm. The apples should be 2–3 layers thick. Fold the border over the apples. Using a pastry brush, paint the exposed pastry border with the melted butter. Brush the remaining butter over the apples. Sprinkle the crust with 2 tablespoons of the sugar and then sprinkle the apples with another 3–4 tablespoons of sugar. If using blackberries, scatter them over the top.

If using a pizza stone, slide the baking parchment directly onto the stone. Otherwise, place the tart on the baking sheet in the centre of the oven. Bake the tart for 45–55 minutes, until the crust is golden brown on the bottom and the apples are beginning to caramelise at the edges. Eat while still warm with some whipped cream or crème fraîche.

CHOCOLATE

What would I be doing if I didn't have my cookery school? I think I would probably have some form of chocolate business. I have long had a fascination with chocolate and it has taken me many places, including to Cocolat in San Francisco (sadly, no longer in business) and to Callebaut in Brussels.

My very first chocolate trip was some years back, chasing a dessert that wasn't working out for me. I had been trying to cook Chocolate Nemesis, the signature dessert of London's River Café, without much luck and had phoned the pastry chef more out of frustration than real hope. It turned out that I wasn't the only one having the same difficulty, so he was sufficiently curious to give me some time. He suggested that I should 'pop in' if I was passing by. I spared him the small matter of the Irish Sea and headed over. Fortune favours the brave. I met Dustin Hoffman and other luminaries as they passed through the kitchen and watched the first screen test of a very young assistant, Jamie Oliver. I found out how the River Café cake tins were producing a particular result and *The Irish Times* even paid (modestly) for a resulting article.

When I came back from a trip to San Francisco, I was all enthused to see what I could do. It was approaching Easter and I turned our whole apartment into a chocolate factory. I was buying chocolate by the half ton. There were moulds stacked high in one room and packaging in the hall. The kitchen counter was covered with a huge piece of marble on which I tempered chocolate, and beside it was a bain marie that I had brought back from Brussels. No food was allowed in the fridge, since chocolate easily picks up the smells and tastes of other foods. The temperature of the house was set to suit the chocolate, not my famished husband, who was delighted to see my ambitions move in other directions when the last Easter egg had been sold. There are people who stop me in the street almost twenty years on and wonder if I'm still doing the Easter eggs, so they must have made some impression!

TEMPERING AND MELTING CHOCOLATE

If you were to melt some squares of chocolate and leave them to set on the counter, they would lose many of the qualities they would normally be prized for. The chocolate would be cakey in texture, would have no shine or snap and wouldn't taste as smooth. Why is this? Cocoa butter, which derives from the cocoa bean itself, is present in all good-quality chocolates in various amounts. When melted, it doesn't regain its stable crystalline form. This often results in a white-ish bloom that you may see on some chocolate that has not been kept in perfect conditions. This indicates that the chocolate has gone out of temper. However, it's still perfectly good to use and can be remelted for use in other desserts. Tempering is an interesting technique but is not required for the desserts in this chapter.

Here are a few tips for working with chocolate that will help you start on your journey.

- Always buy good-quality chocolate. There are many poor-quality chocolates for sale from which the cocoa butter has been removed and replaced with another fat.

- Store chocolate in a cool place, away from heat. Do not store chocolate in the fridge.

- Never melt chocolate over a direct heat. Chocolate can be melted in a heatproof bowl set over a saucepan of hot water. The bowl should not touch the water and the chocolate should be removed as soon as it has melted, otherwise it might burn. The alternative is to melt chocolate in a microwave in short blasts.

Clara's Hot Chocolate Pots

These chocolate pots are more like a hot mousse with a rich chocolate flavour. They aren't difficult to make and the result is amazing.

Serves 6

160g 55–65% dark chocolate, finely chopped

4 tbsp water

3 large eggs, at room temperature

40g caster sugar

whipped cream or vanilla ice cream (page 345), to serve

EQUIPMENT *6 ramekins*

OVEN *Preheat the oven to 160°C, 140°C Fan, 325°F, Gas 3.*

Place the chocolate and water in a heatproof bowl. Melt in the microwave on 600W for 1 minute and in short bursts after that. Stir each time you remove the bowl from the microwave. Alternatively, melt the chocolate in a bowl set over a saucepan of barely simmering water, stirring every so often. Remove as soon as the chocolate is fluid and allow to cool a little.

Place the eggs and sugar in a bowl and beat with an electric whisk or in a stand mixer (which will give more volume). Whisk the eggs until tripled in volume and you reach what is called the ribbon stage (if you lift the beaters and draw a figure of 8 on the surface, it will hold a trail for 10 seconds or more).

Fold a little of the egg mixture into the chocolate. Pour the chocolate mixture back into the whipped eggs and sugar and fold the two together. Pour the mixture into the ramekins and fill almost to the top. The chocolate pots may be made up to this point in advance and refrigerated, covered, for up to 2 days.

Place the chocolate pots in an ovenproof dish and pour boiling water to come halfway up the ramekins. Place in the preheated oven and cook for 20–25 minutes. The pots should be soft and mousse-like. They will also set a little more if left to cool for 5–10 minutes. Serve while still warm topped with some whipped cream or ice cream.

Dark and White Chocolate Mousse

Poured into individual stainless steel rings, with a layer of rum-laced sponge on the bottom, this two-tiered chocolate mousse makes a spectacular dessert. I love the intense, slightly bitter dark chocolate mousse on the bottom and the silky smooth white chocolate mousse on top, but you could equally choose to make one mousse on its own and serve it in a glass.

In this recipe, my strong preference for the dark chocolate mousse is the French Valrhona chocolate called Guanaja 70% (or Manjari 64%) and Ivoire for the white chocolate mousse. A lot of white chocolate is overly sweet, so source the best you can find.

Serves 4–6
  as a two-tier mousse

sponge cake, to line the bases
  (page 329)

FOR THE RUM SYRUP

2 tbsp sugar

1½ tbsp water

1 tbsp dark rum or another spirit or
  liqueur of your choice

**FOR THE DARK CHOCOLATE
MOUSSE**

110g dark chocolate, finely
  chopped

60g unsalted butter

2 large eggs

2 tbsp caster sugar

2 tbsp water

**FOR THE WHITE CHOCOLATE
MOUSSE**

125g white chocolate, finely
  chopped

3 tbsp water

175ml cream

grated chocolate, to decorate or
  hazelnuts in caramel (page 350)
  (optional)

EQUIPMENT *6 x 5cm or 4 x 7.5cm
  stainless steel rings (or use dessert
  glasses)*

To make the rum syrup and sponge cake bases

Place all the rum syrup ingredients in a saucepan and stir to dissolve the sugar. Bring to the boil and then remove from the heat. Leave to cool a little. Slice the sponge into a layer about 5mm thick with a serrated knife. Using one of the stainless steel rings, cut out discs of sponge and use these to line the base of the moulds. Brush some syrup onto each disc with a pastry brush.

To make the dark chocolate mousse

Place the chocolate and butter in a heatproof bowl. Melt in short bursts in the microwave at 600W, or place the bowl over a saucepan of barely simmering water just until melted. Stir every so often during the melting process. Remove from the heat as soon as the chocolate is ready. Set aside.

Place the eggs, sugar and water in a heatproof bowl and whisk together. Set the bowl over a saucepan of lightly simmering water and whisk continuously, ideally with a balloon whisk, until the egg mixture feels warm to the touch. Be careful, as if the eggs get too hot, they can scramble (in which case, you would need to start a new batch).

When warm, remove the bowl from the bain marie and beat with an electric whisk (or in a stand mixer) until the egg mixture is like softly whipped cream. Fold a little of the egg mix into the chocolate and mix together. Spoon the chocolate into the egg mixture and fold the two together. Pour the chocolate mousse into the rings. (I prefer to fill them about two-thirds full if I'm using white chocolate mousse as well.) Refrigerate until the mousse is set. The dark chocolate mousse will probably be firm enough to hold another layer after about 30 minutes.

To make the white chocolate mousse

Place the white chocolate and water in a heatproof bowl. Sit the bowl over a saucepan of barely simmering water and melt slowly, stirring every so often. If you wish to melt the chocolate in a microwave, do so in short bursts on low – no more than 600W. Remove as soon as the chocolate is fluid. Allow to cool a little. If the chocolate becomes too cold, warm it ever so slightly – it should be cool when mixed into the cream, but not cold.

Whip the cream until it's light and fluffy but has not yet reached the stage of soft peaks. This is critical to a smooth, silky result (otherwise the mousse will be grainy). Fold the whipped cream into the white chocolate. Do not overmix. Pour the white chocolate mousse on top of the dark and fill the rings. Leave in the fridge to set for 2–3 hours.

To unmould the mousse, dip a small pointed knife into a jug of boiling water, dry it off thoroughly and then run the knife between the mousse and the ring to release the mould. Alternatively, place the mousses on a heatproof tray or marble counter and use a blowtorch to quickly release the rings. Using a small metal spatula, lift the mousse onto dessert plates. Decorate with grated chocolate or hazelnuts in caramel.

Sponge Cake

This is a basic light sponge, which is used here as a base for the chocolate mousse on page 327. This quantity will make far more than you need for the mousse, so either eat the remainder with raspberry jam, fresh fruit and whipped cream or wrap it in cling film and use another time.

Makes 1 x 20cm sponge cake

3 eggs

85g caster sugar

85g plain flour

pinch of salt

EQUIPMENT *2 x 20cm cake tins or a 34cm x 25cm baking tray*

OVEN *Preheat the oven to 180°C, 160°C Fan, 350°F, Gas 4.*

Line the base of the cake tins, or the baking tray, with baking parchment.

Place the eggs and sugar in a mixing bowl and whisk with an electric beater until the mixture has tripled in volume and is light and fluffy. Continue whisking until the mixture holds a figure of 8 on the surface when you draw a line with the beaters. Sift the flour and a pinch of salt and fold into the egg mixture.

Scrape the mixture into the prepared tin(s) and bake in the middle of the oven for 20–25 minutes. The sponge is cooked when it feels firm and springy in the centre and has begun to shrink slightly away from the sides of the tins. Leave for a few minutes to cool and then turn out onto a wire rack.

This sponge may be made in advance and frozen.

Robert de Niro's Chocolate Hazelnut Cake

There was some commotion when Robert de Niro and Sean Penn booked into a restaurant I was working in. It was de Niro's birthday and he had requested a chocolate cake. This is what I baked for him. On tasting it, I wishfully imagined that he would demand to meet the person who had made it. No such request ever materialised. All I can report is that he did ask for the rest of the cake to take home with him. And I got a name for my chocolate cake.

If the stars you are cooking for have a preference, the hazelnuts can be replaced with almonds or pecans. A perfectly smooth icing may not be achieved on your first attempt.

Serves 8–10

175g hazelnuts
175g dark chocolate
175g butter
175g caster sugar
6 eggs

FOR THE GANACHE

175ml single cream
170g dark chocolate, finely
   chopped

EQUIPMENT *23cm springform pan, greased and lined with a round of baking parchment*
23cm cake base

OVEN *Preheat the oven to 190°C, 170°C Fan, 375°F, Gas 5.*

To toast the hazelnuts

Put the hazelnuts on a baking sheet and toast in the oven for about 6 minutes. Remove from the oven and place the nuts in the centre of a clean tea towel. Scoop up the tea towel, holding it sealed in one hand, and rub the nuts vigorously through the towel with the other hand. Remove the skinned hazelnuts and repeat the process. It's not usually possible to remove every piece of skin. Allow to cool before grinding the nuts finely in a food processor (a food processor is ideal, as it will leave a little texture rather than grinding them into a powder). Do not overprocess or the nuts will become oily.

To make the cake

Place the chocolate in a heatproof bowl. Melt in short bursts in the microwave at 600W or place the bowl over a saucepan of barely simmering water just until melted. Stir every so often during the melting process. Remove from the heat as soon as the chocolate is ready. Allow to cool a little. The chocolate should not be really cold when being mixed with the rest of the ingredients, so warm it slightly if necessary.

Cream the butter and all but 2 tablespoons of the sugar until light and fluffy. Separate the yolks and the whites of the eggs. Gradually add the yolks to the butter and sugar mixture and beat until incorporated. Mix the melted chocolate into the butter mixture with a wooden spoon or spatula.

Beat the egg whites until stiff and gradually add the remaining 2 tablespoons of sugar. Beat again until they hold stiff peaks. (Do not carry on beating after this point, as the egg whites can start to break down.) Fold the whites into the chocolate mixture alternately with the ground hazelnuts, finishing with egg white.

Pour the batter into the lined cake tin and spread it out evenly. Bake for about 40 minutes. Test towards the end of cooking by placing a wooden skewer in the centre of the cake. The cake is ready when moist crumbs stick to the skewer (the centre of the cake is neither completely dry nor runny). When the cake has been removed from the oven, run a small utility knife around the edges of the cake but do not unmould the cake at this stage. After about 10 minutes, run a knife around the edges again, release the outside of the springform pan and remove. The cake will sink a little in the middle as it cools, leaving a slightly crusty higher rim around the edges. The cake will need to cool for a couple of hours before icing.

To make the ganache

If you wish to make the cake even all over, then level the top slightly by removing some of the edges (though I never mind if the cake is slightly sunken in the middle, as it means that there will be extra ganache in the centre). Place a cake base on top of the cake and invert the cake onto it.

Heat the cream in a saucepan. As soon as the cream comes to the boil, remove from the heat and add the chocolate. Stir gently with a spatula back and forth until the chocolate has melted completely. The ganache should be completely smooth, without any flecks of chocolate. Pour into a bowl and allow to cool until it has a consistency similar to pouring yoghurt.

Place a cooling rack over a baking sheet to catch the extra glaze that runs off the cake. Place the cake on the cooling rack. Have by your side a metal icing spatula. Pour most of the glaze in a puddle in the centre of the cake. Ideally, lift up the cake base and tilt the cake from side to side so that the ganache spills over the edges. If the ganache has set a little too much for this, then spread it over the sides with two or three quick strokes of the spatula. Spread the ganache around the sides of the cake. Keep in a cool place until ready to serve.

WHAT IS A GANACHE?

A basic chocolate ganache is a combination of chocolate and cream (or chocolate and butter) that is used as a glaze for cakes and as a base for truffles. The proportion of cream or butter to chocolate varies, but for a cake it is typically equal quantities of chocolate and cream. The ganache may be poured over cakes when cool, or set at room temperature and spread as an icing. If refrigerated overnight, ganache may also be whipped and used as a filling for cakes.

Any leftover ganache from glazing a cake may be refrigerated for several hours and rolled into balls to make truffles. The truffles may then be rolled in cocoa or in very finely chopped nuts.

Chocolate ganache has a tendency to separate or curdle if reheated. This means that the fats will start to separate from the cocoa solids. The natural reaction when you see this happening is to whisk vigorously in the hope that the chocolate and fat will emulsify. This seldom does the trick. A magical trick, which often works, is to add a teaspoon of water to the ganache and to whisk it in.

Chocolate and Pistachio Cake

This cake has a lovely light consistency which resembles that of a chocolate mousse. Nuts are interchangeable in chocolate cakes, so you could use ground hazelnuts, pecans or almonds instead.

Serves 8-10

150g dark chocolate, roughly chopped

150g butter

150g caster sugar

5 eggs, separated

1 tsp vanilla

150g unsalted pistachios, finely ground

EQUIPMENT *24cm springform pan or cake tin*

OVEN *Preheat the oven to 120°C, 100°C Fan, 250F, Gas ½.*

Line the tin with a circle of baking parchment. Grease the sides of the tin with butter.

Place the chocolate and butter in a heatproof bowl. Melt in the microwave in short bursts at 600W, stirring regularly. Alternatively, place in a bowl over a saucepan of barely simmering water just until fluid. Remove from the heat and mix in most of the sugar, reserving 3 tablespoons of sugar to add to the whipped whites.

Separate the egg yolks and the whites. Whisk the yolks and the vanilla into the chocolate mixture. Beat the whites with an electric beater to stiff peaks. Add in the remaining 3 tablespoons of sugar and whisk again until stiff. Mix a large spoonful of the whites into the chocolate mixture. Fold in the ground pistachios alternately with the whites.

Scoop the batter into the cake tin and spread out evenly. Bake in the preheated oven for about 55 minutes, until the cake is totally set when you press the centre very gently. Remove and allow to cool in the tin.

To slice, dip a chopping knife in very hot water, dry the knife and slice cleanly.

NOTE 1 tablespoon of rum can be added to the chocolate when melting it.

SOUFFLÉS

I never used to cook soufflés. Who knows why, but I thought that they were old-fashioned. When my first task at the Michelin two-starred Le Manoir aux Quat' Saisons was at the soufflé oven, I changed my views fairly sharply. We used to do some fairly stunning combinations, but the simple ones, such as Soufflé au Chocolat or Soufflé aux Fruits de la Passion, were hard to beat. As service quietened down, I would sometimes experiment a little. One evening, I made a lychee soufflé, which Raymond Blanc tasted and could not identify as he glided by. He insisted on not being told. Several minutes later he returned, having worked it out, dismayed that it had taken him so long. The joy of small triumphs. (For the record, it never made the menu.)

Coming on duty, my first task would be to make a crème pâtissière, which was the base for all the hot soufflés. The crème pâtissière was also used to fill little tartlet cases that could be spectacularly adorned and served as petits fours or for afternoon tea. Then I would ready myself. There were generally just two dessert soufflés on the menu, but as the orders came in, that was enough to focus on.

At the height of service, the oven door would be flying open and closed as more orders for soufflés came in. That dispelled one myth very quickly: soufflés are much more robust than old cookery books and old cooks would have had me believe – I guess the arrival of the convection oven has helped.

At Le Manoir, there was superb communication between those in the kitchen and those in front of house, but for those at the soufflé oven, there was even more special attentiveness. As soon as I shouted that I was ready, hovering waiters jumped into action. We all knew that the structure of a soufflé waits for no man.

I had previously seen a chef make an incision on the top of a soufflé and pour in a hot sauce. I liked that idea (and still do), but it was very coolly received by the normally unflappable Monsieur Blanc. "Unsightly" was the only response. I watched and listened more and suggested less – a better outcome for us both.

SOME HINTS AND PRINCIPLES FOR
COOKING A SOUFFLÉ

*

Use up older egg whites

Older egg whites work well in a soufflé, so if you happen to have
egg whites in the fridge this is a convenient way to use them up. In a
restaurant, there would always be egg whites in the fridge, clearly labelled
with the day the batch was started. Egg whites would be weighed before
use: 30g egg white is equivalent to the white of one egg.

Create volume

A key element in making soufflés is creating volume with the egg whites.
Separate the eggs one by one and then transfer the clean whites into a
mixing bowl. This way, there is no risk of tainting a whole batch with a bit
of egg yolk. The mixing bowl for the whites must be scrupulously clean,
with no trace of grease, so it's best to use stainless steel or china rather
than plastic.

Don't overbeat

Beating the egg whites incorporates air. The more you whisk, the more
the air bubbles increase, but there is a maximum point of expansion.
Go beyond this point and the egg whites will begin to break down and
release some of their moisture. This happens if you beat the egg whites to
stiff peaks and then carry on beating beyond this point. If the egg whites
do break down, there is no alternative but to start with a fresh batch.

Choose a good-sized dish

The choice of soufflé dish can affect the final result. The smaller the ramekin, the harder it is to cook the soufflé to perfection. I do like individual ramekins over a single large dish. The ones I use are 7cm deep and 9cm in diameter.

Folding

Folding two mixtures together is an important technique in making many desserts. In the case of soufflés, the challenge is to incorporate the beaten egg whites without deflating them.

The first step is to loosen the mix: a scoop of the whisked egg whites is stirred in to lighten the heavier mix. This will make it easier to incorporate the rest of the egg white.

How to fold

Using either a spatula or a wooden spoon, cut through the centre of the mixture and, in a sweeping motion, scoop up some of the mixture at the bottom of the bowl and bring it up to the top, rolling your hand over as you go. With the other hand, give the bowl a little turn, moving in a clockwise direction. Cut through the mixture again and repeat the folding action. Do not overwork the mix.

Let them rise

When the soufflés are ready to go into the oven, sit the dishes on a baking tray and place on a lower shelf in the oven. Too high up and the tops can become too hot. Enjoy watching them rise but remember that the timing is crucial. The pleasure is in digging into the crust and finding a soft centre. Have the icing sugar and a little sieve ready so you can dust them and rush them to the table.

Hot Lemon Soufflé

A soufflé is an event, a drama. It commands awe and attention. Warm, light and yet full of flavour, it's one of the great, elegant desserts and so much easier to make than doubters might believe.

The base for this soufflé is a fresh and tangy lemon curd. The curd can be made several hours or even several days in advance, as long as it is well covered so that it doesn't develop a skin. Then all you have to do is whip the egg whites and fold them in.

Serves 6

TO COAT THE MOULDS
soft butter
caster sugar

FOR THE LEMON CURD
200g caster sugar
100g butter
160ml lemon juice (from about 4–5 lemons)
7 egg yolks (reserve the whites for later)
grated rind of 3 lemons

FOR THE EGG WHITE BASE
8 egg whites
100g caster sugar
icing sugar, to dust over the top
whipped cream, to serve

EQUIPMENT *6 individual soufflé dishes or ramekins, about 7cm deep and 9cm wide (though you can use smaller ramekins)*
OVEN *Preheat the oven to 220°C, 200°C Fan, 425°F, Gas 7.*

Using a pastry brush, butter the inside of the soufflé dishes. Put 2 tablespoons of sugar into the first ramekin and rotate so that the sugar adheres to the butter. Pour the excess sugar into the next dish and continue until all the soufflé dishes are buttered and sugared.

To make the lemon curd

Place the sugar, butter and lemon juice in a medium saucepan and heat until the butter is melted and the sugar has dissolved. Remove from the heat and whisk in the egg yolks, one by one. Place the saucepan back on the heat and cook, stirring continuously over a low to medium heat, until the mixture thickens. Do not allow the mixture to boil. When the lemon curd has thickened (it will thicken more when it cools), pass it through a strainer into a bowl and stir in the lemon zest. Place some cling film directly on the surface and allow to cool. Keep at room temperature if you are planning to cook the soufflé within a couple of hours; otherwise, refrigerate when it has cooled. (Return to room temperature before using.)

To make the soufflé

About 30 minutes before serving, preheat the oven.

Beat the egg whites until they reach soft peaks and then sprinkle in the sugar. Beat again to soft peaks. Mix about a quarter of the egg whites into the curd. Fold the remaining egg whites into the lemon curd just until incorporated. Do not overmix or the egg whites will deflate.

Fill the soufflé dishes to the top and smooth the surface with a metal spatula so that it's completely level with the edge of the dish. Run your thumb around the edge of the ramekin as you rotate the souffle dish – this prevents the soufflés from catching on the edge as they rise.

Place the soufflé dishes on a baking tray, spacing them well apart. Place in the oven and cook for about 10 minutes for individual servings. The timing is only a guideline. What you are seeking is a soufflé that is set on the outside and still soft and almost creamy in the centre. Remove from the oven, dust with icing sugar and serve immediately with some whipped cream.

Passion Fruit Soufflé

I love passion fruit. I am happy to cut one in half and dig in with a spoon to get at that indescribable sharp-sweet taste. More usually I would be using the juice for any number of desserts. I think it's a perfect taste for a soufflé.

I presumed that there was nothing I could do with the seeds until I had a student with a parrot. It turned out the parrot went crazy for the seeds, so I took pleasure in saving them for him (we foodies must watch out for each other).

Serves 6

TO COAT THE MOULDS
soft butter
caster sugar

FOR THE SOUFFLÉ
280ml passion fruit juice
200ml crème pâtissière (page 32),
    at room temperature
8 egg whites
80g caster sugar

EQUIPMENT *6 soufflé dishes, about 7cm deep and 9cm wide*
OVEN *Preheat the oven to 220°C, 200°C Fan, 425°F, Gas 7.*

To prepare the soufflé moulds, butter the inside of the moulds with a pastry brush using softened butter. Place a few tablespoons of sugar into the first mould, rotate the mould so that it adheres to the butter and then transfer the excess to the next mould. Continue to the last mould and then discard the remaining sugar. Set aside until ready to use.

Boil the passion fruit juice until it has reduced to 120ml (8 tablespoons). Allow to cool. Add the reduced passion fruit juice to the crème pâtissière and mix well.

Beat the egg whites until they reach soft peaks and then sprinkle in the sugar. Beat again to soft peaks. Whisk a few tablespoons of the egg whites into the crème pâtissière to lighten it. Using a spatula, fold the remaining egg whites into the crème pâtissière just until incorporated. Do not overmix or the egg whites may deflate a little.

Fill the soufflé moulds to the top. Scrape the surface with a metal spatula so that the top is totally flat. Run your thumb around the edge of the soufflé as you rotate the soufflé dish. This prevents the soufflé from catching on the rim and helps it to rise more easily. Place the soufflés on a baking tray and place in the oven. Cook for about 12 minutes, or until risen and set on the outside but still slightly creamy in the centre. Serve immediately. If the soufflés are set the whole way through, they won't taste the same. Soft, creamy centres are what you're aiming for. When you shake the soufflés, if they wobble alarmingly they aren't ready – if they still wobble a little in the centre, they're cooked.

Crème Pâtissière

Makes 250ml

250ml milk

1 vanilla pod

3 egg yolks

50g caster sugar

15g plain flour

Pour the milk into a saucepan. Split the vanilla pod in half lengthways and scrape out the seeds. Add the seeds and the pod to the milk. Heat until just below boiling point and then set aside for at least 20 minutes to allow the vanilla to infuse.

Bring the milk back up to the boil. Put the egg yolks and sugar in a stainless steel bowl and whisk until completely combined. Continue whisking while adding the flour until the mixture is completely smooth.

Remove the vanilla pod from the milk and pour the warm milk directly onto the egg yolk mixture, whisking all the time. Return to the saucepan and bring to the boil, stirring continuously with a wooden spoon. Once the custard boils, reduce the heat and simmer for a further 5 minutes, stirring continuously. Remove from the heat and pour into a container. Place cling film directly on the surface of the custard and allow to cool. Refrigerate until ready to use. The crème pâtissière can be made in advance and stored for 3 days.

HOW TO MAKE CONCENTRATED VANILLA SUGAR

This is a great way to use up every part of the expensive vanilla bean. Rinse the vanilla pods thoroughly after use and allow them to dry at room temperature. They will become quite brittle. When you have gathered a few vanilla pods, grind them in a coffee grinder with an equal weight of caster sugar until they are reduced to a powder. Strain through a very fine mesh strainer to remove all the crunchy vanilla bean bits. Use this concentrated vanilla sugar to flavour whipped cream, desserts and biscuits. The sugar is very intense, so it should be added to some of the existing sugar in a recipe as a natural flavouring.

ICE CREAM

There is a temptation to make ice cream on a commercial basis when you realise how easy it is. If it goes well for you, please remember the early encouragement you received here. Homemade ice cream is far superior to anything you can buy and allows you to experiment with all sorts of ingredients.

The first step is to buy an ice cream maker. Fancier models have their own internal freezing systems and are essential if you're catering for big numbers or you want to make two or three different flavours on the same day. However, they are big, heavy and expensive. The one I use and recommend is the basic one-litre Donvier ice cream maker. It has an inner canister that needs to be put in the freezer a day before the ice cream is made and taken out when you have prepared an ice cream base. You have, at your cold fingertips, the most efficient way of freezing the mixture into ice cream. All it takes is a few hand churns over a 15-minute period, and the ice cream is made.

SERVING TEMPERATURE FOR ICE CREAM

Ideally, ice cream should be served just one degree away from melting – this way, the flavour is at its best. It does not make sense to go to the trouble of making ice cream and then to serve it rock hard. It needs to melt quickly on the tongue so that the flavour explodes in your mouth. Check the ice cream well in advance of serving – remove it from the freezer and place in the fridge to thaw a little (set a timer though). You may do this a couple of hours before serving and place it back in the freezer. It generally remains at much the same consistency an hour or two later.

Banana Ice Cream

This is the simplest ice cream I know and also one of the lightest. The amount of cream proportional to the volume is tiny and all you need to do is whizz all the ingredients in a liquidiser. It's essential to have really ripe bananas, otherwise the ice cream will taste rather bland. The lemon adds a lovely freshness. Serve with some crispy biscuits alongside.

Makes 1 litre

300g skinned, ripe bananas

100g caster sugar

juice of 1–2 lemons, sieved

300ml full cream milk

150ml cream

Purée the bananas, sugar and lemon juice in a liquidiser. Pour in the milk and cream and whizz again. Taste and add more lemon juice if necessary. Pour into a bowl, cover with cling film and chill in the fridge for an hour or two before churning in an ice cream maker.

NOTE The banana mixture should not be left in the fridge for too long or the bananas will slowly discolour, even with the addition of lemon juice.

Greek Yoghurt and Honey Ice Cream

Pastry tutor at the school Sandy Sabek-Wyer is always looking to bring balance to a dessert plate. The freshness of her Greek yoghurt ice cream makes this an ideal counterpoint to desserts at the sweeter end of the spectrum.

Makes 1 litre

150g caster sugar

150ml water

500g Greek yoghurt

2 tbsp honey, or to taste

In a small saucepan, heat the sugar and water to make a stock syrup. Set aside to cool.

In a large bowl, mix the Greek yoghurt and cooled stock syrup. Add honey to taste. Place in the fridge until well chilled, then churn in an ice cream maker.

Vanilla Ice Cream

The base for this ice cream is a classic crème anglaise, an egg custard made from egg yolks, milk, cream and sugar.

You can make many variants from this basic method. Heat raisins in a little rum for a rum and raisin ice cream; add finely chopped candied ginger and a little ginger syrup for candied ginger ice cream; or drizzle in some melted 70% dark chocolate towards the end of the churning and you have chocolate chip ice cream.

Makes 1 litre

500ml single cream
200ml milk

1 fresh vanilla bean
6 egg yolks
130g caster sugar

Place the cream and milk in a saucepan. Split the vanilla bean in half lengthways, press it flat with a knife and scrape out the little black seeds. Put the seeds and the pod itself into the cream and milk. Slowly bring up to the boil, then remove from the heat.

In a medium-sized bowl, beat the egg yolks and sugar together with a hand whisk just until combined. Have a sieve to hand beside the hob. Pour the hot cream and milk onto the egg yolks, whisking all the time. Pour this mixture back into the saucepan. Cook over a low to medium heat, stirring with a wooden spoon and making sure that you also get into the corners of the saucepan. Cook for a few minutes, until the custard is very lightly coating the back of the spoon. If you draw a finger across the back of the wooden spoon, the custard should hold a clear line. (The crème anglaise really only thickens properly when it's cold.) If you have a thermometer, the custard is ready when it reaches 70–85°C, 160–185°F. Do not let the custard boil or it may curdle.

As soon as the crème anglaise is ready, pass it through a sieve back into the bowl. Reserve the vanilla pod (see page 342). Allow to cool and then refrigerate until well chilled.

To make the ice cream, pour the crème anglaise into an ice cream maker and churn.

ADDING INTEREST

Glazed Blueberries

fresh or frozen blueberries

caster sugar

a dash of crème de cassis
  (blackcurrant liqueur) or water

Heat a dry frying pan until hot. Place a layer of blueberries in the pan and then sprinkle with a generous dusting of caster sugar. Add a dash of crème de cassis or water to the pan to create some syrupy juices. If using frozen berries, add them to the pan still frozen. Frozen blueberries retain water, so you may not need any extra liquid. Shake the pan for a minute or two, until the sugar melts and the blueberries look glazed.

Sugared Pecans

When making a caramel sauce, the rule is that you do not stir the sugar after it has come to the boil. In this technique you do exactly the opposite, stirring the sugar and water syrup in order to make it crystallise. This creates a sugar coating for the pecans so that you get toasty, sugary nuts.

100g pecans

30g caster sugar

1 tbsp water

OVEN *Preheat the oven to 160°C,*
  140°C Fan, 325°F, Gas 3.

Place the nuts on a baking tray and toast in the oven for 5–6 minutes.

Heat the sugar and water in a saucepan, stirring to dissolve the sugar, and bring up to the boil. Add the warm toasted pecans and stir until the sugar starts to crystallise and coats the nuts completely. The sugar should be white – do not allow it to go darker. Transfer straight away to a baking tray. Spread out the nuts and allow to cool. When cold, store in an airtight container.

Praline

Praline is made from nuts that are bathed in caramel and then allowed to set till rock hard. The praline may be broken into chunks or whizzed in a food processor to fine crumbs. Sprinkled over ice cream, added to buttercreams in cakes or on a dessert plate to add texture, this technique yields many options. Praline can be made with different nuts, such as hazelnuts, pecans, pistachios or peanuts.

60g caster sugar
60g pecans (or other nuts)

Line a tray with a silicone mat or a sheet of baking parchment. Heat a dry frying pan or saucepan and sprinkle in the sugar in an even layer. Cook over a medium heat until the sugar starts to caramelise. The sugar will not caramelise evenly, so every so often, mix the liquefied sugar with a heatproof spatula or a wooden spoon to allow for even colouring. Once the sugar has turned golden all over, add in the whole pecans and stir to coat with the caramel. Be careful with the heat towards the end of the cooking – if the caramel becomes too dark in colour, it will taste bitter. Pour onto the lined tray and leave to set and become hard – this will only take about 5 minutes. Break into chunks by bashing with a rolling pin or a pestle. Alternatively, when broken into chunks, whizz in a food processor to make a praline powder.

Caramel Sauce

This sauce is fabulous with ice cream, apple cake, fruit tarts and many other desserts.

100g caster sugar
50ml water
200ml cream

50g unsalted butter
pinch of sea salt, such as Maldon

Combine the sugar and water in a saucepan. Heat the syrup and slowly bring up to the boil, stirring to dissolve the sugar. Continue boiling until the sugar begins to turn golden. Do not stir the syrup at any point after it comes to the boil. The caramel generally cooks unevenly, so as the colour changes, you may swirl the pot a little to encourage the caramel to become more even in colour. Continue cooking until the caramel is a rich golden colour all over and then add the cream. The caramel will splutter and foam a little (you can turn down the heat at this

point), so wait a minute or so for the foam to subside and then continue cooking on a low heat until the shards of caramel have dissolved completely. Stir to make sure that the caramel is smooth, then whisk in the butter and remove from the heat. Add a pinch of sea salt (a bigger pinch if you would like a salted caramel sauce). Once cold, the sauce can be stored in the fridge for up to 2 weeks.

Hazelnuts in Caramel

12 skinned hazelnuts
 (or more if you wish)

150g caster sugar

100ml water

1 tsp glucose

EQUIPMENT *Wooden cocktail sticks*
Blu-Tack

Press a wooden cocktail stick into each hazelnut. Stick small pieces of Blu-Tack under a hanging cupboard. Have a bowl of cold water beside the cooker.

Heat the sugar, water and glucose in a saucepan, stirring once or twice to dissolve the sugar. Bring up to the boil and simmer until the syrup thickens and turns into a caramel. Swirl the saucepan gently as the colour starts to change. When the caramel is lightly golden all over, dip the base of the saucepan briefly into the bowl of cold water in order to stop the cooking process. Remove the pan from the water and let the syrup cool for about a minute.

Holding the cocktail stick, dip the hazelnuts, one by one, into the caramel until the nut is completely coated. Stick each cocktail stick into a piece of Blu-Tack and suspend the caramel-coated nuts in the air so that the caramel falls down and creates a long caramel tail. Continue with the rest of the nuts. The nuts will hold for several hours provided the glucose is used. Use these nuts to garnish chocolate cakes, mousses or other desserts. Once cold, transfer carefully to an airtight container lined with baking parchment, keeping each hazelnut separate.

Index

353

Weighing and Measuring

For consistency, I have used American tablespoon measurements throughout the book. American spoon measures are available in all kitchen stores or online.

All spoon measurements are level.

5ml = 1 teaspoon and *15ml = 1 tablespoon.*

Ounces to grams

OUNCES	GRAMS
½ oz	10 g
¾ oz	20 g
1 oz	25 g
1½ oz	40 g
2 oz	50 g
2½ oz	60 g
3 oz	75 g
4 oz	110 g
4½ oz	125 g
5 oz	150 g
6 oz	175 g
7 oz	200 g
8 oz	225 g
9 oz	250 g
10 oz	275 g
12 oz	350 g
1 lb	450 g
1 lb 8oz	700 g
2 lb	900 g
3 lb	1.35 kg

Dimensions

INCHES	METRIC
⅛	3 mm
¼	5 mm
½	1 cm
¾	2 cm
1	2.5 cm
1¼	3 cm
1½	4 cm
1¾	4.5 cm
2	5 cm
2½	6 cm
3	7.5 cm
3½	9 cm
4	10 cm
5	13 cm
5¼	13.5 cm
6	15 cm
6½	16 cm
7	18 cm
7½	19 cm
8	20 cm
9	23 cm
9½	24 cm
10	25.5 cm
11	28 cm
12	30 cm
16	40 cm

Pints to Litres

IMPERIAL	METRIC
1 fl oz	25 ml
2 fl oz	50 ml
4 fl oz	100 ml
6 fl oz	175 ml
7 fl oz	200 ml
8 fl oz	225 ml
10 fl oz	300 ml
12 fl oz	350 ml
14 fl oz	400 ml
15 fl oz	450 ml
16 fl oz	475 ml
18 fl oz	530 ml
1pt (20 fl oz)	570 ml
1¼ pt (25 fl oz)	700 ml
1½ pt (30 fl oz)	900 ml
1¾ pt (35 fl oz)	1 ltr

American Cup Conversions

AMERICAN	IMPERIAL	METRIC
1 cup flour	5 oz	150 g
1 cup caster/ granulated sugar	8 oz	225 g
1 cup brown sugar	6 oz	175 g
1 cup butter	8 oz	225 g
1 cup sultanas/raisins	7 oz	200 g
1 cup ground almonds	4 oz	110 g
1 cup uncooked rice	7 oz	200 g
1 cup grated cheese	4 oz	110 g
1 stick butter	4 oz	110 g

Oven Temperature

GAS MARK	°F	°C
1	275°F	140°C
2	300°F	150°C
3	325°F	170°C
4	350°F	180°C
5	375°F	190°C
6	400°F	200°C
7	425°F	220°C
8	450°F	230°C
9	475°F	240°C

If using a fan oven you will need to reduce the oven temperature in a recipe by 20 degrees.

Liquid Conversions

IMPERIAL	METRIC	AMERICAN
Imperial	Metric	American
½ fl oz	15 ml	1 tbsp
1 fl oz	30 ml	1/8 cup
2 fl oz	60 ml	¼ cup
4 fl oz	120 ml	½ cup
8 fl oz	240 ml	1 cup
16 fl oz	480 ml	1 pint

Acknowledgements

Creating this book has been a fascinating experience from which I have learned so much. It started with friends who took the time to read excerpts and to urge me on. For their encouragement and suggestions, thanks to Paddy, Annie, Ann Marie, Judy, Georgia, Hilary, Chandana and Dermot.

For her stunning book design, my thanks go to Libby Carton. She was a natural choice. She has done all the design work for the school since the day we opened and she had a strong sense of how I wanted this book to look. She says that she follows my ideas, but in fact she only ever uses them as a rough starting point. I never doubted that the layout of the book would far exceed my expectations. She and her husband were opening a brewery (watch out for their Kinnegar beer!) at the same time as this project. Such is their attention to detail, it's no surprise that this is the best beer I have ever tasted.

An enormous thank you to my copy editor and proofreader, Kristin Jensen, for her extraordinary contribution, for working late at night when deadlines had to be met and for her ever-encouraging voice. I had no idea what a copy editor would bring. I do now.

For the food styling, I took the risk of working with a very close friend. Irish fashion designer, Liz Quin, has a wealth of experience planning and designing new collections for each season. We approached the book as she would a fashion shoot, with boards on the wall pinned with ideas, building up a sense of the book as a whole and then each individual shot. Her willingness to take me on this journey, despite all the demands of her own work, was unforgettably generous.

To my wonderful photographer, Joanne Murphy, who approached each shot, whether early in the morning or late in the afternoon, with the same energy and focus, I owe a huge debt. She was always such a pleasure to work with. Her keen eye, her never-ending patience and her desire to continue until we were all happy with a shot made such a contribution.

There were so many dishes to be tested and meticulously recorded. Aoife McCarthy planned all the testing and prepared all the dishes for the photo shoots. For her endless good humour, her support and patience and all her hours of commitment, I am enormously appreciative.

I am grateful to the team at the school over the years, personified by the drive and energy of Gerry Devlin, Lorna Doherty and Sally Herron. A particular thanks to the current team who have contributed so much to the cookery school on a daily basis and who have held the fort while this project took my attention: John and Sandy Wyer, Suzanne McElligott, Maria Huston and Grainne Wall.

I am grateful to the many chefs down through the years who have come to the school. A particular thanks to those who have become regular visitors, such as Paul Flynn, Neven Maguire, Rossa Crowe, Atul Kochhar, Sunil Ghai, Matthew Albert, Oliver Dunne, Niall O'Sullivan, Paul Kelly and Stephen Gibson, all of whose friendship I now value.

There are two shops nearby where I love to browse and admire their wonderful wares and taste. Eileen Kelly in the Blue Door in Monkstown and Philippa Grant in Eden Home and Garden in Blackrock, thanks for your interest in this project and for lending props that added so much to the photos.

A final thanks to my husband, Richard, who nourished the project from the outset, and to my mother-in-law Muriel Booth who, at 93, still continues to nourish us all.

About the Author

Lynda Booth is a hugely experienced chef who has worked in simple bistros and Michelin two star restaurants (with Raymond Blanc in Oxford). She is the owner and director of Dublin Cookery School, the current Irish Cookery School of the Year (Irish Restaurant Awards). Lynda runs weekend and evening classes for those looking for fresh inspiration. Her particular pride is the three month full-time course which attracts students from all over the world. For this course, she invites national and international chefs to join her carefully selected team of tutors.

From Lynda's Table is her first book.

To find out more about Dublin Cookery School, visit the website on www.dublincookeryschool.ie.

Dublin
Cookery
School

From Lynda's Table by **Lynda Booth**
Published in 2013 by DCS Publishing

DCS Publishing, 2 Brookfield Terrace, Blackrock
Co. Dublin, Ireland

Text © **Lynda Booth** 2013
Additional text by **Richard Booth**
Food Photography © **Joanne Murphy** 2013
Photos pages 6 & 9 © **Gary Belcher** 2013
Photo page 366 © **Simon Burch** 2013

A CIP catalogue record for this book is available
from the British Library.

Food Styling by **Liz Quin** and **Lynda Booth**
Designed in Ireland by **Carton LeVert**

Printed and bound in Italy by **Graphicom S.r.l**
Colour origination by **Altaimage**, London

ISBN 978-0-9926951-0-1